Pen & Sword

A Journalist's Guide to Covering the Military

Pen & Sword

A Journalist's Guide to Covering the Military

By Ed Offley

Marion Street Press, Inc.

Library of Congress Cataloging-in-Publication Data

Offley, Edward.
  Pen & sword : a journalist's guide to covering the military / by
Edward Peyton Offley.
     p. cm.
Includes index.
  ISBN 0-9665176-4-4
  1. Journalism, Military. I. Title: Pen and sword. II. Title.
PN4784.M5 O44 2001
070.4'49355--dc21

                              2001007001

Cover photo by Dave Ekren, *Seattle Post-Intelligencer*
Cover design by Michelle Crisanti
Edited by Ed Avis

ISBN 0-9665176-4-4
Printed in U.S.A.
Printing 10 9 8 7 6 5 4

Marion Street Press, Inc.
PO Box 2249
Oak Park, IL 60304
708-445-8330
www.marionstreetpress.com

Dedication

This book would have been impossible without the support and help I received from six colleagues during my years as a military reporter: George Hebert and the late Perry Morgan at *The Ledger-Star* in Norfolk, Va., who launched me into the military beat and gave me an unparalleled opportunity to cover the U.S. armed forces at a pivotal time of their recovery from the Vietnam era; Virg Fassio, J.D. Alexander and Bob Schenet at the *Seattle Post-Intelligencer*, who invited me to continue this specialty, first as an editorial writer, then later as military reporter; and to Steve Aubin, formerly of the Center for Defense Journalism at Boston University, who provided invaluable help to this project.

But my special thanks goes to my wife, Karen, and daughters Elaine and Andrea, for their love and support.

Table of Contents

How to...cover a serviceman's death
It can be heartbreaking, but writing about a serviceman's death is an important community service.

Broadcast Challenges:
Tech issues make the job tougher
TV and radio play increasingly vital roles in coverage of the military, but broadcasters face special challenges.

How to...Cover the nuclear story
The Soviet Union may be dead, but the nuclear story lives on. In fact, it may be more important now than ever.

Using the Freedom of Information Act:
It's your nuclear weapon
FOIA letters are sometimes necessary to pry out information. Here's how to use them.

The Internet, Information Technology and Military Coverage:
Be sure to mine this mother lode
Modern technology has made covering the military easier. This chapter concludes with a list of useful web sites.

Going to War I: Realtime
Covering major incidents and operations
Even during peacetime the military frequently engages in actual low-intensity operations that the media must cover.

**Chronology of U.S. Military Operations: 1981-2001 **

Preface

A Nation At War

The decade-long post-Cold War era ended in a cataract of fire and death on Sept. 11, 2001, as terrorists hijacked four civilian airliners and, employing them as suicidal missiles, struck the World Trade Center in New York and the Pentagon in Arlington, Va., across the Potomac River from the nation's capital (a fourth airliner that crashed in Pennsylvania after several passengers attempted to overpower the hijackers was believed to have been headed for the U.S. Capitol).

Out of the chaos, bloodshed and destruction, the American people appeared more united than at any time since the aftermath of Dec. 7, 1941, when the Japanese Navy mounted a sneak attack against the U.S. Pacific Fleet at Pearl Harbor. But in the first weeks after the stunning terrorist strike, it was clear that the United States— with an ad hoc coalition of other nations — was heading to war.

President George W. Bush and his then-eight-month-old administration quickly set wheels in motion for a multi-layered military campaign (along with economic and political actions) to uproot the terrorist networks and retaliate against any nations that either harbored or supported them. He braced Americans for a protracted and difficult effort that he said will take years — rather than months or weeks — to carry out. That particular story, a global package of dispatches from multiple fronts, was still unfolding as this book went to press. It is a war with a home front as well, given the protracted anthrax poisoning incidents that have killed four people and sickened over a dozen more.

One immediate aftermath of the Sept. 11 disaster was a stunning reversal in American journalism priorities. For a decade after the 1991 Persian Gulf War, coverage of the armed forces, defense and intelligence issues and even foreign affairs had steadily dwindled as a result of economic trends and business decisions that forced print and broadcast operations to slash manpower and costs. Of equal significance, the nation itself had turned away from an interest in foreign and military news after victory in the desert, and the political slogan, "It's the economy, stupid," aptly defined journalism priorities up to the moment the twin towers of the World Trade Center came crashing down.

"[W]e are paying the price of our complacency — the price of a decade-long flight from seriousness in the way we view public affairs," *Newsweek* columnist Jonathan Alter eloquently wrote in his magazine's special edition report on the attacks. "The habit of thinking that international events have no significance at home has been exposed as just as dangerous as pre-World War II isolationism."

For American journalists in particular, the stunning events of Sept. 11, 2001 surely will be seen as a major turning point in coverage priorities. After a decade of neglect, reporters and editors and producers are clamoring to cover military events with the intensity and seriousness of purpose to match that of their predecessors at Normandy in 1944, Inchon in 1950, the Ia Drang Valley in 1965 and 73 Easting in the Iraqi desert in 1991.

But the road ahead for military reporters, never easy, will be tougher than ever. They will likely be attempting coverage in an atmosphere of operational security and military classification unprecedented since the one-day total news blackout imposed by then-Secretary of Defense (and now Vice President) Dick Cheney at the commencement of the ground offensive against Iraq on Feb. 24, 1991.

Based on my experience as a military reporter over the past two decades, I anticipate that many journalists will be rushed into the military beat totally unprepared for wartime coverage. Knowledge is fungible, and most reporters today have never had any previous contact with the military. That is a recipe for frustration, bewilderment and error.

The military constitutes an entirely separate culture within the larger boundaries of American society (its five uniformed services resembling more a roster of different tribes assembled in loose confederation rather than a single entity), and those who volunteer to cover a wartime campaign will not have much of a chance to catch up.

It is my sincere hope that this book will be a useful roadmap and guide that will assist the newly arrived reporter on the military beat in carrying out a grave and important task: Serving as an independent and honest link between the military at war and the wider civilian society it is sworn to defend.

Ed Offley
Springfield, Va.
November 2001

Introduction
Scenes from the military beat

The four MiG fighters roared out of the pre-dawn darkness, their engines at full throttle as they swept past the two U.S. Navy warships at masthead height.

On the dimly lit navigation bridge of the U.S. Navy guided missile frigate *USS Reuben James*, a team of officers and sailors on watch peered intently at radar screens and gazed through binoculars at the land mass rising out of the sea ahead. A full moon low on the western horizon threw a golden splash of light on the dark waters off to port, and a radio speaker came to life with the voices of Russian sailors on ships up ahead.

"Aircraft to starboard," a lookout shouted, and the MiG-21s screamed past the warship's mast a second time.

It was four a.m., and the *Reuben James* had just penetrated Soviet territorial waters.

This was a military reporter's dream assignment: To accompany and write about two U.S. Navy ships and their crews of 560 men on a 1,100-mile voyage into naval history. The *Reuben James* and the Aegis cruiser *USS Princeton* were not going into battle this morning on Sept. 10, 1990. Rather, they were conducting a mission of friendship and history as the U.S. Pacific Fleet paid its first visit in 53 years to the Soviet Navy bastion at Vladivostok.

The three-day trek up from Yokosuka, Japan, to the shores of Peter the Great Bay marked a dramatic reversal from the first military field coverage I had undertaken for the *Seattle Post-Intelligencer* just three years earlier.

In November 1987, I had traveled from Seattle to the outer Aleutian Islands to observe a major U.S. Navy fleet exercise that tested the Reagan administration's controversial "maritime strategy" by which the Pentagon planned to wage war on the Soviet Siberian littoral in response to a superpower clash elsewhere in the world. There, reporters had talked with aviators and sailors as the nuclear aircraft carrier *USS Enterprise* and several dozen other 3rd Fleet warships practiced combat operations in the Bering Sea. An admiral's press conference had been delayed when the giant carrier suddenly took an evasive maneuver to avoid colliding with a Soviet spy ship within sight of Adak Island. The Arctic waters, Navy officials said, were shoaling with Soviet submarines.

The following year, on a two-week assignment to South Korea, I had watched similar signs of the grim military standoff between American and Soviet forces. From the "primary flight" control tower of the carrier *USS Midway* in the Sea of Japan, I watched flight deck crewmen hurriedly launching F/A-18 Hornets and A-6E Intruders to intercept, if needed, a group of Soviet aircraft coming south out of Vladivostok into that small, but strategically vital, body of water. The announcer's voice echoed through the carrier, "Now launch the Alert 5 aircraft," confirming that reality had just intruded on the 1988 "Team Spirit" wargame where American and South Korean forces regularly honed their combat skills to deter communist aggression in the real world. A shadowy EP-3 signals-intelligence aircraft — the same type of surveillance aircraft that would make world headlines 13 years later in a confrontation with Chinese fighters off Hainan Island — monitored the radio transmissions of the Russian pilots and kept the carrier informed while it patrolled the Sea of Japan.

But that morning in September 1990 brought a different encounter to the fore. The Soviet aviators overhead carried a different message to the crews of the *Reuben James* and *Princeton*, and to the U.S. Navy where it was operating in all oceans of the world: a new era was dawning. "Welcome American sailors," proclaimed one banner from a Soviet coastal patrol boat emerging from the predawn haze. "Let's leave mistrust astern," another sign said. Soviet sailors in their teens waved their hats in unison, and their American comrades manning the rail, on cue, did the wave.

For the next five days, at formal ceremonies, informal parties and spontaneous gatherings throughout the Russian seaport, American and Soviet sailors made manifest the thaw in superpower tensions that signaled the end of the Cold War.

Opportunity calls

For the past 20 years I have had the great opportunity to work as a military reporting specialist covering the day-to-day life of military personnel from post ceremonies and routine training exercises to overseas maneuvers, peacekeeping operations and war.

When colleagues ask me why I enjoy a reporting job that can be as maddening and frustrating as none other in journalism, I cite my experience in Vladivostok as the type of assignment that makes all of the doublespeak, unreturned phone calls, bureaucracy and frustration worthwhile. There have been others:

■ On an Air Force resupply mission to the South Pole base camp — a 22-hour nonstop flight that required three separate in-flight refuelings — I was able to see the sun rise twice on the same day, and watch a rainbow form inside the windowless cargo fuselage as the side hatches were opened to the minus-150 degree temperature outside.

■ In a covered aircraft revetment in Taif, I studied the expressions of sheer excitement and joy of two Air Force fliers just returned from their first night combat mission over Iraq.

■ Crouching in a shallow trench in the pine woods of Louisiana, I watched through night-vision goggles as an armada of special-operations helicopters seemed to rise out of the trees as they hurtled toward a landing zone with an entire Army Ranger battalion in combat gear.

■ Several hundred feet below the surface of the Pacific Ocean, I watched the clockwork precision as the crew of a Trident missile submarine simulated the launch of 24 nuclear-tipped ballistic missiles in less than seven minutes.

■ At the border village of Panmunjom, I stared into the face of an armed North Korean army soldier two feet away on the other side of the line separating a free and prospering South Korea from the impoverished but militarized North.

■ In a shattered airport control tower in Mogadishu, I watched three young airmen just past their teens ignore the random gunfire outside as they coordinated a massive aerial supply campaign by the light of a battery-powered lantern.

But the rewards are not limited to interesting assignments, foreign travel and the adrenaline rush of a Scud missile attack. There is the satisfaction that comes when in-depth research pays off with the confirmation of a long-suppressed Cold War incident. (Did you know the United States once dropped an atomic bomb on Canada?)

There is the stronger fulfillment of coming to the assistance of a military service person or veteran who has suffered wrong-doing or inattention at the hands of the bureaucracy.

There is the sheer fun of exposing a phony self-described POW who never served a day in uniform.

And there is the potential that the facts that you uncover could significantly — and positively — affect an ongoing military policy debate.

The very nature of the military precludes ready access to ordinary citizens, yet its size, budget and life-and-death responsibilities span the globe and touch every citizen and taxpayer. Civilian understanding of the military is further hampered by a cultural separation between civilian and military communities, by the complexity of its high technology, by the rituals of military groups, and by the alienation by some civilian elites from the entire notion of a military role in American society. To the degree that American journalism is responsible for monitoring and charting the major institutions of our society, the military beat is a critically important specialty.

Today, the Defense Department finds itself at war with international terrorism while simultaneously grappling with a looming budgetary crisis that threatens a much-needed transformation of military structure, weapons and information technology.

To rephrase the old recruiting slogan: American journalism needs a few good military reporters. This book is offered as a road map for those reporters who volunteer for that difficult, complex but ultimately rewarding assignment.

Chapter 1

The U.S. Military Today
It's not your father's service

The U.S. military at the start of the 21st Century is the most powerful fighting force in the world, and its units operate across the globe in a wide spectrum of missions, ranging from defense against a North Korean invasion of South Korea to peacekeeping in Kosovo, from "no fly" combat air patrols over Iraq to a growing war against terrorists worldwide.

But at the start of a new century and decade, the armed forces also are bracing for a possible revolution in strategy, force employment and organization unprecedented in the past five decades. The transformation is being pushed by a combination of external factors, particularly the need to realign the U.S. military to confront an entire new array of threats, and a resource crisis caused in great part by the military's obsolete organizational structure and inefficient business practices.

A decade after the end of the Cold War superpower standoff with the former Soviet Union, the U.S. military today has shrunk considerably but still remains a vast and globe-spanning enterprise. Its roster consists of 1.37 million active-duty personnel, another 672,000 civilian employees and 1.35 million men and women serving in the reserves and National Guard. The Pentagon controls 18 million acres of land and operates 250 major bases and installations. The Defense Department has a current inventory of 15,000 aircraft, 250,000 vehicles and more than 1,000 seagoing vehicles, including 325 naval warships.

At any given moment the Pentagon has nearly 250,000 soldiers, sailors, airmen and Marines deployed overseas. To take a single snapshot of the U.S. military in one week in May 2001:

■ The Navy had deployed 105 ships — 33 percent of the fleet — and 48,286 sailors overseas, including 16 submarines, four aircraft carrier battle groups and five amphibious-ready groups with embarked Marine Corps combat units. This included 18 ships with 13,961 sailors and Marines operating in the Persian

Gulf; 21 ships and 12,963 sailors and Marines serving in the Mediterranean Sea, and another 38 ships with 19,355 sailors and Marines deployed in the western Pacific.

■ More than 140,000 Army personnel were stationed overseas or serving on foreign deployments at any given day in 2001. That constitutes nearly 30 percent of the ground service's active-duty roster of 479,426 soldiers, part of the total personnel roster of 1.2 million servicemen and women which also includes 206,836 reservists, 357,469 National Guard personnel, and 224,902 civilian employees. Soldiers overseas included about 70,000 in Europe, 29,000 in the Western Pacific (primarily Japan and South Korea), and another 3,500 serving in the Persian Gulf.

■ The Air Force, with a total of 355,654 personnel, operated 64,400 of them at overseas bases, while flying hundreds of airlift and combat training missions from the continental United States to overseas bases each day.

■ The U.S. had personnel operating in 130 foreign countries, ranging from as few as five personnel in Albania to 69,000 in Germany. These included 6,300 personnel serving as part of the international peacekeeping force in Kosovo, and another 3,300 soldiers with the six-year-old Bosnia peacekeeping operation. More than 18,000 U.S. military personnel were in Queensland, Australia, participating in the multi-national "Operation Tandem Thrust '01" war game along with Canadian and Australian personnel. Another 4,973 U.S. military personnel from the continental United States, Okinawa and Hawaii were participating in the 2001 "Cobra Gold" multi-national training exercise in Thailand along with Thai and Singaporean troops.

■ To pay for this, the Pentagon was spending about $305 billion in the 2000 fiscal year defense budget, an amount greater than that spent by the NATO Alliance members, Japan and South Korea combined. Defense spending ranged from B-2 stealth bomber production to day care facilities for 200,000 military dependent children. As in each month, the Defense Department executed about 920,000 contracts or purchase actions, wrote 5

Soviet sailors ignore a photographer while standing at a rigid brace during welcoming ceremonies for the U.S. fleet in Vladivostok. (Photo: Ed Offley, *Seattle Post-Intelligencer*)

million payroll checks, and recruited 207,000 new employees (while separating another 170,000 for retirement or discharge). The fraction of the Pentagon budget earmarked for infrastructure and support functions — approximately $200 billion of the $300 annual appropriation — was larger than the gross domestic product of 152 of the world's 190 nations.

But these statistics only showed part of the picture. The U.S. military today is in serious trouble. As former vice chairman of the Joint Chiefs of Staff Adm. William A. Owens recently observed in his book, *Lifting the Fog of War*, (with Ed Offley, Farrar, Straus & Giroux, New York, 2000):

> The armed forces have been cut by 40 percent in the last decade, but are still largely structured as they were during the Cold War. The unrelenting pace of overseas deployments, humanitarian missions and other unscheduled operations are straining military units and personnel to the breaking point. Combat readiness, the measurement of a unit's ability to carry out its wartime

mission, is declining throughout the military. The services are struggling with unanticipated personnel shortages due to a sharp decline in first-term enlistments and an exodus of experienced, mid-level career specialists.

This is further straining military units that are being forced to operate with as much as a 10 percent shortage in the number of personnel required to fill their ranks. And the Pentagon faces a crisis in its attempt to modernize the force as a result of insufficient funds to purchase the next generation of warships, combat aircraft and other military hardware to replace earlier generations of equipment that will become obsolete within the next decade or two.

Since 1989 the Pentagon budget itself has been cut by 25 percent (and the procurement subsection earmarked for new weapons and equipment was slashed by 70 percent). The end of the Cold War led the White House and Congress to cut the total force by 1 million active-duty and reserve personnel, a 33-percent cut. In the past decade the Pentagon reduced the Army from 18 to 10 divisions, a 44-percent reduction; shrank the Navy's aircraft carrier force from 15 to 11 flattops, a 26 percent drop; and what had been a 600-ship Navy in 1986 had plummeted to 325 ships

---

American involvement in major 20th Century wars
(See chapter 13 for chronology of minor conflicts)

World War I
U.S. involvement: 1917-1918
Main combatants: U.S., Great Britain, France, Italy, Russia vs. Germany, Austro-Hungary, Turkey

World War II
U.S. involvement: 1941-1945
Main combatants: U.S., Great Britain, France, Russia vs. Germany, Italy, Japan

Korean War
U.S. involvement: 1950-1953
Main combatants: U.S., Republic of Korea vs. North Korea, China

Vietnam War
U.S. involvement: 1965-1973
Main combatants: U.S., South Vietnamese vs. Viet Cong

Gulf War
U.S. involvement: 1990-1991
Main combatants: U.S. vs. Iraq

(and was slated to shrink even more) by 2001.

While no single country can match U.S. combat power today, and experts say it will be decades before the United States faces a serious "peer rival" who can assert military parity against this nation, the decisions on military reform and reorganization that will be made in the next 5-10 years will determine whether the Defense Department succeeds in preparing the nation's future military capabilities to deal with an increasingly volatile, dangerous and unpredictable security environment. While the feared crisis is perhaps a decade away, the solutions to that crisis will likewise require a decade or more to organize and carry out.

Former Pentagon acquisition chief Dr. Jacques Gansler described the current situation as a "death spiral" resulting from the annual migration of $10-15 billion from the Defense Department's procurement accounts to pay for unplanned maintenance and repairs on old and obsolete military equipment. As more funds have been required to maintain the current force, with less and less money available for modernization and replacement, the military finds itself operating with a physical infrastructure (from bases to aircraft, ships and weapons) that is heading for obsolescence across the board within the next decade. Other experts have coined the phrase "defense train wreck" to describe a nightmare scenario in which the United States experiences a virtual collapse of its military capability because of the cost of replacing the aging inventory with state-of-the-art weapons and systems.

This is a crisis well known to the small handful of fulltime military journalists, to the U.S. military leadership, and to the loosely-knit community of defense experts in Washington, D.C. think-tanks and congressional defense committees. But to many Americans, defense issues remain a peripheral concern of abstract importance far removed from their own daily lives.

During the height of the 2000 presidential race between Democratic nominee Al Gore and Republican nominee George W. Bush, one prominent political analyst attempted to characterize the significance of military and defense issues in the race. "It's not a major issue, it's not a front-burner issue — it's on the back burner, but that's the good news," said Dr. Larry Sabato, who has studied presidential campaigns for over 20 years. "It [defense] wasn't even on the stove in 1992 or 1996."

The incoming Bush administration in the winter and spring of 2001 clearly signaled that it planned to instigate a series of in-depth reviews of U.S. military strategy, force structure, modernization and business practices that could lead to unparalleled changes in the military. (A separate review of the sprawling U.S. intelligence community has also been launched.) To the shock of many in the armed services and Congress, Bush and newly-confirmed Secretary of Defense Donald H. Rumsfeld announced that any significant increases in defense spending would have to await the findings of the comprehensive review of the Defense Department.

Rumsfeld himself in his Senate confirmation hearings noted that deep reforms were overdue. "The legacy of obsolete institutional structures and processes and organizations does not merely create unnecessary [defense] costs," Rumsfeld told the Senate Armed Services Committee. "[I]t also imposes an unacceptable burden on national defense. In certain respects, it could be said we are in a sense disarming or 'underarming' by our failure to reform the acquisition process and to shed unneeded organization and facilities."

Although the formal findings of the Pentagon "top to bottom" review were still being reviewed at mid-year, press reports confirmed that the new Defense Department leadership was preparing for the most profound changes in the U.S. military since the end of World War II in 1945. Press reports indicated the shifts would include:

■ Dropping the goal that U.S. forces should be able to win two major regional wars almost simultaneously, a planning assumption that has dictated the size and structure of the armed services since before the 1991 Persian Gulf War, including the "end strength" (total personnel) of each service, the number of aircraft carriers, Army and Marine divisions, and operational Air Force combat wings.

■ Eliminating up to two-thirds of the nation's nearly 7,300 strategic nuclear warheads, but without first reaching a reciprocal arms deal with Russia.

■ Abandoning the 1972 Anti-Ballistic Missile Treaty with the (defunct) Soviet Union and pressing for both theater and national missile defense systems.

■ Shifting the primary focus of U.S. defense planning from Europe to the Asia-Pacific basin, where long-range Air Force bombers and Navy war ships might be more important than large Army ground forces.

■ Investing less modernization money in "platforms" — tanks, ships and aircraft designed for the Cold War and European combat — and spending more on lighter, more agile weapons, sensors, unmanned aerial vehicles and long-range, precision-guided munitions.

■ Preparing to expand the U.S. military's combat power into space as a defensive capability to protect the galaxy of military and civilian satellites on which both the Pentagon and private sector depend today for worldwide communications.

■ Privatizing hundreds of thousands of the military's administrative and maintenance jobs such as personnel who perform maintenance on aircraft and other combat equipment.

■ Pressing Congress for additional base closure commission hearings to rid the Pentagon of scores of excess military bases in the continental United States. (This was heading for congressional approval as this book went to press.)

These are not only the fundamental fault lines on which the transformation of the U.S. military will occur. They are also the major themes of the dominant news stories — over and above the ongoing campaign against terrorism — that will likely be written and broadcast in the next decade by military reporters at the Pentagon and local news organizations.

Industrial-era force in a cyberspace era

The current structure of the U.S. military reflects several centuries of human history and military organization intermingled and layered atop one another. The Army structure of brigades and battalions was first introduced to European armies during the Napoleonic era, while the service's new inter-vehicle information system — a low-powered communications network that enables groups of tanks or combat vehicles to plot all "friendly" vehicle locations in real time — reflects the service's commitment to using information technology on the battlefield. The Navy has done away with the hand-held sextant in favor of the Global Positioning System satellite network for precise navigation, but still ties its warships up to the pier the same way the Phoenicians did: With sailors straining on hemp ropes.

Even the most cursory study of the existing U.S. military system finds a strange combination of tradition and innovation that reflects the mixture of bureaucratic inertia and creative innovation that are both hallmarks of the American armed services.

Both the current Defense Department and military services themselves have steadily evolved from the original Army and Navy called for in the U.S. Constitution. The Army, Navy and Marine Corps are older than the nation itself, all three having been founded in 1775. The War Department was formed in 1789; nine years later the Navy formed its own department to manage Naval and Marine Corps affairs, with the Army remaining under the War Department. It remained that way until the end of World War II. In 1947, Congress passed a transforming National Security Act that created the modern defense establishment, placing the military services under the direct control of the Secretary of Defense, who held Cabinet rank. In addition, the legislation created an independent U.S. Air Force out of the wartime U.S. Army Air Corps, and established the Central Intelligence Agency to handle national intelligence-gathering functions. In 1949, Congress passed an amendment to the Act both establishing the agency as an executive department and renaming the former Department of War the Department of Defense. This structure has remained essentially unchanged to this day. (The one significant reform implemented during the late innings of the Cold War was the 1986 Goldwater-Nichols military reorganization act that centralized military administrative authority in the chairman of the Joint Chiefs of Staff, replacing a system in which the four service chiefs and chairman had an equal vote.)

Military structure basics
Who are these people?

It would take a separate book larger in size than this one to provide a detailed analysis of the organization and lines of authority of the Defense Department and its many components. Fortunately, the novice military reporter has immediate access to a wealth of information via the internet that can provide for a quick self-study on the particular military service(s), service branches and components, and other subordinate agencies that are pertinent to his or her coverage requirements (see Appendix 2 and Chapter 12, The Internet, Information Technology and Military Coverage, for specific references).

The following description is for basic familiarization to those who have never studied military structure and organization.

Civilian control of the military

Under the constitutional provisions establishing the executive branch, the leadership and control for military operations resides with the National Command Authority — a term used to collectively describe the president and the secretary of defense. The president, as commander-in-chief of the armed forces, is the ultimate authority over their employment. The office of the secretary of defense carries out the secretary's policies by tasking the three military departments for "providing" tasks such as budget, personnel policies, training and procurement, and the chairman of the Joint Chiefs of Staff for planning and coordinating deployments and operations.

The U.S. Army

The Army's mission is to defend the land mass of the United States and its territories, commonwealths and possessions and overcome any aggressor that imperils our nation's peace and security. As part of the evolving Defense Department policies mandating effective multiservice, or "joint" operations, the Army is structured so that it can operate effectively as a single-service combat or noncombatant force, or as part of a Joint Task Force with other military service components.

Led by a civilian secretary of the Army, the senior uniformed officer is the Army chief of staff, who is a member of the Joint Chiefs of Staff and who directs a Pentagon headquarters to supervise his service's administration, budget and planning.

From squads to corps

The current Army force structure is based on the triangular building block concept designed by Army leaders prior to World War II, as the following description of an infantry division, its subordinate components and higher echelons will show:

The *squad* is the basic element of ground combat, consisting of 8 to 15 soldiers divided into two or three fire teams. Led by a staff sergeant, the infantry squad in offensive ground operations advances on a front of 50 to 100 yards, and can defend a piece of territory 200 yards wide and deep. Squad weapons include the M-16 rifle, M-203 grenade launcher, M-249 Squad Automatic Weapon, and M-60 machine gun.

The *platoon*, commanded by a 2nd lieutenant, consists of three rifle squads and a heavy weapons squad (machine guns or mortars). Other specialists include radio operators and medics. On offense, controls an area 100 to 150 yards across.

The *company* consists of three or four platoons with a total of 400-500 soldiers, usually commanded by a captain. Three of the platoons are infantry while the fourth platoon has heavy weapons such as machine guns or light anti-tank rockets.

The *battalion*, commanded by a lieutenant colonel, is the Army's smallest unit that can maneuver and fight independently. Ranging in size between 600-1,500 soldiers, a battalion can contain between three and five companies, including tanks or artillery. The battalion fights on a front up to two miles across.

The *brigade*, with between 2,000-3,500 troops, has at least three combat battalions and other attached support units as needed including intelligence, artillery or combat engineers. It is commanded by a full colonel.

Note: Combat task forces are normally established within brigade or division-sized forces to handle the particular battlefield missions. For instance, a *battalion task force* might include a company of tanks from an armored brigade supporting two infantry companies from an infantry brigade, assisted by a company of attack helicopters from an aviation brigade.

The *division* is the primary Army combat organization, consisting of at least three combat brigades of about 3,000 soldiers apiece (infantry, mechanized infantry or armor) and supplemented with other, specialized brigades such as artillery, aviation, combat support or intelligence. Divisions have between 15,000-18,000 personnel depending on unique organizational requirements. The division is commanded by a major general with two brigadier generals as assistant division commanders. There are numerous variants of the divisional structure, ranging from the heavy armor division with its tank and mechanized infantry units, to the "light" 82nd Airborne Division and 10th Mountain Division which are organized around infantry units relying on air transport to deploy quickly to the battlefield.

There are four active corps headquarters commands in the U.S. Army responsible for directing multi-divisional operations in event of a major theater war. Commanded by a lieutenant general and identified by their Roman numeral title, they are I Corps at Fort Lewis, Wash., responsible for conducting Joint Task Force or Army operations in the Pacific theater (as well as training reserve and National Guard units); III Corps at Fort Hood, Tex., responsible for the Army's heavy armor and mechanized divisions and an ongoing "digital" transformation of the ground force; the V Corps, Heidelberg, Germany, responsible for Army units in Europe including Balkans peacekeeping mission troops; and the XVIII Airborne Corps, Fort Bragg, N.C., responsible for the Army's "first response" units such as the 82nd Airborne Division, 101st Air Assault Division and 10th Mountain Division. During Operation Desert Storm in 1991, the U.S. Army ground campaign included the XVIII Airborne Corps and the Germany-based VII Corps (subsequently deactivated) and their subordinate divisions.

Numbered Army headquarters commands are still utilized as major theater administrative headquarters. For example, the 8th U.S. Army is the major component commander for all Army units in South Korea, while the 3rd U.S. Army headquarters at Fort McPherson, Ga., is the ground force component commander for the U.S. Central Command.

Other Army formations include the *armored cavalry regiment,* a mini-division organized around heavy tank and infantry fighting vehicles that serves as an advance screen for a deployed corps and its divisions; and brigade-sized *special forces groups* consisting of three battalions that break down into companies or 12-man special forces *A-teams* for counter-insurgency and special operations in designated geographical areas.

Critical issue: The overarching issue confronting the U.S. Army leadership is to overcome a nascent military and political movement within the Defense Department that would de-emphasize U.S. military ground power in favor of naval/Marine and aerospace force. To do that, the Army has launched a dual-track transformation plan that will make the service more mobile and lethal in the decades ahead. The "digital division" plan, which has been underway since the mid-1990s, aims at expanding combat power and command-and-control effectiveness by embedding the latest in information technology hardware throughout a division's chain of command. A more profound transformation program unveiled in August 2000 aims at re-equipping Army combat units with lighter and more easily-deployed wheeled combat vehicles as opposed to heavy M-1A1 tanks, infantry fighting vehicles and self-propelled artillery that have to be either stored on cargo ships or pre-positioned in crisis areas such as Korea or Kuwait. Both initiatives have sparked widespread debate within the Army, Pentagon and Congress over their ultimate cost and value, and are expected to take several decades to complete.

The U.S. Navy

The Navy's mission is to maintain, train and equip combat-ready naval forces capable of winning wars, deterring aggression and maintaining freedom of the seas. It does so in close formal partnership with the U.S. Marine Corps, both of which are controlled by the Navy Department and its civilian secretary. In time of war, the U.S. Coast Guard — the nation's fifth uniformed service — transfers from the Transportation Department to the Navy Department for operational control.

The Navy is organized into a Shore Establishment and Operating Forces, both of which report administratively to the senior uniformed naval officer, the Chief of Naval Operations. The Shore Establishment consists of the Navy's Pentagon headquarters and a host of agencies ranging from the Naval Sea Systems Command, responsible for designing ships, nuclear propulsion and weapons; to the Naval Supply Systems Command, which operates the service's depots and supply processes. The Operating Forces consist of the Atlantic and Pacific Fleet headquarters, U.S. Naval Forces Europe and U.S. Naval Forces Central Command, which control the Navy's five numbered fleets, as well as subordinate type commanders (e.g. COMNAVAIRPAC, the Pacific Fleet Naval Air Forces, is responsible for the bases, aircraft carriers and shore-based carrier squadrons operating various combat and support aircraft).

The numbered fleets, which are assigned operational missions in specific geographical areas under the appropriate Unified Command headquarters, include the U.S. 2nd Fleet in the Atlantic; U.S. 6th Fleet in the Mediterranean; U.S. 5th Fleet in the Persian Gulf/Southwest Asia region; U.S. 7th Fleet in the western Pacific; and U.S. 3rd Fleet in the eastern Pacific.

As will be discussed below, there is a separate operational chain of command where Navy and Marine Corps units are "chopped," or formally placed under the control of, a specific Unified Combat Command when they deploy overseas. For instance, when the destroyer *USS Cole* was preparing to deploy from Norfolk, Va., to the Mediterranean and Persian Gulf in 2000, it was under the administrative control of the U.S. Atlantic Fleet and its subordinate administrative headquarters, Naval Surface Forces, U.S. Atlantic Fleet. But upon arrival in the Mediterranean, the *Cole* formally became an operating unit of the U.S. 6th Fleet headquartered in Gaeta, Italy, and when it crossed into the Red Sea via the Suez Canal and entered the harbor at Aden, Yemen, the destroyer shifted to the operational control of the U.S. Central Command and its naval component, the Bahrain-based U.S. 5th Fleet.

In 2001, the Navy inventory included 11 aircraft carriers, including eight *Nimitz*-class nuclear-powered carriers (with a ninth under construction) and three conventional-propulsion flattops. Its surface force included 27 *Aegis*-class guided missile cruisers, 40 *Burke*-class and 22 older *Spruance*-class destroyers, and 32 active-duty *Perry*-class guided missile frigates. The

Navy's submarine service included a force of 18 *Ohio*-class guided missile submarines, four *Virginia*-class nuclear attack submarines (all under construction), two advanced *Seawolf*-class nuclear attack submarines (with a third under construction) and 51 *Los Angeles*-class attack subs. In partnership with the Marine Corps, the Navy today operates a fleet of 36 amphibious ships to deploy in the form of Amphibious Ready Groups with battalion-sized Marine Expeditionary Units.

Other Operating Forces elements include the Naval Special Warfare Command, responsible for training and deploying combat-ready SEAL Team commandos; the Military Sealift Command and its array of 119 noncombatant, civilian-crewed supply and support ships; and the Naval Reserve Force and its 23 warships, including the carrier *USS John F. Kennedy.*

Critical issue: The most serious problem confronting the Navy today is a serious backlog in new ship and aircraft procurement during the 1990s which, if not reversed, will result in a steady shrinking of the fleet and its air arm as older ships and aircraft inevitably retire due to obsolescence. In 2000, Navy leaders and defense experts said the fleet inventory of 325 ships was below the minimum number of 360 ships calculated as required to carry out the Pentagon's existing deployment requirements (including 12 carrier battle groups and 12 amphibious-ready groups). Experts calculate to maintain that number of ships over time, the Defense Department needs funds to construct on average 8.5 ships a year, but during the 1990s the number fluctuated between 6-8 new construction contracts per year. Similarly, the Navy's inventory of carrier-based F-14 Tomcats, S-3 Vikings and EA-6B Prowlers were inexorably flying toward their design-life obsolescence as the Pentagon wrestled among three planned new tactical aircraft programs — the Navy F/A-18E/F Super Hornet, Air Force-Navy Joint Strike Fighter and Air Force F-22 — which combined had a total pricetag of over $350 billion, a monetary amount many experts said is simply too large to fully fund.

The U.S. Marine Corps

The call "Send in the Marines!" has been sounded more than 200 times since the end of World War II, an average of once every 90 days. In 1999 alone, Marines provided humanitarian assistance to earthquake victims in Turkey, were among the first U.S. ground troops to enter Kosovo and formed the core of U.S. peacekeeping efforts in East Timor. The Marine Corps maintains expeditionary forces in readiness, provides sea-based, integrated air-ground units for contingency and combat operations, and suppresses or contains international disturbances.

With an active end strength of 171,142 active-duty personnel and 39,000 reservists, the Marine Corps remains the smallest of the four combat services. But due to the shifting geopolitical environment of the 1990s that saw a rise in the number of crises and emergencies requiring U.S. military intervention at short notice, the Marine Corps evaded the large-scale cuts that were imposed on the Navy, Army and Air Force.

Administratively led by the Navy Department and civilian Navy secretary, the Marine Corps' senior officer is the commandant, who is a member of the Joint Chiefs of Staff. The Marine Corps is administratively organized into three active-duty divisions and subordinate units of more than 40,000 personnel apiece (the 1st Marine Division, Camp Pendleton, Cal.; the 2nd Marine Division at Camp Lejeune, N.C.; and the 3rd Marine Division at Camp Courteney, Okinawa), along with the reserve 4th Marine Division. However, for combat operations, the Corps task organizes its units into division-sized Marine Expeditionary Forces (containing both ground and combat aviation units), brigade-sized regimental combat teams, and smaller Marine Expeditionary Units of about 2,200 personnel each with an attached "composite" squadron of supply and attack helicopters. In 2001, the Marines operated seven MEUs (three at Camp Pendleton, three at Camp Lejeune and one on Okinawa) earmarked for forward deployment aboard Navy amphibious ships.

Critical issue: The Marine Corps' most pressing problem in 2001 was the serious state of decline of its aviation arm as a result of obsolescence of a number of aircraft, and controversy over the development of the revolutionary hybrid MV-22 Osprey aircraft which takes off and lands like a helicopter but flies like a fixed-wing aircraft. The fatal crash of two Ospreys six months apart, and subsequent allegations that maintenance records had been falsified to present a better-than-actual readiness record, prompted a number of experts to warn that the program might be cancelled.

The U.S. Air Force

The Air Force provides America a rapid, flexible, and when necessary, a lethal air and space capability. It can deliver forces anywhere in the world in less than 48 hours. It routinely participates in peacekeeping, humanitarian and aeromedical evacuation missions and is actively patrolling the skies above Iraq and

National Guard and Reserve: Key players

The U.S. military has long relied heavily on part-time soldiers, sailors, airmen, Marines and Coast Guardsmen to fill the wartime ranks of the armed services. In June 2001 there were 1.35 million reservists and National Guardsmen as a potential reinforcement to the active-duty roster of 1.37 million personnel.

The Army Reserve (431,447), Army National Guard (367,157) and Navy Reserve (206,167) are the largest three reserve categories.

The Reserve Component, as it is formally known, consists of three building blocks: Reserve Units belonging to the five uniformed services who train and serve as an organization; Individual Ready Reservists who are subject to recall to active duty and assignment to a unit in event of an emergency or war; and the National Guard, whose members in peacetime report to the governors of the states and territories but train in units for a wartime mission under Defense Department control should the president formally "federalize" them to active duty.

Reservists and National Guardsmen have played key roles in nearly all major American military endeavors. For example, 169,000 Army reservists served in World War I, 15 Naval Reservists earned the Medal of Honor during World War II, and Air National Guardsmen flew 39,530 combat sorties during the Korean War.

Bosnia. Air Force crews annually fly missions into all but five nations of the world. Its job is to defend the United States through control and exploitation of air and space.

Led by a civilian secretary of the Air Force and a four-star Air Force chief of staff, the air service today fields a total force of 355,654 personnel who operate or support a fleet of 4,440 aircraft across a broad field of 66 different categories, including bombers, fighters, cargo aircraft, helicopters, electronic warfare and surveillance aircraft, air-to-ground gunships and trainers. The Air Force is also responsible for the land-based strategic missile force, and recently assumed primary responsibilities for managing future defensive and offensive operations in space. The air

Under the Pentagon "Total Force" policy enacted in the early 1970s toward the end of the Vietnam War, the Defense Department reorganized the Reserve Component, shifting a large number of critical wartime specialties from the active force to the reserves and National Guard. This included many combat service support, military intelligence, civil affairs and psychological operations units.

This served a two-fold purpose: Since these specialties are not needed in peacetime, the Defense Department saves a lot of money relying on part-time reservists to fill the ranks; but on a deeper level, the wartime generals and admirals wanted to ensure that — unlike in Vietnam — if the nation ever had to fight a major war again, no president could avoid confronting the American people with the need for a widespread mobilization affecting both the civilian and military communities.

Over 200,000 reservists and National Guardsmen were called to active duty in the 1991 Persian Gulf War. As of mid-October 2001, the Pentagon had activated 29,387 reservists and Guardsmen from 237 units in 44 states, the District of Columbia and Puerto Rico to serve in Operation Enduring Freedom.

Local reserve and Guard units can be located in the U.S. government pages of your telephone book or by contacting local military base public affairs offices. Each state has a separate Military Department that administers Army and Air National Guard units.

service also has a lead role in the emerging Pentagon effort to devise a national defensive and offensive capability for cyberwar.

Its active-duty fleet in 2001 included 21 B-2 stealth bombers, 73 swept-wing B-1 Lancer bombers and a residual force of 85 1960s-era B-52H bombers. Fighters included the 1970s-era F-15 and F-16, the 1980s-era F-117A stealth fighter, and the new F-22 Raptor, of which only several test models had been built. The air mobility arm consisted of 43 (out of 120 planned) C-17 Globemaster III cargo planes, 122 aging C-141B Starlifters (which are programmed for retirement by mid-decade) and 81 giant C-5 Galaxy cargo planes, which are a critical airlift asset because of their ability to deliver outsized cargo. The Air Force Reserves and Air National Guard maintained a smaller fleet of 446 aircraft spread across the same categories of combat and support functions.

The smallest operational organization in the Air Force is the squadron, which usually has between 12 and 30 assigned aircraft, but can have as few as two and as many as 67 aircraft in specific cases. The dominant administrative unit is the wing, normally assigned to a single Air Force base, which may have between two and five squadrons operating either a single type of aircraft or a variety of aircraft. As a result of a continuous high operational tempo throughout the 1990s, the Air Force in 2000 unveiled 17 new "Aerospace Expeditionary Force" wings formally staffed with different squadrons to carry out combat or airlift missions overseas on a pre-scheduled basis. These include 10 combat AEF wings, two "on-call" combat wings on a quasi-permanent alert status, and five air mobility wings.

The missile force consisted of seven numbered space wings that operated the Peacekeeper and Minuteman intercontinental ballistic missiles, conducted satellite launch operations in Florida and California, and controlled the military satellite networks.

Critical issue: Delayed modernization of major aircraft systems was the most important problem for the Air Force in 2001, particularly as both the F-22 Raptor — deemed the service's highest-priority program — and multi-mission Joint Strike Fighter were candidates for Pentagon and congressional scrutiny (and possible cancellation) due to ongoing reviews of the military strategy and service missions. Other concerns included a push to obtain more C-17 airlift aircraft to sustain the service's mobility requirements, and development of both Unmanned Aerial Vehicles and new space systems.

The multi-service unified commands

Operational control of the U.S. military combat forces is held by the commanders-in-chief of the Unified Combatant Commands. The chain of command runs from the president to the secretary of defense to the Unified Commanders-in-Chief. Orders and other communications from the president or secretary are transmitted through the chairman of the Joint Chiefs of Staff. A Unified Combatant Command is composed of forces from two or more services, has a broad and continuing mission and is normally organized on a geographical basis. The number of unified combatant commands is not fixed by law or regulation and may vary from time to time. The current commands are:

European Command

The U.S. European Command is responsible for all U.S. military activities in Europe, most of Africa and Israel, Lebanon and Syria, and the South Atlantic Ocean. Headquartered at Heidelberg, Germany, its components include U.S. Air Forces Europe, U.S. Army Europe and U.S. Naval Forces Europe, with the U.S. 6th Fleet, two Army divisions and six Air Force wings permanently deployed overseas. (Most of these units are also integrated into the NATO Alliance command structure.) Operations include enforcing the Iraq "no fly" zone from Turkey, and peacekeeping operations in Bosnia and Kosovo.

Central Command

The U.S. Central Command oversees the balance of the Middle East, parts of Africa and west Asia, and part of the Indian Ocean. Headquartered at MacDill Air Force Base, Fla., its components include the U.S. 5th Fleet in Bahrain, III U.S. Army at Fort McPherson, Ga., and 9th Air Force at Shaw Air Force Base, S.C. Current operations include permanent training with Kuwaiti forces and enforcement of the southern Iraq "no fly" zone from Saudi Arabia and deployed Navy warships.

Southern Command

The U.S. Southern Command, headquartered in Miami, guards U.S. interests in the Southern Hemisphere, including Central America, South America and the Caribbean. Its current operations include an array of counter-drug missions in the Caribbean, Central and South America.

Pacific Command

The U.S. Pacific Command covers 50 percent of the Earth's surface including the Pacific Ocean, Indian Ocean, Australia and Alaska. Its components include the U.S. Pacific Fleet (which controls half of the Navy) and two numbered fleets, the U.S. 7th Fleet headquartered in Yokosuka, Japan, and the U.S. 3rd Fleet based in San Diego, Calif. The Pacific Air Forces include four numbered air forces (the 5th Air Force at Yokota Airbase, Japan; 7th Air Force at Osan Airbase, South Korea; 11th Air Force at Elmendorf Air Force Base, Alaska; and 13th Air Force at Andersen Air Force Base, Guam). Together they control nine Air Force fighter, air base and composite wings with 378 aircraft and over 44,000 personnel. The U.S. Army Pacific component includes the I Corps headquarters at Fort Lewis, the 25th Infantry Division based in Hawaii and a brigade in Alaska. In addition, the U.S. Forces Korea Command includes the 2nd Infantry Division as well as the 7th Air Force and a naval headquarters. Current operations include the defense of South Korea and Japan.

Joint Forces Command

The U.S. Joint Forces Command, headquartered in Norfolk, Va., has a unique mission. While the other combatant commands are categorized either as geographic (e.g., U.S. European Command) or as functional (e.g., U.S. Space Command), the Joint Forces Command is a hybrid of both categories.

Its main effort centers on the functional role as the chief advocate for "jointness" — inter-operability and coordination among the four combat services — and is the leader in ongoing efforts to transform U.S. military strategy, tactics, weapons and information technology. But the Joint Forces Command also retains geographical responsibility for the North Atlantic and adjacent Arctic and subarctic waters.

The Joint Forces Command, with a headquarters staff of 645

active-duty and 386 reserve personnel, has control over 437,047 active-duty personnel and another 778,000 reservists based in the continental United States in four subordinate — component — commands: the U.S. Army Forces Command at Fort McPherson, Ga.; the U.S. Atlantic Fleet, headquartered at Norfolk; the Air Force Air Combat Command, headquartered at Langley Air Force Base, Va.; and the Marine Corps Forces Atlantic, also headquartered at Norfolk.

The four-star officer serving as commander of Joint Forces Command also wears another hat as the Supreme Allied Commander Atlantic, a major NATO Alliance military command, with 400 headquarters staff members from 17 of the 19 NATO nations. In this role he is responsible for alliance military operations throughout the Atlantic Ocean region.

Space Command

The U.S. Space Command, headquartered at Peterson Air Force Base, Colo., launches and operates satellites; supports joint-service military forces worldwide with intelligence, communications, weather, navigation, and ballistic missile attack warning information; engages adversaries from space; assures U.S. access to and operation in space; and denies enemies that same freedom. Its Air Force, Navy and Army components support the multi-service command headquarters on a wide variety of missions, including space launch operations, satellite network management, North American aerospace defense (including ballistic missile early warning), and a new mission to organize and carry out cyberspace defensive and offensive operations.

Special Operations Command

Created in 1986 under legislation reorganizing U.S. military authority, the multi-service U.S. Special Operations Command, headquartered at MacDill Air Force Base, Fla., provides counter-paramilitary, counter-narcotics, guerilla, psychological warfare, civil education, and insurgency capability. Its components include the Air Force Special Operations Command at Hurlburt Field, Fla., the U.S. Army Special Operations Command at Fort Bragg, N.C., and Naval Special Warfare units at San Diego, Cal. and Little Creek, Va.

Transportation Command

The U.S. Transportation Command, headquartered at Scott Air Force Base, Ill., is responsible for moving things and people around the world, specifically providing air, land and sea transportation for the Department of Defense in time of peace and war. Its components include the Air Force Air Mobility Command, U.S. Army Military Traffic Management Command, and Military Sealift Command.

Strategic Command

The Strategic Command, based at Offutt Air Force Base, Neb., deters conventional and nuclear attacks on the U.S. and its allies. Its forces include land-based bombers, intercontinental ballistic missiles and sea-based Trident nuclear submarines and support assets.

How to...
Understand military rank

To the outsider, military rank is at once baffling and yet readily understandable once you learn the basics.

Despite different specific rank titles, each of the armed services has three tiers of personnel. They are commissioned and warrant officers; noncommissioned officers (sergeants and petty officers); and junior enlisted personnel.

The enlisted and officer manpower rosters for each of the services resembles a pyramid, with the number of personnel of each rank shrinking as you ascend the chain of command. For instance, the Air Force in June 2001 had a total of 280,007 active-duty enlisted personnel of which 130,220, or 46 percent, were in the lowest four ranks: Airman Basic (E-1), Airman (E-2), Airman 1st Class (E-3) and Senior Airman (E-4). The next five rank tiers — noncommissioned officers — continue the pyramidal structure: There were 69,634 Staff Sergeants (E-5), 42,139 Technical Sergeants (E-6), 29,463 Master Sergeants (E-7), 5,731 Senior Master Sergeants (E-8) and only 2,820 Chief Master Sergeants (E-9).

The officer cadre in each service has a similar pyramidal shape. For the Air Force, the lower three officer ranks in 2001 — 2nd Lieutenant (0-1), 1st Lieutenant (0-2) and Captain (0-3) — comprised 39,105 of the service's 68,689 commissioned officers, or 56 percent of the total. And as you ascend the rank structure from Major (O-4) to four-star General (O-10), the number of personnel in each category also declines sharply. There were 15,405 Majors, 10,081 Lieutenant Colonels (O-5), 3,832 Colonels (0-6), 137 Brigadier Generals (0-7), 80 Major Generals (0-8), 38 Lieutenant Generals (0-9) and 11 four-star Generals (0-10).

One interesting set of facts that emerges from these numbers is the increasing competition for promotion as you climb the rank structure. For instance, two out of every three Captains are promoted to Major, while the number of Majors selected for Lieutenant Colonel is slightly less, at 64 percent. But the number of Lieutenant Colonels advanced to Colonel sharply diminishes: Only 38 percent of Lieutenant Colonels can expect to advance to Colonel.

Special notes on addressing Navy petty officers

Enlisted personnel earn specialty designations in their particular jobs. In the Army, Marines and Air Force these designations are not indicated in their insignia nor are they used when addressing the individual.

However, Navy enlisted petty officers have their specialty, called a "rating," indicated with a special insignia underneath the eagle on their badge. When writing a Navy petty officer's title before his or her name, you may simply write the rank (e.g., PO2 for a petty officer second class). However, you may choose to indicate both the individual's rank and rating by writing out the entire title. For instance, if Frank Jones is a petty officer second class and a yeoman, you may identify him as Yeoman Second Class Frank Jones. On internal Navy documents you will often see an individual's rank and rating identified only with the appropriate rating initials followed by a numeral 3, 2 or 1 (for third, second or first class) or C, SC or MC (for chief, senior chief or master chief). For example, if Mary Smith is an intelligence specialist and a senior chief petty officer, she will be identified as ISSC Smith. See http://www.chinfo.navy.mil/navpalib/allhands/ranks/ratings/ratings.html for a chart of Navy ratings.

Making flag rank is even more competitive by an entire order of magnitude: Only 3 percent of Colonels can expect to pin on the single star of a Brigadier General. But if an officer surmounts this most difficult of all promotion obstacles, he or she will have more than even odds to become a two-star general. About 58 percent of the service's Brigadier Generals receive promotions to Major General. From there, it is nearly even odds to attain three-star rank: The Air Force has 38 Lieutenant Generals selected from a pool of 80 Major Generals, or 47 percent. To attain the supreme rank as a four-star general, the odds tighten again to slightly more than one in four, with 11 four-star general slots for which those 38 Lieutenant Generals compete.

Footnote: Officers who go on to become 3- and 4-star admirals and generals are not selected by promotion boards, but instead are recommended for promotion either by committees composed of their service's senior 3- and 4-star counterparts, or by the chairman of the Joint Chiefs of Staff or even the secretary of defense and president. As one Marine general told put it, "At that level, there is a job opening (requiring a 3- or 4-star officer) and the job comes looking for you." For instance, a three-star general responsible for his service's budget and plans would likely be selected by the Air Force uniformed leadership in coordination with the civilian secretariat, while the nominee for chairman, Joint Chiefs of Staff is selected by the secretary of defense and president. All 3- and 4-star generals and admirals require confirmation by the U.S. Senate.

There is one unavoidable source of confusion for those encountering the military rank structure for the first time: The commonality of specific terms employed for different ranks, and the use of the same title for different ranks in different military services. You will find the term *Lieutenant* in six different military titles: 2nd Lieutenant (0-1) (Army, Air Force, Marines); 1st Lieutenant (0-2) (Army, Air Force, Marines); Lieutenant (0-3) (Navy/Coast Guard); Lieutenant Commander (0-4) (Navy/Coast Guard); Lieutenant Colonel (0-5) (Army, Air Force, Marines), and Lieutenant General (Army, Air Force, Marines). Then there is the rank of *Captain*, which in three of the services is a mid-level officer (0-3) (Army, Air Force, Marines), but a senior officer (0-6) in the other two (Navy and Coast Guard). And, of course, the rank title of every enlisted person in the Army, Air Force and Marine Corps between the rank of E-5 and E-9 contains the word *Sergeant*; while Navy and Coast Guard NCO ranks E-7 through E-9 are a variant of the term *Chief Petty Officer* (see accompanying chart).

I have found that there is only way to overcome this semantic chaos: Study the rank chart long enough that you assimilate the specific titles for each rank.

Commissioned officers

These are men and women who upon graduation from a military service academy, or civilian college and an officer training program such as Officer Candidate School or Reserve Officer Training Corps, become commissioned officers in the Army, Navy, Air Force, Marine Corps and Coast Guard.

There are also a limited number of warrant officers in the Army, Navy, Coast Guard and Marine Corps (but not Air Force) who receive these special commissions after rising through the enlisted ranks. In addition, a small number of senior enlisted personnel may receive commissions as limited duty officers (usually the lower three ranks) because they hold an important technical specialty.

There are ten ranks for officers corresponding to the separate pay grade description of 0-1 (the lowest) to 0-10 (four-star rank). As they acquire time in service and professional experience, officers proceed up the rank structure, serving at that level for a number of years as they hold down jobs commensurate with a particular rank. Promotion boards consisting of senior officers regularly convene to select individual officers for elevation to the next rank. A synopsis of officer rankings is as follows:

Ensign/2nd Lieutenant and Lieutenant (Junior Grade)/1st Lieutenant

Upon receiving their commissions, junior officers serve for their first four or five years in positions that are comparable to management trainee functions at a large corporation. For example, Navy and Air Force fliers spend nearly two years in various flight schools before joining operational squadrons, while Air Force, Army and Marine lieutenants receive advanced training (e.g. Army Ranger school) before commanding small units such as platoons or "flights" under the close supervision of more senior officers and assisted by senior enlisted personnel.

Lieutenant/Captain

Promotion to this rank usually occurs between 3-10 years after commissioning. Scope of responsibilities ranges from command of an Army infantry or armored company (several hundred soldiers), to command of a ship's division. During this time they are engaged in their primary military specialty such as flying aircraft, operating warship systems or combat equipment. They will also serve at least one three-year staff assignment ranging from ROTC instructor, junior aide to a senior officer, or staff officer in the Pentagon or field headquarters.

Lieutenant Commander/Major
These career officers, with anywhere between 10 and 20 years in service, may hold more senior operational commands such as executive officer of a Navy destroyer or attack submarine, or brigade or divisional staff positions.

Commander/Lieutenant Colonel
This is the first rank for many prime combat unit commands. A Navy or Coast Guard Commander is the commanding officer of all but the largest warships, and his or her counterpart in the ground services would command either an infantry battalion or Air Force or Navy squadron. Promotion to this rank normally comes after 15 years of service.

Captain/Colonel
This is the ultimate rank attained by a majority of commissioned officers, and is usually attained after 22-25 years of active duty. Colonels and Captains (0-6) command Army brigades, Navy and Air Force aircraft wings and Navy aircraft carriers.

Rear Admiral (LH)/Brigadier General
A small percentage of Colonels and Captains will be selected for one-star rank, which comes usually after 25 years in the service. Navy Rear Admirals (lower half) command carrier battle groups, while Brigadier Generals serve as assistant Army or Marine Corps division commanders. Those holding this rank also serve in senior Pentagon staff positions.

Rear Admiral (UH)/Major General
Two-star flag officers reach this rank usually as they approach the 30-year mark in their careers. In the Army and Marine Corps, they command divisions, while in the Air Force and Navy they hold senior administrative command posts.

Vice Admiral/Lieutenant General

Promotion to three-star rank usually comes after three to five years as a Major General or Rear Admiral (UH). Officers in this rank command Navy numbered Fleets, Air Force numbered Air Forces and Army corps headquarters commands, as well as senior deputy staff positions at the Pentagon or Unified Military Commands.

Admiral/General

The 33 four-star generals and admirals in the U.S. military serve in two broad arenas: They comprise the chairman and vice chairman, Joint Chiefs of Staff as well as the four 4-star uniformed service leaders (Army and Air Force chiefs of staff, chief of naval operations and Marine Corps commandant), or their deputies. They also hold down the command slots of the nine Unified Combatant Commands (such as the U.S. European Command and U.S. Strategic Command) and the major service component commands (U.S. Pacific Air Forces, U.S. Atlantic Fleet). Other four-star officers command unique headquarters such as the Combined Forces Command Korea or the Navy's Nuclear Propulsion Program.

Enlisted Rank Insignia

Army	Marines	Navy/Coast Guard	Air Force
Paygrade - E-1 (No insignia)			
Private Say: Private Write: PV	**Private** Say: Private Write: Pvt. .	**Seaman Recruit** Say: Seaman Write: SR	**Airman Basic** Say: Airman Write: Amn
Paygrade - E-2			
Private E-2 Say: Private Write: PV2	**Private First Class** Say: PFC Write: PFC	**Seaman Apprentice** Say: Seaman Write: SA	**Airman** Say: Airman Write: Amn
Paygrade - E-3			
Private First Class Say: Private Write: PFC	**Lance Corporal** Say: Lance Corporal Write: LCpl	**Seaman** Say: Seaman Write: SN	**Airman First Class** Say: Airman Write: A1C
Paygrade - E-4			

Army Specialist is an alternate E-4 rank for Corporal.

Specialist
Say: Specialist
Write: SPC

Army	Marines	Navy/Coast Guard	Air Force
Paygrade - E-4			

Corporal Say: Corporal Write: CPL	**Corporal** Say: Corporal Write: Cpl	**Petty Officer Third Class** Say: Petty Officer Write: PO3	**Senior Airman** Say: Airman Write: SrA
Paygrade - E-5			
Sergeant Say: Sergeant Write: SGT	**Sergeant** Say: Sergeant Write: Sgt	**Petty Officer Second Class** Say: Petty Officer Write: PO2	**Staff Sergeant** Say: Sergeant Write: SSgt
Paygrade - E-6			
Staff Sergeant Say: Sergeant Write: SSG	**Staff Sergeant** Say: Sergeant Write: SSgt	**Petty Officer First Class** Say: Petty Officer Write: PO1	**Technical Sergeant** Say: Sergeant Write: TSgt

Army	Marines	Navy/Coast Guard	Air Force

Paygrade - E-7

Sergeant First Class Say: Sergeant First Class Write: SFC	**Gunnery Sergeant** Say: Gunnery Sergeant Write: GySgt	**Chief Petty Officer** Say: Chief Write: CPO	**Master Sergeant** Say: Sergeant Write: MSgt

Paygrade - E-8

Master Sergeant Say: Master Sergeant Write: MSG	**Master Sergeant** Say: Master Sergeant Write: MSgt	**Senior Chief Petty Officer** Say: Senior Chief Write: SCPO	**Senior Master Sergeant** Say: Sergeant Write: SMSgt

Paygrade - E-9

Sergeant Major Say: Sergeant Major Write: SGM	**Sergeant Major** Say: Sergeant Major Write: SgtMaj	**Master Chief Petty Officer** Say: Master Chief Write: MCPO	**Chief Master Sergeant** Say: Chief Write: CMSgt

Officer Rank Insignia

Army	Marines	Air Force	Navy/Coast Guard
Paygrade - O-1			
(Gold)	(Gold)	(Gold)	
2nd Lieutenant Say: Lieutenant Write: 2LT	**2nd Lieutenant** Say: Lieutenant Write: 2nd Lt.	**2nd Lieutenant** Say: Lieutenant Write: 2nd Lt.	**Ensign** Say: Ensign Write: ENS
Paygrade - O-2			
(Silver)	(Silver)	(Silver)	
First Lieutenant Say: Lieutenant Write: 1LT	**First Lieutenant** Say: Lieutenant Write: 1st Lt.	**First Lieutenant** Say: Lieutenant Write: 1st Lt.	**Lieutenant Junior Grade** Say: Lieutenant Write: LTJG

Army	Marines	Air Force	Navy/Coast Guard

Paygrade - O-3

(Silver)	(Silver)	(Silver)	
Captain	**Captain**	**Captain**	**Lieutenant**
Say: Captain	Say: Captain	Say: Captain	Say: Lieutenant
Write: CPT	Write: Capt.	Write: Capt.	Write: LT

Paygrade - O-4

(Gold)	(Gold)	(Gold)	
Major	**Major**	**Major**	**Lieutenant Commander**
Say: Major	Say: Major	Say: Major	Say: Commander
Write: MAJ	Write: Maj.	Write: Maj.	Write: LCDR

Paygrade - O-5

(Silver)	(Silver)	(Silver)	
Lieutenant Colonel	**Lieutenant Colonel**	**Lieutenant Colonel**	**Commander**
Say: Colonel	Say: Colonel	Say: Colonel	Say: Commander
Write: LTC	Write: Lt. Col.	Write: Lt. Col.	Write: CDR

Army	Marines	Air Force	Navy/Coast Guard
Paygrade - O-6			

(Silver)	(Silver)	(Silver)	
Colonel	**Colonel**	**Colonel**	**Captain**
Say: Colonel	Say: Colonel	Say: Colonel	Say: Captain
Write: COL	Write: Col.	Write: Col.	Write: CAPT
Paygrade - O-7			

(Silver)	(Silver)	(Silver)	
Brigadier General	**Brigadier General**	**Brigadier General**	**Rear Admiral Lower Half**
Say: General	Say: General	Say: General	Say: Admiral
Write: BG	Write: Brig. Gen.	Write: Brig. Gen.	Write: RADM (LH)
Paygrade - O-8			

	(Silver)		
Major General	**Major General**	**Major General**	**Rear Admiral Upper Half**
Say: General	Say: General	Say: General	Say: Admiral
Write: MG	Write: Maj. Gen.	Write: Maj. Gen.	Write: RADM

Army	Marines	Air Force	Navy/Coast Guard

Paygrade - O-9

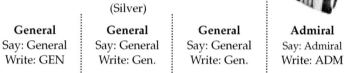

(Silver)

Army	Marines	Air Force	Navy/Coast Guard
Lieutenant General Say: General Write: LG	**Lieutenant General** Say: General Write: Lt. Gen.	**Lieutenant General** Say: General Write: Lt. Gen.	**Vice Admiral** Say: Admiral Write: VADM

Officer Ranks - O-10

Army	Marines	Air Force	Navy/Coast Guard
			★★★★

(Silver)

Army	Marines	Air Force	Navy/Coast Guard
General Say: General Write: GEN	**General** Say: General Write: Gen.	**General** Say: General Write: Gen.	**Admiral** Say: Admiral Write: ADM

Warrant Officer Rank Insignia

(The Air Force has no warrant officers.)

Army	Marines	Navy/Coast Guard
	Paygrade - W-1	
(Silver/Black)	(Gold/Red)	No W-1 rank in Navy/Coast Guard
Warrant Officer 1 Say: Mister/Miss Write: WO1	**Warrant Officer 1** Say: Mister/Miss Write: WO	
	Paygrade - W-2	
(Silver/Black)	(Gold/Red)	(Gold/Blue)
Chief Warrant Officer 2 Say: Mister/Miss Write: CW2	**Chief Warrant Officer 2** Say: Mister/Miss Write: CWO2	**Chief Warrant Officer 2** Say: Mister/Miss Write: CWO2

Army	Marines	Navy/Coast Guard
	Paygrade - W-3	
(Silver/Black)	(Silver/Red)	(Silver/Blue)
Chief Warrant Officer 3 Say: Mister/Miss Write: CW3	**Chief Warrant Officer 3** Say: Mister/Miss Write: CWO3	**Chief Warrant Officer 3** Say: Mister/Miss Write: CWO3
	Paygrade - W-4	
(Silver/Black)	(Silver/Red)	(Silver/Blue)
Chief Warrant Officer 4 Say: Mister/Miss Write: CW4	**Chief Warrant Officer 4** Say: Mister/Miss Write: CWO4	**Chief Warrant Officer 4** Say: Mister/Miss Write: CWO4
		Paygrade - W-5
(Silver/White)	(Gold/Red)	No W-5 rank in Navy/Coast Guard
Chief Warrant Officer 5 Say: Mister/Miss Write: CW5	**Chief Warrant Officer 5** Say: Mister/Miss Write: CWO5	

Chapter 2

The Military Press Today
Know an F-16 from an M-16? You'll succeed

Ten years after the 1991 Persian Gulf War, when print and broadcast journalists became the butt of sitcom jokes for their incompetence, arrogance and lack of preparedness to cover a major military operation involving hundreds of thousands of American troops, the state of military reporting has changed little, and if anything, has declined further. What happened a decade ago when war broke out on Jan. 16, 1991, remains a model of how the American print and broadcast media cover the military even today. It is also a grim harbinger of what may come as the United States moves against the terrorists and their sponsors in the wake of the attacks against the World Trade Center and the Pentagon on Sept. 11, 2001.

At the opening of the allied air campaign against Iraq, the cadre of several dozen fulltime military reporters still working at the Pentagon (many of their Pentagon colleagues had already deployed to Saudi Arabia) climbed aboard a specially-assigned C-141 military transport jet that flew them to Dhahran and Riyadh. The next morning, senior officials held the first of what would become daily press briefings at the Pentagon televised live worldwide as the rush of events in the Gulf continued.

But who was there to ask the questions? With the deployment of most of the Pentagon press corps, the Defense Department issued temporary credentials to a mob of stand-ins hastily impressed for military coverage by their Washington bureau chiefs and station managers. From my own direct observations via satellite television (later confirmed by hair-curling anecdotes from press colleagues and military contacts), the fill-in reporters were universally unfit for the assignments they had been given. They knew nothing about the allied ground, air and naval force that had been assembled by the U.S. Central Command over the past five months in the Persian Gulf region; they knew nothing of the strategies and tactics that the military had honed throughout the 1980s to carry out multiservice and multinational military operations; they knew nothing about the weapons and armaments assembled in the region — except that, of course, none of them were going to work; they had neither contacts nor sources to help them identify and hone any inquiries that would have helped inform the American people as to how their sons and daughters were girding for battle. And most revealing of all, they seemed oblivious to how stupid they looked when attempting to hector the Pentagon briefers on worldwide television. One veteran colleague contemptuously referred to them as "the invasion of the food editors."

In the Gulf region itself, a similar situation devolved. An estimated 1,300 reporters — of whom at most a hundred had any military coverage background — swamped the press center in Dhahran, Saudi Arabia.

In 1991, retired Associated Press Pentagon correspondent Fred Hoffman — a veteran at that time of 28 years of military coverage — watched the newcomers perform, and came away nauseated: "I listened to the (Pentagon and Riyadh) briefings and I watched the briefings every day ... This is going to set back military relations with the press, way back because of the impression it gives to military officers that the press is a collection of ignorant dodos and hip-shooters." Reporter Henry Allen of *The Washington Post*, appalled at what he saw in the Pentagon briefings, indicted the military reporter wannabes as a pack of "fools, nit-pickers and egomaniacs." He went on, "They don't seem to understand the military, either. Meanwhile, the military seems to have their number, perfectly."

During the frenzied, high-pressure weeks of the air and ground campaigns, the U.S. military leadership manipulated the stand-in reporters at the Pentagon while strictly controlling access and information to the press contingent in the Gulf. Their control effort was strongly aided by the dog-eat-dog competition among the major news outlets — who had established a standing committee (read "cartel") to control which reporters would be allowed into the small number of combat pool slots available. Thus, during one week at Dhahran, a senior editor for *The Army Times* newspaper — an independent publication that covers the U.S. Army fulltime — was informed by the committee that his staffers would not be given access to the print media combat pool on grounds that *The Army Times* did not meet the committee's

After extensive background interviews, hours of studying the aircraft manual and completing the Navy aviation physiology and water survial program, the civilian reporter can document what it is like to fly a low-level attack mission. (Photo: Cary Tolman, *Seattle Post-Intelligencer*)

definition of a newspaper, while at the same time a lifestyles writer from the fashion magazine *Mirabella* was handed a pool slot so that she could write about sexual tensions between male and female soldiers.

The same situation was likely to reoccur in the fall of 2001 as the United States assembled an international coalition to retaliate against terrorist organizations worldwide in the aftermath of the attacks on the World Trade Center in New York and the Pentagon that left more than 6,000 people dead or missing: A stampede of ill-prepared reporters rushed to a story lacking the basic background or experience to cover it effectively.

Lessons learned — the PAO revolution

As has been documented elsewhere in after-action reports compiled by several media research foundations, in 1991 the military succeeded in manipulating and controlling the unruly and ill-informed press contingent in the Gulf. And the initial feeling among senior military leaders was that the harsh treatment was justified. One Navy report from 1991 concluded that the Gulf War briefing fiasco deeply impressed military officials thinking about coverage in the next crisis or war: "We were in a 'win-win' situation," Marine Brig. Gen. Richard Neal, the well-recognized Central Command briefer in Riyadh, told the *PA Communicator*, an internal Navy PAO newsletter. "Due to the nature of their (reporters') questions, everything the press did was wrong in the mind of 'Joe Six-pack' out there in the public." The *PA Communicator* article explicitly cited a now-famous *Saturday Night Live* parody of the Pentagon press briefing as evidence that the military, and not the media, had won the hearts and minds of the American public.

It did not take long for the military leadership to discover that its Persian Gulf War triumph over the news media had been a Pyrrhic victory, that the story of American heroism and military competence in the Iraqi desert had largely gone untold because of the access restrictions and the early collapse of the communications system for transmitting stories from the field. Navy and Air Force officials would later privately admit that they had shot themselves in the foot by preventing in-depth coverage of their operations. The Marine Corps, which has a long tradition of proactive press relations, was a major exception to the rule, and welcomed the press to its field command centers and combat units as it mounted the flank attack into Kuwait.

In the aftermath of the war, the Pentagon scrapped the onerous system of pools and press controls, and the military services individually went through their own versions of what has been called, a "revolution in public affairs." In part, this reflected the honest realization that, in one admiral's phrase, the news media "is not the enemy, but rather the battlefield" for the peacetime battles over force cuts, budgets, weapons procurement and other vital issues.

How the U.S. Navy succeeded in transforming its relations with the press is a textbook example for the military as a whole. Under the public affairs leadership of Rear Adm. Kendall Pease, who served as chief of naval information under three separate chiefs of naval operations in the 1990s, the Navy underwent both an internal and external transformation of how it works with the news media. Internally, Pease expanded the service's own training program to prepare upcoming leaders to work effectively with the press (including how to survive ambush interviews). Externally, Pease and his staff won the Navy leadership's support to embrace a pro-active press stance and to open up previously closed areas (such as submarines) to coverage.

While this reflected in part a gradual relaxation of operational security that had long characterized naval operations during the Cold War, it also stemmed from a cold-blooded assessment by Pease and his colleagues that the Navy needed to reach out to an American public that was becoming less familiar with the military each passing year. The consequences of the end of the draft in 1973, coupled with the inevitable shrinking of the U.S. armed forces by 40 percent during the 1990s, made such outreach essential if the Navy (or any other service) was to retain its political and budgetary support in Congress and each administration.

The Army (and NATO) innovated in press relations during the 1995 intervention on Bosnia.

When Task Force Eagle deployed from Hungary into Bosnia, the Pentagon launched what one subsequent report would term "a bold and innovative plan in military-media relations." Journalists were "embedded" in the Germany-based Army units earmarked for deployment. They traveled with the units and remained with them in Bosnia for two or three weeks after their arrival.

This constituted a full reversal from the earlier pool arrangements in the Gulf that allowed only brief and transitory visits with deployed units. Now, the journalists were considered to be part of the military unit itself, a concept that had not been seen since World War II. A total of 33 journalists, including 24 Americans, took part in the plan.

"The rationale for embedded media was to foster familiarity on the part of the journalists with the unit and its soldiers," one participant later wrote. "The assumption was that as the reporters grew to know the unit and its soldiers, there would be a more positive attitude on the part of the soldiers toward the military's mission." Except for one incident where a brigade commander was quoted alleging that Croats were racist, which sparked several days of intense press scrutiny, the media deployment was deemed a success by all parties.

It was within this context that the sudden explosion of the Internet and widespread availability of powerful computers added an entire new dimension to the relationship between the generals and the journalists.

Two personal vignettes further underscore the immensity of change that the Navy and other military services implemented in press relations between the mid-1980s and mid-1990s:

■ In 1987, when the Pentagon ordered a squadron of Navy Reserve minesweepers to duty in the Persian Gulf (during the height of the Iran-Iraq War), officials imposed a total ban on information about the impending deployment. The squadron happened to be based about a half-mile from one newsroom in Seattle and while no one would confirm the wooden ships were preparing to sail, reporters could watch the working parties loading supplies from the newsroom window. Still, when they were invited to "cover" the departure, the Navy invited the press to the pier where they locked us up in a fenced-in area too far from the scene to record any questions and interviews. The story was replete with phrases such as "declined comment" and "tight-lipped officials."

■ In 1996, when mainland Chinese ballistic missiles began bracketing the island of Taiwan, the Pentagon was ordered to rush two aircraft carrier battle groups to the region. One of them, the *USS Nimitz*, was based in Puget Sound, Wash., and constituted a major local impact to a growing international crisis. It took only one phone call for Navy public affairs officials to arrange a direct interview via satellite telephone of the carrier group commander, ship's captain and carrier air wing commander, all of whom had been briefed that it was acceptable for them to discuss the broad outlines of their upcoming mission with a reporter. Thanks to the revolution in Navy public affairs — and, admittedly, the Navy's political interest in getting the story out rather than suppressing information — a reporter was able to construct a lead sentence in his article that read, "When combat aircraft from the carrier *USS Nimitz* appear on mainland Chinese air-defense radars tomorrow night...."

Lessons unlearned — the news media

The issue of press competence in military coverage has been sidestepped in many of the after-action critiques that have circulated between the nation's news executives and Pentagon officials in the years since the Gulf War. The major newspapers and TV networks, who have professional military reporters in their ranks, have turned a blind eye to the overall industry weakness, preferring to focus their efforts on getting access and stories to their own military specialists.

One media study concluded — in carefully understated tones — that the news media had failed to prepare in advance for the Persian Gulf War: "While most reporters (and editors) assigned to this conflict had little or no prior experience with war coverage on the scale of the Persian Gulf conflict, they knew instinctively that this was likely to be 'the story' of the decade and they wanted to be there," the Gannett Foundation (later Freedom Forum) study noted. "The organizations they worked for were also committed to covering the war and, in fact, some media outlets that rarely send people abroad committed resources to cover this story."

In 1992, representatives of the news media and military formally hammered out a post-Gulf War agreement to govern coverage of future military operations. The Pentagon agreed to scrap the controversial pool system and to direct field commanders to provide reporters maximum access subject to specific operational and logistical constraints. For its part, the news media pledged to send experienced military reporters to cover future conflicts. This latter promise has been a shamefully unmet pledge.

Both newspapers and broadcast outlets have for the past decade struggled with severe economic pressures that have resulted in fewer fulltime international news bureaus, a reliance on third-nation journalists for initial coverage in a foreign crisis, a decimation of the number of fulltime military reporting specialists, and a continued decline in budgets for in-depth coverage and travel. Moreover, the national security and defense beats have declined in prestige within the journalism profession since the end of the Cold War even while the pace of military operations and the number of international crises involving U.S. military forces have continued unabated.

For a brief period in the late 1990s, it appeared that the "dot.com" revolution might create the opportunity for specialized online news sites dedicated to military and defense coverage, but the subsequent collapse of the NASDAQ stock index and widespread bankruptcies in that business sector in 2000 have delayed the emergence of such a journalistic capability.

As we saw in Somalia in 1992-93, Haiti in 1994, Bosnia in 1995 and Kosovo in 1999, coverage of military operations again and again fell to a dwindling number of fulltime specialists and an outsized mob of untrained general assignment reporters unprepared for the story they were about to meet. This stems from two parallel trends that have taken hold in the journalism profession during the last decade: (1) An unwillingness or inability for many news organizations to invest in and sustain the relatively high cost of a fulltime military beat, and (2) a disinclination by many news executives to provide dedicated coverage to the armed forces out of an unspoken consensus that military affairs in the post-Cold War era simply did not justify the effort, expense or newshole allocation.

While the U.S. military has been trimmed about 40 percent in size since the end of the Cold War and Operation Desert Storm, the roster of fulltime military journalists dwindled even more. A 1995 study by the author found that the number of fulltime military reporters had fallen from around 120 in 1989 to as few as 65 just six years later. At the Pentagon, officials say the fulltime cadre of television network, wire service and military trade publications regularly covering events has shrunk to only 20 or so.

Military leaders today assume that in event of crisis or major news event, they will be confronted by reporters who are unschooled in the specific details or technological background of the military story they are covering. For their part, military officers don't mind. "A blank slate doesn't have much of a comeback" to military-provided information, one senior public affairs officer said.

The technological revolution

The reporter entering the military beat for the first time — or even merely covering a specific military event — has one advantage his colleagues a mere decade ago did not enjoy: access to information via cyberspace. (For specific tactics on how to use the internet and other digital applications to cover military stories, see Chapter 12.)

The explosion of digital computer information technology (IT) that is transforming American society and the military is also revolutionizing the way in which the journalism industry is able to cover military operations. It has already sparked countermoves by the Pentagon both to exploit the new technology for its institutional interests while attempting to preserve operational security. Some aspects include:

■ As internet and e-mail capability continues to spread throughout the news media to include smaller, community-oriented publications and broadcast outlets, the Pentagon is able to expand its grassroots public affairs presence using computerized "home town" news releases, feature profile news releases and even digital imagery.

■ Coverage of peacetime military subjects has become easier — especially for news organizations outside Washington, D.C. — because of the Pentagon's commitment to use its internet websites to promulgate timely information ranging from briefing transcripts to unclassified publications. A similar profusion of other federal and non-governmental websites such as the General Accounting Office, Congress' Thomas system, and scores of policy think-tanks and research institutes, have expanded the scope of rapid information-gathering possible for reporters assigned to military and national security subjects.

■ News media organizations versed in "computer-assisted reporting" have also been able to increase their quality of reporting on issues employing DoD computer databases for information on important issues.

■ The profusion of new IT devices — from ultra-light laptop computers to "videophones" that can pump a digital image over a telephone line — is providing journalists with more powerful tools to conduct field coverage independent of the military, including direct uplinks from portable laptop computers to commercial communications satellites that avoid any dependency on military communications networks. This is particularly true in crisis areas where American journalists already have an established presence before the arrival of American forces.

■ Both the military and media are learning to cooperate and effectively work together under a news cycle that is even more intense than the 24-hour-day-seven-day-week pattern that began on cable television and now also exists on the internet. Both institutions will have to learn how to manage the enormous strains to "get it right" while avoiding release of information that could threaten the success of the operation and the lives of American service people.

■ In the absence of a particular TV image, news organizations have an arsenal of computer-driven graphics at their fingertips, including actual satellite imagery from commercial satellites, animated simulations and static visual depictions to serve as gap-fillers during coverage of a critical military operation.

■ The administration and Pentagon will find themselves competing with outside experts and analysts in the diplomatic and public relations aspects of a conflict. Even the enemy, whether a hostile state or sub-national ethic group, will be able to wage a public-relations campaign in cyberspace as the battlefield struggle proceeds. The Pentagon will learn to use cyberspace as it previously used live television to send its message "around" the news media directly to the American people and global bystanders.

The Pentagon will likely expand its use of the internet to provide information in event of specific incidents or crises, though it also is being careful to remove sensitive information that could help terrorists. After the terrorist bombing of the destroyer *USS Cole*, the collision between the submarine *USS Greeneville* and the Japanese vessel *Ehime Maru*, and the collision between a Navy EP-3 and Chinese F-8 fighter, public officials created dedicated websites linked to the main military news portals that provided a continuously updated flow of text, still and video imagery as the military responded to each event.

Technology and a pro-active military public affairs strategy will in the end help to offset the institutional barriers preventing print and broadcast reporters from mastering complicated military stories. But the final result will still depend on the reporter's commitment to become literate in military subjects and not rely on a smile or a sneer to mask a gaping ignorance.

How to...

Weed out phony POWs, fake heroes and other wannabes

The Air Force base was honoring one of its own.

For the formal observance of POW/MIA Day in Alaska in September 2000, Eielson Air Force Base officials did not have to go far to find a living symbol of American servicemen who had suffered in captivity.

It turned out that one of the Alaska base's senior civilian employees had not only been a POW in Vietnam, but was one of a very small handful who managed to escape from his tormentors.

Jim Spohn, 55, the superintendent of information management at Eielson, agreed to be interviewed by Capt. Don Lewis for the base newspaper, and was the featured guest of honor at the formal POW/MIA memorial ceremony at the base. Lewis' article was picked up by the Air Force Online News Service – an internal newswire whose product is used by base newspapers and websites worldwide. Shortly afterwards, civilian reporter Beth Ipsen of the local *Fairbanks News-Miner* newspaper published a similar profile of the quiet civil servant and his incredible ordeal 35 years earlier. Her story traveled worldwide on the Associated Press newswire.

Spohn told Capt. Lewis that he was serving in South Korea with the 833rd Ordnance Co. at a base near the city of Taejon when, in December 1965, he was temporarily assigned to another Army unit along the demilitarized zone that separates North and South Korea. Just several days later, Spohn said, he was placed in a group of soldiers and flown to South Vietnam as part of an advance guard of the 1st Cavalry Division, which was then preparing for combat deployment to Vietnam. The assignment was supposed to last only two weeks, he recalled.

"We'd been in the country less than 72 hours when we entered an area that was just cleared by the infantry," Spohn said. "There were 12 of us with M-1s strapped to our backs, not one of us trained in guerrilla warfare. The Viet Cong had a tremendous network of tunnels through the countryside. They're fairly small people, so they could squeeze through the smallest holes. We never saw them until they were on top of us — 50 to 60 of them all at once."

According to Spohn's recollection, ten of the 12 Americans were killed during the ambush itself, and Spohn and another soldier were taken prisoner. The other soldier died of his injuries the next day, Spohn said.

"I thought I was going to die, that they were going to try to get whatever they wanted to know from me, and then kill me," he told Lewis. Spohn added that to confuse his captors he only spoke German to them.

Spohn claimed that in three months of captivity he lost 62 pounds, but one night was able to free himself from the ropes used to bind his arms and legs and overpower a guard. He said he fled into the jungle and wandered around for two weeks until he was rescued by a patrol of Australian soldiers.

Recovering in a hospital in Japan, Spohn says he was visited by an officer one day who handed him a Purple Heart medal. "That one [medal] really means something to me," Spohn said in the Air Force interview. "It means I spilled my blood on the ground for our country."

Spohn left the Army in 1968 and enlisted in the Air Force in 1971. He retired as a senior master sergeant in 1989.

Lewis, writing to the internal Air Force readership, noted, "It is important time is taken to recognize these people. As a nation, some of them are mourned on Memorial Day, some of them are cheered on Veterans' Day, and now, on Sept. 15, remember some of them on POW/MIA Day. Some of those people will remain a memory forever."

Spohn's story was an uplifting and inspiring account of courage under fire. It was also a total fabrication that fooled not only a civilian newspaper reporter but the Air Force's own internal news media. But not for long.

When word of the POW story reached Chuck and Mary Schantag in the small town of Skidmore, Mo., the two researchers immediately smelled a rat. Co-founders along with Ron and Pam Peterson of the non-profit POW Network, the Schantags have spent the past 12 years exposing false veterans, phony POWs and imitation generals who have fooled public officials, reporters and other citizens with false claims of military heroism.

In an interview with the author, Mary Schantag said the entire structure and pattern of Spohn's account raised immediate doubts as to its veracity:

He claimed to have been transferred to another Army unit in Korea, then immediately attached to a third unit going to Vietnam without any written orders to that effect. Anyone who has spent even a week in the military knows that you cannot be transferred, go on leave or be discharged without generating multiple copies of the orders changing your status, position or assignment.

He claimed to have been armed with an M-1 Garand rifle (which was used by the Army in World War II and Korea). Army soldiers in Vietnam all carried the M-16 rifle.

He claimed that his provisional unit was sent on combat patrol only after being in-country for three days. While later in the war some individual combat replacements would find themselves rushed into the field immediately upon arriving, normal practice for managing newly-arrived soldiers was provide them refresher combat training and a "break-in" period before sending them on to combat units.

The events of the alleged ambush, captivity, escape and rescue as described by Spohn contained a common thread: Verification of the account through interviews with former comrades or witnesses was physically impossible: First, Spohn was transferred from his Army unit to a second outfit in Korea, then immediately dispatched to Vietnam with a group of strangers. Then he was the only survivor of the massacre. Then he was rescued, not by an American unit, but by Australian troops. Then he woke up in a military hospital in Japan. Spohn said he never received any records of his transfer, combat, rescue or hospitalization, which Vietnam veterans say would be impossible. Moreover, the only Australians in Vietnam in 1965 were a small contingent stationed near the South Vietnamese capital.

Spohn later admitted that he could not recall the names of any fellow soldiers in Korea or Vietnam who could verify any part of his story.

Spohn said he earlier tried to get copies of his service records but was told they had been destroyed in a massive July 1973 fire at the National Personnel Records Center in St. Louis, Mo. In fact, the blaze, as POW researchers well know, did not destroy Vietnam-era records at all, but destroyed Army service records dating from 1912 through 1960, and a small number of Air Force files dating from 1947 to 1964.

Spohn never changed his story that he indeed had been a POW, even as unofficial investigations kept proving the contrary.

Capt. Lewis, the Eielson spokesman who had originally interviewed Spohn for the base newspaper, later obtained permission from Spohn to study the self-described POW's military and medical records (much of which is releasable only to the former serviceman or woman under the federal Privacy Act).

"I can conclude there is no evidence I have found to support his claim of his service in Vietnam or capture in the timeframe he alleges — or at any other time frame for that matter," Lewis told reporters. "There is no evidence of any trauma, disease or anything that would indicate that he suffered in a prisoner of war camp."

The Schantags and Petersons (and the Air Force, had it realized it earlier) had a weapon that has never failed them in their quest to unmask phony POWs. It is called PMSEA (for Personnel Missing in Southeast Asia), a comprehensive roster of military POWs and MIAs from the Vietnam War compiled by the Pentagon in the mid-1970s. While POW activists and Pentagon officials have quarreled bitterly for the last quarter-century over the fate of several hundred MIAs, the one thing both sides agree on is that the PMSEA list is totally accurate and complete.

"In the 30 years that the Pentagon has held its roster there never has been an occasion where anyone not listed by the Pentagon had evidence that he had been held [as a POW]," Mary

Schantag said.

Jim Spohn's name was not on the PMSEA roster.

As a result of the POW Network's challenge, embarrassed Air Force and *Fairbanks News-Miner* editors had to retract their previous stories and write follow-up articles on the controversy explaining that there was no available information in service archives to support Spohn's claim.

The controversy over Jim Spohn and his unfounded POW claim goes far beyond one veteran's assertion about his wartime experience, Mary Schantag said in a 2001 interview. "Every time we expose a new one, it seems like we get reports of two or three more," she told *The Baltimore Sun*. "It just keeps growing and growing and growing," she said, to the point that fake POWs and battle heroes sometimes outnumber the real ones.

The POW Network, which maintains a roster of "phonies" at its Internet website, www.pownetwork.org, has unmasked nearly 700 false POWs in its decade of work. In the same article in *The Baltimore Sun* with Mary Schantag, retired Capt. Larry Bailey, a former Navy SEAL commando — who helps manage a database of phony SEALs at the website www.cyberseals.org. — said nearly 7,000 phony SEAL commandos had been unmasked between 1995 and 2001. (That comes close to the total number of Navy personnel — 10,000 — who have served in the SEAL program since its inception in 1962, and its precursor, the Navy frogman program, that began in World War II.)

So while a reporter new to the military beat might have no concern over being conned by a false POW or fictitious veteran with an amazing tale to tell, the sad truth is that this is one of the most common blunders in military reporting. Not only newcomers to the military beat, but many of the "best and the brightest" in American journalism have fallen for these hoaxes.

History of deceit

The span of deceit is as broad as American society itself. It involves criminals who invent the psychological torments of Vietnam service to explain their failures in life. It involves ordinary people who feel driven by insecurity to invent a heroic past. It even involves people who served honorably (if not heroically) but felt driven to fictionalize their records. And it can even involve active-duty service personnel who do the same.

Falsely posing as a former POW or battle hero — while morally reprehensible — is not by itself illegal: Barroom bragging is still covered under the First Amendment. However, falsely wearing the Medal of Honor has been made a federal crime that can land you a one-year prison term and/or a $100,000 fine. So too, forging documents to support military medals or decorations, or falsely wearing a military uniform and medals, is a misdemeanor that can bring a maximum six-month prison term.

But despite these sanctions, false heroes and phony POWs are never in short supply. Consider the following stories:

■ Former President Lyndon Johnson throughout his political career wore a lapel pin depicting the Silver Star medal he received from Gen. Douglas MacArthur for heroic acts in an Army bomber in the Pacific. (A congressman who received a Navy commission after Pearl Harbor, Johnson was flying as an observer when Japanese fighters allegedly attacked his aircraft during a bombing raid.) Veterans of the bombing raid long voiced doubts over the incident and raised concerns over the veracity of the award, but their accounts were ignored by the news media for decades — even as Johnson attained the presidency and became a politically controversial figure who escalated American combat involvement in the Vietnam War. It wasn't until 2001 that CNN aired archived records and interviews with crewmen on the aircraft that showed Johnson's aircraft was not even involved in the combat incident for which he received the third-highest award for bravery in combat: It had turned back from the mission with a mechanical malfunction long before fighting took place.

■ In Pennsylvania, the Panther Valley School District superintendent lost his job when he was exposed as an impostor who'd been falsely boasting about his exploits as a Navy SEAL commando. A federal judge sentenced Raymond Aucker to two years probation and 200 hours of community service at a veterans hospital in Iowa for falsifying his military records.

■ At Fort Lewis, Wash., Army chaplain and Vietnam veteran

Maj. Gary Probst was a familiar and comforting figure for the families of the soldiers, including the elite 2nd Ranger Battalion. When the airborne Rangers were dispatched to Panama in December 1989 for "Operation Just Cause," Probst was one of several officials made available to reporters — including the author — to describe the family service network and "chain of concern" established to keep family members informed of the ongoing combat mission and to provide assistance wherever needed. A quiet man who talked eloquently about helping the Ranger family members, Probst himself was a reassuring sight with his Army Ranger tab and Special Forces insignia, as well as the master paratrooper badge and expert field medic insignia. Six months later, Army officials were stunned to learn that the chaplain had never served in Vietnam nor was he eligible to wear a single one of those devices. Facing multiple court-martial charges (it is a crime for active-duty personnel to wear medals or badges for which they are unqualified), Probst copped a plea and was quietly booted out of the Army.

■ Then there was the baffling case of Ed Dailey, a Korean War veteran who confessed to the Associated Press and numerous other news media organizations in 1999 that he had participated in a deliberate massacre of South Korean civilians at the village of No Gun-ri in 1950. Following worldwide publicity (NBC News flew Dailey to the site of the alleged massacre for a tearful reunion with shooting survivors from that era), the Associated Press — which won the 1999 Pulitzer Prize for the No Gun-ri report — and the other news outlets were deeply embarrassed when archival records were found confirming that Dailey was not in Korea at the time of the incident, and never received the battlefield commission nor multiple decorations and medals he has long claimed. Dailey, who did serve in Korea with the 1st Cavalry Division, was apparently so hungry for fame and publicity that he was willing to confess to a war crime he didn't commit (and which the Army later determined did not happen).

How to spot a phony POW or false hero

The veteran you are about to interview claims to have been a prisoner of war. Or that he received the Medal of Honor. Or holds other high awards and decorations. Or that he was involved in secret assassination missions behind the lines. Or that he retired with the rank of colonel or general. How can you determine whether any of this is true, including his status as a veteran?

There is a simple three-step process you can follow.

1) Require a full set of identification papers and military documents before you agree to the interview.

Many phony veterans merely make up their biographies from thin air, but others have been known to forge documents and even to commit "identity theft" of actual POWs or veterans. So it is necessary not only to check out the interviewee's claims but to compare his documentation against that of the military archives.

You should begin by informing the veteran that because all too many phony veterans have deceived the news media in recent years about their wartime experiences, it is a sad necessity that you have to confirm the veteran's identity and his official records before you may proceed. To do that you need to obtain a transcript of military service from the National Personnel Records Center in St. Louis, Mo. — the component of the National Archives that handles all military personnel records.

You should insist on the following: A copy of his birth certificate or passport, driver's license, Form DD-214 (summary of military service at discharge), and a copy of the General Order for each award or medal. You should also obtain his Social Security number.

2) Apply for his official military records from the National Personnel Records Center.

You should require from him a letter authorizing you as the media representative to receive a copy of all releasable information from the NPRC, or have him fill out a Form 180 request for information. You can download a .pdf version of NARA Form 180 at www.nara.gov/regional/mprsf180.html. If the veteran declines to do this, you have the option of calling off the article or proceeding anyway.

If he declines and you wish to proceed, the following information in every serviceman's file is releasable to the public under the federal Freedom of Information Act (see Chapter 11):

■ Name

■ Age (date of birth)

■ Dates of service

■ Source of commission (for officers)

■ Rank/grade and date attained

■ Marital status

■ Promotion sequence number

■ Salary*

■ Office phone number*

■ City/town and state of last known address and date of this address

■ Serial/service number (those issued prior to the use of the Social Security number as the service number)

■ Decorations and awards

■ Place of birth; date and geographical location of death; and place of burial+

■ Military and civilian education level

■ Photograph (or photocopy if only one photo is available)

■ Place of induction and separation

■ Duty assignments (including geographical location)

■ Dependents (including name, sex, and age)

■ Records of court-martial trial (unless classified)

■ Education/schooling (military)

■ Future assignments which have been finalized *

■ Duty status #

Notes:

* These items obviously relate to active-duty personnel and are not likely to be found in the records at the NPRC.

For records at the NPRC this generally means discharged or retired.

+ If person is deceased, these items also may generally be released.

Send your FOIA Request (See Chapter 11) to:

National Personnel Records Center
Military Personnel Records
9700 Page Ave.
St. Louis MO 63132-5100

Caution: NPRC officials warn that there is usually a backlog of between 4-10 weeks due to the large volume received.

Another word of caution: Some phony POWs and false heroes have gone so far as to forge the documentation authorizing their medals (primarily in order to obtain VA benefits under false pretenses). It is not enough, for example, to take at face value the signed and chronologically numbered General Order document that stipulates the granting of a military medal. It is sometimes necessary to make a FOIA request to the National Archives and Records Service, www.nara.gov, or the historical branches of the specific military service involved.

3) Check out the POW and veterans networks

One of the most effective organizations dedicated toward unmasking phony POWs and military heroes is the nonprofit POW Network. You can contact the POW Network by going to their website at www.pownetwork.org or calling (660) 928-3304. The POW Network contains a large archive of phony POWs, some of whom have attempted to dupe reporters, veterans groups or individuals in more than one location.

The POW Network has assembled a number of official rosters which will be useful in determining the veracity of the veteran's claim, including:

■ The PMSEA Roster of all Vietnam-era POWs

■ Roster of all Medal of Honor recipients and citations

■ Roster of all living Medal of Honor recipients

■ Legion of Valor website (Membership limited to recipients of the Medal of Honor, Distinguished Service Cross, Navy Cross, and Air Force Cross)

■ CyberSEALS: Rosters of unmasked phony SEALS

In addition, the POW Network has hyperlinks to a number of military alumni organizations that monitor false claimants, including the Army Ranger Association, Naval Special Warfare Command (SEALs), *USS Pueblo* incident and more.

For information on the Navy SEAL program — the elite commando unit that attracts a large number of phonies — contact the private organization cyberSEALS at www.cyberseals.org. Another networking source is nightscribe.com (www.nightscribe.com/Military/SEALs/wannabee_seals.htm) which has a roster of other activists dedicated to rooting out phony SEALs.

Texas financial adviser B.G. "Jug" Burkett, a Vietnam veteran who served with the 199th Infantry Brigade, has become a one-man research institution into the proliferation of phony POWs and military heroes. His 1998 book, *Stolen Valor* (Verity Press), should be on the desk of every reporter who may cover military or veterans' issues. The 692-page book is not only a harsh indictment of how American society allowed the image of the Vietnam veteran to be hijacked by Hollywood and a long parade of criminals falsely posing as Vietnam veterans, it offers many case studies of how reporters not only fell for outrageous false stories, but in many cases refused to run corrections after the false veteran was later unmasked. In addition, Burkett has included in *Stolen Valor* the official Pentagon rosters of returned Vietnam POWs, and recipients of the Medal of Honor, Air Force Cross, Navy Cross and Army Distinguished Service Medal — a ready checklist when approached by someone claiming such a distinction. To contact Burkett or to order a copy of *Stolen Valor*, contact his website at www.stolenvalor.com.

In addition to the mainstay veterans organizations, many combat and support units assigned to Vietnam have active unit alumni associations that regularly host reunions and seminars. They can readily be located on the internet through various webrings dedicated to veterans affairs, and their records are invaluable in verifying or knocking down a veteran's claims. Moreover, you can easily find a veteran who is expert on the alleged incident or battle in which your would-be hero claims to have been involved.

Chapter 3

Organizing the Military Beat
Three strategies to get started

So you want to become your newspaper or TV station's military reporter. Where to begin? If the experience of numerous military reporters interviewed for this manual is a guide, you, your line editor and management superiors should first devise and implement three separate strategies:

A strategy for defining your beat coverage

This is a formal "charter" for military coverage, defining the scope of military activities on which you will concentrate, the geographical boundaries of primary coverage, and an initial outline of topics and story subjects that you intend to monitor in the first 12 months of your beat. It should address editorial management issues such as a beat budget and travel.

A strategy for personal preparation

This consists of the personal steps you need to take to obtain entry-level knowledge of military organization, particularly focusing on the bases, commands, military leaders and issues of direct local interest.

A strategy for beat organization and sustainment

From the outset, maintaining your beat will be as important as opening and expanding contacts with the military commands you will cover. This strategy encompasses the "logistics" of the military beat, including your file and desktop organization, schedules, tickler files and time management.

How to begin

For illustration's sake, let's assume that you are a reporter with a daily newspaper that is planning to open a full-time military beat. You are interested in the job, but have little or no experience in working with the military on stories. Your experience as a reporter has given you the confidence to tackle challenging new assignments, but in moments of candor, you realize that you don't know a colonel from a corporal. Still, you and your editors have decided that local and/or regional military activities warrant full-time coverage and you have tentatively agreed to take a crack at it. Let's do it, your editor says. Congratulations! You are now a military reporter, following in the hallowed footsteps of Richard Harding Davis, Ernie Pyle, Homer Bigart and Charlie Aldinger.

Now what the hell do you do? Strategize!

Coverage strategy for the military beat

Writing your "charter" for the military beat, a formal memo setting out your priorities, areas of coverage and — equally important — limits of coverage, is one of the most important tasks you will undertake at the outset of creating the position. It will provide a structure of understanding between you and your editors that will minimize conflict and confusion during the initial months when you have to devote as much effort toward backgrounding and source development as to article writing itself. Some elements of this should include:

Institutional coverage: What are the bases and military commands that you will cover? Will you shadow only the major base in your city or region? All military organizations located within your state? Or the entire U.S. military establishment? Will your beat focus on the uniformed military (e.g. bases, commands and personnel) or will you also cover the defense industry, veterans groups, and quasi-military organizations such as the NOAA, Maritime Administration or Army Corps of Engineers? When subjects on the military beat intersect with other beats (e.g., environmental stories), which reporter will get the assignment?

Geographical boundaries: What are the physical boundaries of your beat? Will you stay close to home, monitoring military activities in your region alone? Will you follow local units as they travel out of state or overseas for maneuvers, training or actual operational deployments? Will you chase Pentagon stories from afar (it can be done), and monitor congressional issues from your

Live from the pier: A minor ceremony can become a major news event when a senior Pentagon official presides. Then-Under Secretary of the Navy H. Lawrence Garrett III (later promoted to Navy secretary) answers questions from Seattle-based print and TV reporters during a visit to the Bangor Submarine Base in 1988. (Photo: U.S. Navy)

hometown? Can you expect out-of-country assignments to cover military crises such as Operation Desert Storm or Kosovo?

Budget and travel: The military beat can be one of the most expensive beats on a newspaper (just ask editors who shipped reporters and photographers to the Persian Gulf War where inhaling and exhaling easily cost $500 per day). What will be your expenses and travel costs to create the military beat? For the first 12 months of activity? You should budget for specialty publication subscriptions, other reference materials, any special gear you'll use in the field (see Chapter 14); you should plan on at least two or three out-of-town coverage trips per year, including a backgrounder visit to Washington, D.C. for source development. Use your company's travel agency to cost out several "notional" trips (e.g. two weeks to Europe, 10 days at the National Training Center in Southern California) to present a fine-grain travel budget estimate. Press hard for emergency contingency travel funds in the event of that unexpected major incident that comes out of left field to consume your publication's time and energy.

Product: What do your editors expect from you once the military beat is up and running? Will you appear only in the front and local news sections, or will you also be asked/invited to write features, or even op-ed analysis pieces? What is their expectation on general assignment work from you? Are you available for general assignment emergency coverage only, or can any assistant city editor hijack you on request? What is their anticipation on the mix of spot daily stories, longer enterprise articles, or long-range investigative projects? Will you have formal staff backup support for the beat while you are out of town on assignment or on vacation?

Professional development: What can you expect from your newspaper in the way of opportunities for increasing your knowledge about the military as you continue in the beat? Will your superiors guarantee you an annual backgrounding trip to the Pentagon and other Washington, D.C. institutions? If there is a major military command headquarters out of your region that heavily impacts local bases, do you have a green light for a fact-finding trip there as well? Are occasional military war college seminars or other confabs something you can plan on — or something only to dream about?

Tenure: How long will your appointment as a military reporter run? Is it an open-ended assignment, or will you anticipate transfer and relief after two or three years?

Personal strategy for the military beat

Your personal preparation for writing and covering military topics should include:

■ A self-organized course in basic military concepts, organization, history and current issues primarily through reading and local backgrounders.

■ A step-by-step task list to organize the military beat to conform to the strategy on coverage which you and your editors have agreed to, including a compiled roster of bases and commands you will cover, their public affairs representatives, and military and non-governmental contacts elsewhere that can provide entry-level information for you.

■ A detailed canvass of local, regional and national-level experts, academic contacts, think tanks and other non-military organizations that monitor military issues and can serve as independent sources on military stories.

■ A clear timetable for your organizational efforts. If you are organizing a full-time beat from thin air, you should give yourself at least four weeks "off deadline" to identify your immediate coverage area, make initial contact with military officials, receive briefings and study background materials.

Military beat maintenance and sustainment

This is actually a strategy for maintaining the military reporter's sanity. Based on my own experience, the military beat is the most paper-pile and megabyte-creating position in the newsroom (the environmental beat and medical beat draw a close second, but their reports seem more neatly bound and covered, therefore stack more easily). Every reporter learns from his or her mother to be neat and tidy, but I cannot overemphasize the need for controlling from the outset what will be a continuous river of materials terminating in your mailbox. Two weeks into your new job, you will already be inundated with wire report printouts, faxes, junk mail, news releases, subscription publications and your own growing mountain of notes. I took two weeks off work to conduct the first interviews for this manual and came back to find a 37-inch hillock of mail on my desk (I measured it with a yardstick). Now, if you are the type of reporter who flourishes in a sea of loose paper, fine; I'm not. Your initial concerns on the beat (source contacts, backgrounders, etc.) should not divert you from immediately setting up mechanisms that will enable you to route, file, archive and retrieve pieces of paper quickly. Essential desktop tools include:

■ A calendar and tickler file to track your schedule.

■ A business card notebook that can hold and alphabetically file cards, or a large Rolodex, and a digital version in your computer such as Microsoft Outlook or some other contact manager.

■ A telephone log (8 x 11 spiral notebook is okay).

■ Enough filing shelf space to create your own beat/subject archive. I have found it useful to create a file on every military unit and base, co-located with a file on the local facility's parent command. But in a separate drawer I create individual subject files, stored alphabetically. When a subject file is no longer needed, you can cull it for whatever permanent stuff you want to keep and then re-file that under the base/unit file that applies.

■ A suitable collection of desktop manuals, reference books and almanac editions of military magazines for that quick look-see.

■ An ironclad schedule for clipping, photocopying and filing, and tossing material — at least once a week — or you can kiss this particular strategy goodbye.

■ And one item of gratuitous advice (colleagues think me obsessed, but it works): Decide once and for all whether your filing system will be 8 x 11 or 8 x 14, and photocopy to that size only. Not only does this make the physical act of creating and organizing files easier, it facilitates neatness, which facilitates a more pleasant environment. There is a need for pleasantness in a job with so many unpleasant moments just ahead.

How others survived

Do you still find the prospect of being tossed into the military beat terrifying? If you say yes, you are in good company.

Several experienced and distinguished journalists and public affairs officials interviewed for this manual found themselves thrust into the military specialty with little warning or preparation. Somehow, they survived, endured, and prevailed.

Louis A. "Pete" Williams, currently a senior reporter for NBC

News, became a household name as assistant secretary of defense/public affairs for then-Secretary of Defense Dick Cheney during 1989-93, specifically for his calm, professional TV press briefings during the 1990 U.S. invasion of Panama and Operation Desert Shield/Desert Storm less than a year later.

Williams, as press secretary to then-Wyoming Rep. Cheney, found himself promoted from a one-person congressional spokesman to command of more than 120 military public affairs specialists (with a protocol rank of four-star general, no less) when President George H. W. Bush tapped Cheney to lead the Defense Department in early 1989. The downside, Williams said, was that he had less than two weeks to prepare for an intense, crisis-driven job speaking on behalf of an organization that spans the gamut from nuclear weapons to MRE rations, and where press statements are forged in committees whose members battle over the placement of a semicolon.

Named chief Pentagon spokesman at the age of 37, Williams readily admitted he had scant military knowledge and no direct background dealing with military topics when he moved with Cheney to the Pentagon.

"I just knew, I had a cold sweat every night, that I was going to be in a (Pentagon press) briefing and George Wilson (the long-standing *Washington Post* military reporter) was going to be sitting in the front row eyeing this young guy who just came in and he was going to say, 'WHAT ABOUT THAT PROBLEM WITH THE M-93?' and I'd say, 'It's a great tank,' and he'd say, 'It's a rifle, kid.'" So Williams set out to do what his journalistic counterparts have to do: Cram study. He volunteered for what the military calls "the firehose treatment" of briefings, background sessions and other ways in which information is imparted.

"One day you are talking with a guy who knows that there is a left-handed thread on every bolt of the AIM-9 missile, that's his life, he speaks to you in that level of detail, and it's just absolute gobbledygook," Williams recalled with a laugh. "This building does not speak English."

Williams said he can sympathize with new military reporters, especially the ones tossed onto the beat at the Pentagon level, where they must not only handle day-to-day military crises, but master the nuances of defense politics, procurement issues and congressional defense committees.

"I think first of all covering the Pentagon is very hard, it's a huge organization, it's doing so many things," Williams explained. "Certainly you can't depend on the meager gruel that we handed out from our office, that's a starvation diet."

Veteran military reporters recall the same sense of bewilderment and shock.

"It was terrible," recalled *Washington Post* reporter Molly Moore, who covered the Defense Department during the 1991 Persian Gulf War, when asked how her first days on the Pentagon beat had gone. "It has the reputation of being one of the hardest beats on our paper."

"This is a beat reporters run away from," said former Associated Press Pentagon reporter Fred Hoffman, who held the post for nearly 30 years before retiring in 1984. "When I was getting ready to retire, literally people were running the other way so as not to be tapped for that beat. This is not a beat that a lazy reporter can thrive in despite the mythology about the great (military) propaganda machine. There is less 'news' generated by the Defense Department than State or the White House. But it is a reporter's beat."

Moore agreed: "At my paper, most reporters are terrified of the military beat. It's viewed as so mammoth and impenetrable that most people don't even try."

Jack Dorsey thought he'd give it a try when the military reporting slot opened up at his newspaper in the Hampton Roads naval complex in southeast Virginia. Given the concentration of military bases and commands in the Hampton Roads area, *The Virginian-Pilot* (at that time operating in friendly competition with its afternoon sister newspaper, *The Ledger-Star*), deploys a team of reporters and editors to handle military subjects.

Having covered most of the standing beats, Dorsey said he was ready for a challenge. And, as a former police-beat reporter, he had experience with uniformed government officials who tend to mistrust the press.

The hardest lesson to impart for new military reporters is that it will take years — not months, not an occasional splash of a story — for the hard work, dogged research and continuous reporting to pay off, veterans like Hoffman and Dorsey contend.

"A new reporter on that beat can't just jump in there and

think he's going to whip the world and be a Jack Anderson," Dorsey said. "You just can't do it. You need the public affairs officers and you need the blessings of the admiral because ... you can't get on a Navy ship or a Navy plane or an Air Force plane if they don't like you."

The correct strategy, Dorsey said, is to earn their respect while maintaining your reputation as a tough but fair — and independent — journalist. Dorsey's advice — geared toward a long-term strategy of establishing mutual confidence between military institution and reporter — is for the novice to consciously avoid arrogance or "a chip on your shoulder."

"Go into that beat with a positive attitude," Dorsey suggests. "You'll find out soon enough whether or not they are crooks or dishonest."

Peter Copeland, who held famed World War II reporter Ernie Pyle's job as military reporter for the Scripps-Howard News Service, suffered culture shock on his first day at work covering the military.

Copeland entered the Pentagon for the first time in January 1989 with little knowledge of the military and a personal belief that it was a dead-end job. "The Cold War was winding down and the story was going to be 'How does the military get smaller?'" he said. "It turned out that I had two wars in two years," he said, referring to the 1990 U.S. invasion of Panama and Operation Desert Storm a year later.

Copeland's first deadline assignment was the equivalent of a dive into the deep end of the pool with lead ankle weights. Six thousand miles away, a pair of Navy F-14 fighters had just shot down two Libyan warplanes that had made threatening moves toward them as they patrolled above the Mediterranean Sea. A Pentagon press briefing was announced to explain the encounter.

"I was totally lost, didn't even know where the Pentagon was," Copeland recalled. "I got into the briefing room and they started talking about jinking the bogeys and the Sparrows left the rail. I didn't know anything, but I saw everyone taking notes so I wrote it all down. Afterwards I went up to this older reporter and I said, 'I'm Peter Copeland from Scripps-Howard and I don't understand any of this.'" The experienced journalist — George Wilson of *The Washington Post* — patiently led his novice colleague through the twists and turns of military slang (a bogey is an unidentified aircraft, a Sparrow is a radar-guided air-to-air missile, and the rail is the fuselage or wing attachment where the missiles are mounted.) "Forever grateful" to the older man's help, Copeland filed his story and went on with his apprenticeship, which matured with his on-scene reporting from the Desert Storm ground war in February 1991.

That Copeland, Moore, Dorsey, Williams and others managed to survive their first encounter with the military is obvious. And the way they did it is no mystery — hard work, taking the work an assignment at a time, not being afraid to tell a source that they didn't understand some of the terminology or concepts, an open mind, and plenty of empty notebooks.

That three of the four had no prior military experience (Dorsey had a brief stint in the National Guard), or prior formal training in military subjects, did not present an insurmountable obstacle to their indoctrination.

"You attend these (explanatory) briefings with the overhead projectors and you get this 'tell you two things at once' syndrome," Williams reminisced. "You're trying to read that (overhead slide) while they talk to you about something entirely different. You think, 'Am I supposed to read this or listen?' I was feeling particularly lost at one of these briefings one day and I leaned across and said (to a general), 'What is C-cubed-I?' and he said, 'I don't know either.'"

"It's sink or swim," Copeland agreed.

Williams overcame his night sweats to become an eloquent government spokesman whose daily work required him to coordinate Pentagon policy announcements with Cheney, Chairman of the Joint Chiefs of Staff Gen. Colin Powell, as well as White House and State Department officials.

Moore and Copeland flourished in their respective military beats and turned out distinguished stories from the Persian Gulf War, subsequently rising to become a foreign news reporter and Washington bureau chief, respectively. Dorsey continues to anchor the military reporting of his Norfolk newspaper, and in his second decade at that slot continues to break military stories of national significance.

How to...

Cover an aircraft crash

It is the one military story that can demand immediate, in-depth coverage at any location on the globe, for military aircraft carry out thousands of peacetime missions worldwide each year.

By its very nature, a military air crash forms a very difficult "bolt from the blue" news story that can catch a military reporter (or any reporter) unprepared. There are several variations of this scenario that require instantaneous response by a news organization:

Local crash: Either a locally-based aircraft or transiting aircraft from an out-of-area command goes down in your coverage area, with or without casualties.

Distant crash: A locally-based aircraft goes down in a distant location.

People only: Local servicemen are involved in a distant crash involving an aircraft not from your area, either as aircrew or passengers.

The reality that exists in the immediate hours following the loss of a military aircraft is quite simple: You and the military officials responsible for the aircraft and any investigation into its loss are in a neck-and-neck race for the bare facts. That aspect of the event — even more than bureaucratic protectionism or efforts to shield accident victims' families from the press — will guarantee that a half-hearted attempt to cover the story will produce nothing, and even a Herculean try will most likely gather up only the bare minimum data essential to tell your readers or viewers what has taken place.

This case study focuses on spot coverage of a controversial Navy A-6E crash that occurred in May 1988.

A plane is down

The first report of a downed Navy bomber came in early morning over the regional Associated Press wire from the city of

Chehalis in southern Washington state: An A-6E Intruder from Whidbey Island Naval Air Station was missing and presumed down in the foothills of Mount St. Helens.

The immediate response by a *Seattle Post-Intelligencer* reporter was to canvass Whidbey Island Navy officials and civilian law enforcement officials known to be involved in the crash search. That preliminary sweep turned up few details for the story itself, but clearly indicated that obtaining the facts needed for a spot story was going to be more difficult than normal.

An official with the Lewis County sheriff's department told the AP that a two-man Intruder had crashed shortly before midnight while flying through a mountain valley east of the city; witnesses had reported a distant fireball and explosion. The 53-foot-long subsonic jet, which operated from aircraft carriers and carries a bomb load 1/3 that of a B-52, was a first-generation "stealth" bomber, in that its radar and other navigation gear were designed to enable the plane to fly below effective radar coverage against enemy targets. (The Navy retired the A-6E from service in 1996.)

Peacetime crashes of the 1960s-era aircraft based at the naval air station outside Oak Harbor (and a corresponding base near Norfolk, Va.) were an inevitable occurrence, given the Navy's need for realistic training and the multitude of things that can (and do) go wrong in any complex aircraft system — especially one like the A-6E that was entering its third decade in the 1980s. In fact, the Navy lost 9 of the aircraft in 1986.

What made the previous night's crash different — and more newsworthy — was this: It was the second A-6E crash in a 21-day period on a 10-mile stretch of that same training route. Clearly, the close timing of the two mishaps would drive several questions by the press and Navy investigators: Were the two losses somehow connected, either to the particular training route, training regime or seasonal factors such as weather? Was some as-yet unidentified flaw in the aging A-6E fleet to blame? Had budget cuts impaired the safety of training or maintenance efforts at the base? Or did a combination of these issues come into play?

The immediate issue, an hour after word of the crash came out through the AP wire, was not how, but where, to cover the story.

The telephone canvass of Navy officials and civilians revealed:

■ The Navy base in Oak Harbor had been completely sealed off to the press. Neither public affairs officials nor senior Navy officers were available for interviews, either at the main gate or over the telephone. A senior Navy contact privately explained that this had been done because the Navy — correctly — anticipated a firestorm of media coverage, because investigators were just beginning to get organized for the crash probe, and because the next of kin were still being identified and contacted.

Thus, the two-hour drive from Seattle to Oak Harbor would produce, at very best, random "reaction" interviews from Navy or civilian bystanders who could be induced to talk on the city's sidewalks — a recipe for emotion but few facts.

■ Lewis County law enforcement and search-and-rescue officials, while not formally constrained from talking to the press, were also unavailable since the teams were still deployed and radio contact through a switchboard operator in Chehalis was spotty.

This is an obvious marker to emphasize whenever a military aircraft goes down outside federal property: Eyewitnesses and civil search and rescue workers are often the only on-scene observers, and should be tracked down with a higher priority than military officials, who more times than not know less about the crash than the reporter who has made a half-dozen preliminary telephone calls.

■ Access to the crash site was a question mark, since that initial round of phone interviews revealed that searchers had only found the wreckage at daylight four hours earlier. A quick study of detailed topographical maps of the region in the newspaper's library — and an air chart showing the military low-level route leading from the Pacific coastline up the mountain valley — indicated that the aircraft was probably down on unrestricted state forest land or undeveloped private logging acreage.

The good news was that there seemed no immediate legal

barrier to approaching the crash site. The bad news was that there seemed to be no way into the area save by logging roads that would require heavy-duty four-wheel-drive vehicles, hours of driving and a genius at land navigation.

Had the incident not immediately raised the issue of a possible connection between the two plane losses 21 days apart, the realistic editorial decision would have been to restrict spot coverage to telephone interviews. But given the potential safety issues and public concern, newspaper management got out the checkbook and authorized a chartered helicopter flight to get a reporter and photographer into the valley to obtain whatever data on-site observation would provide. It was a calculated risk, a major expense, and the correct decision.

Five hours later, after a gut-wrenching series of low-altitude, low-speed approaches into the fog-shrouded mountain valley, the helicopter pilot and reporter both spotted a circular, 20-yard-wide burn on a near-vertical wooded ridge several hundred feet above Riffe Lake, the point of impact for the A-6E as it sped up the Cowlitz Valley at speeds exceeding 400 knots.

The payoff for on-scene coverage included:

■ Confirmation of the specific crash location itself, the obvious loss of life of the two crewmen, and visual details essential to the narrative element of any news story.

■ Visual indications that the bomber was well wide of its predetermined aerial corridor at the time of the crash (the low-level route passed over the lake, not the ridgeline that formed a vertical barrier in the face of the plane). This enabled a staff graphics artist to render an accurate map of the crash and route map for the next day's edition.

■ Evidence, gleaned from nearly a half-hour of observation in multiple passes over the site, that military and civilian searchers had only reached the crash site, but had made no obvious attempt to retrieve debris.

■ Aerial photography of the crash site and search teams at work.

Tips for spot coverage

Obvious contacts: A military aircraft crash outside the boundaries of a military base or reservation can be covered promptly by the simple legal fact that civilian witnesses and emergency-response officials first on the scene are not constrained from talking to the press. In event of such a local, external crash, your obvious initial contacts should include: the city police or county sheriff department and emergency management office in the locality where the plane has gone down; the regional office of the Federal Aviation Administration; the regional, or even national, office of the National Transportation Safety Board; any sub-locality civic leaders or law enforcement officials, e.g. a township or village closest to the site. Also, locate on a state map the two or three closest municipal airports and contact their managers to see if any local private pilots may have either seen the crash itself or overflown the site. They often are the eyewitnesses with the closest frame of reference.

Do contact the PAO and as many senior military officials at the base where the aircraft originated its mission, if known, and if not, call every base with an airfield in the state. Not only will this help determine the aircraft's origination or destination promptly, but often other bases will rush search-and-rescue helicopters or other equipment to the crash site, and this will form a basic element of your spot coverage.

Expect delays in information release: Military officials are not withholding information out of embarrassment or insensitivity to your deadlines. In a developing crash response, the PAOs and even most operational leaders are immediately frozen out of the information pipeline so that the mishap investigators can intensify their acquisition of data without fear of premature disclosure of privileged information. Don't expect release of the names of fatalities or injured crewmen for at least 12-24 hours after the crash becomes known, for the military — correctly — has an obligation to track down and inform the fliers' next of kin first. And given the geographic dispersion of military personnel, that might mean the parents of a 25-year-old pilot must be located on the other side of the country. And even harmless facts may not be forthcoming simply because the military on-base officials haven't got them.

Here are some of the minimum essential facts that you should expect press officials to release:

The first day:

■ Formal confirmation of a missing aircraft or crash.

■ Description of the aircraft type and model, its manufacturer and number of crew aboard (passenger and crew manifests are included as an element of every military flight plan).

■ Description, if unclassified, of the aircraft's mission, transit route, cargo and destination. Confirmation, if so, that there are classified portions of the mission.

■ Other background information pertinent to the incident — the aircraft's unit; home base if different from originating point or destination; the unit's normal peacetime and combat missions; the total number of assigned aircraft in the unit and on base as a whole; the unit commander's name and rank.

■ General historical data on crashes involving this aircraft type. The base PAO will usually have a file listing previous crashes involving aircraft from that base only; service PAOs at the Pentagon or regional commands will have to be approached if your story requires a service-wide accounting.

Second day, to several weeks:

■ Request an immediate callback from the base PAO to identify the name, rank and hometowns of the aircrew when their identities have been released; anticipate this within a day or two of the crash to be used as a normal follow-up story.

■ Additional operational details of the flight and mission that were not available the first day; status of investigation, retrieval of debris and remains; legal issues such as civilian requests for property damage claims; indication of any above-normal command response to the crash.

■ Confirmation that the search for wreckage or survivors has been called off, if the mishap occurred at sea or in extremely remote region.

■ Information on memorial services or other commemorations for the lost fliers. The tightly-knit community on a military base will feel the pang of loss much more strongly than a diverse, less-cohesive civilian community of the same size would. A common-sense approach is to inform the PAO officer that your newspaper or station is interested in covering such services, and request that the PAO act as an intermediary with the families. That will avoid misunderstandings that could add stress to the survivors, and risk alienating other members of the base with which you deal. Make the request only once, and heed the response.

Three to six months:
Request under the federal Freedom of Information Act a copy of the service's legal investigation into the crash. This document includes a full "findings of fact" section itemizing the known condition of the aircraft, its mission and results of the crash probe, as well as conclusions and recommendations sections. Also included are "endorsements" by officials in the military chain of command who, after a review of the probe, may change or add to the recommendations. Certain information — including description of physical injuries and legal punishments meted out to surviving crewmen — are withheld under the Privacy Act.

It will speed up your access to the file if you can obtain through the local PAO the aircraft identification number, e.g. Navy Bureau Number, to include with your FOIA request which will contain the date, location and other pertinent identifying data on the crash.

Again, a common-sense and integrity-building step is for the reporter about to rehash the details of the mishap to contact — either directly or through PAO intermediaries — the surviving relatives of the dead or injured crewmen and advise them of your story. To not do so is to risk dealing them another emotional jolt as the grisly details of their loved one's death suddenly appear.

Military services conduct separate "safety board" probes of aircraft crashes, using separate investigators. Personnel testify fully and without fear of court-martial or other punishment to the safety panel, whose specific, delimited charter is to identify any shortcomings in safety, training, maintenance or operation of the aircraft that require corrective efforts through the service's aviation safety programs. These reports are exempt from release under the Freedom of Information Act, but the military safety centers occasionally will release abstracted data on aircraft safety issues that could be pertinent to a follow-up story.

Be prepared

Much of the information needed for spot coverage of an aircraft crash can, and should, already be in your files — particularly since public affairs officers, being human, might not be as dependable as expected when you ask them in the 20th hour of the crisis to rummage through *their* files and come up with the factsheets in time for your deadline.

Your background files should include:

■ PAO contact telephone numbers — including their cellular telephone numbers — for all military bases.

■ Basic military service factsheets of all aircraft based in or known to operate in your coverage area, plus adequate file photographs of same.

■ Information on any low-level training routes, military operating areas (MOAs), bombing or electronic warfare ranges, or other locations where aircraft congregate.

■ Copies of pertinent military crash-investigation rules and procedures, particularly the PAO guidelines for handling inquiries after a mishap.

■ Names of local and state law enforcement, emergency-response and aviation officials broken down by locality. If your outfit monitors police and fire frequencies with scanners, search for a statewide directory of all government transmission frequencies so that if you must drive into a remote or unfamiliar part of your state, you can dial in unscrambled transmissions that may provide update information or clues to a crash site location.

Chapter 4

The Public Affairs Officer
Your front door to information

Now that you have been appointed military reporter, and you and your editor have drafted your beat coverage plan, it's time to make initial contact with the local military commands. You've identified the major military bases in your primary coverage area and through your newspaper archives, telephone directory and other references you have compiled a preliminary roster of the commands that you will be covering as a primary task of your beat.

Now it's time to meet the single most important person you will deal with in your first months as military reporter: the local public affairs officer. He or she (we'll assume a male from now on) is a career military officer in his late 20s to mid-40s who is the primary public affairs officer (PAO) for the major base in your area. His responsibility, among others, is to serve as the go-between with you and the senior commander, his staff, and the operational military units and tenant commands on the base.

His telephone number is in the phone book, or is one quick transfer from the base operator.

These are a few of the critical points you should know before you make that important first contact:

A matter of preparedness

The Defense Department has a well-organized public affairs infrastructure that extends from the E-Ring of the Pentagon to the local base, Navy ship and Air Force squadron level. Facing that nationwide network are a mere handful of military reporters. (The Pentagon PAO complex and the process by which news is "cycled" from the local to the Pentagon level, and other key dynamics of the reporter-PAO relationship, are addressed in Chapter 7.)

As one new to the beat, have no delusions about your level of preparedness compared to that of your counterpart on the other side of the military base fence. He is ready for you, and you are, at best, scantly prepared to deal with him. If you think mere personal charm, bluster or reading a single background clip from your paper's archives will level the playing field, think again.

Common interests and unavoidable conflicts

The military reporter and the local PAO share many common interests. You are interested in obtaining through him a run-down of the local base's organization, mission and leadership. You need to master the "basics" of his installation and command. You want to establish a good working relationship with the PAO and his superiors. You want his office to serve as a front-door channel to the base, its commander and operational units, both for self-generated stories as well as crisis assistance. Your local PAO wants you to have all that as well.

Assuming that your "charter" calls on you to plan for comprehensive coverage of the base — including a range of non-controversial news stories as well as adversarial coverage when events dictate — you will be working up-front with the PAO and his staff for the routine exchanges that define the working relationship between any beat reporter and his institutional contacts. But somewhere on your bulletin board you might write yourself a brief reminder that ultimately, you and the PAO have radically different goals, simply because you are representing two independent, institutional viewpoints. As chief spokesman for a base, its commander and organizations, the PAO's ultimate duty is to protect his institution and service from public embarrassment or damage.

This is the policy goal of the Fort Lewis, Wash., public affairs office, headed by a lieutenant colonel and staffed by more than a dozen military and civilian workers:

> Effective two-way communications with interior and exterior audiences, on mission accomplishments and other subjects of common interest *to gain support for Fort Lewis* (italics added).

That mission statement does not describe the goals of famed war correspondent Ernie Pyle, much less Woodward and

Seattle-area reporters throng around Fort Lewis spokesman Capt. Martin Eckert during a media availability following the 2nd Ranger Battalion's airdrop in Panama on Dec. 20, 1989. (Photo: Grant M. Haller, *Seattle Post-Intelligencer*)

Bernstein.

Your goal should be self-evident, for it is every beat reporter's goal: Full-court coverage, from change of command ceremonies to deep-cover investigative projects, good news and bad. The challenge, as you will know from your other journalistic assignments, is to maintain honest communication and professional respect even when you and the PAO, and the military commanders he represents, find yourselves in a head-to-head confrontation.

Lines of force: the PAO's world

On paper, the public affairs officer is but one of a handful of military officials who work directly for the senior commander on an Army or Air Force base, Marine Corps facility or Navy command. In reality, the PAO's position is a mirror-image of your own. Where a military reporter is constantly negotiating with his editors for newshole, travel money, project approval and an overall green light to do his business, the PAO, in the real world, must establish a personal and professional rapport with his commanding general or admiral to carry out that senior officer's PAO plan for the command. Within the context of their job responsibilities, PAOs are a lot like reporters in that they often work suspended between the ideal and the actual.

Who are those guys?

In the Army, public affairs is a secondary job specialty that comes after an officer has served 7-8 years in a combat arms or support branch. The Navy and Air Force, on the other hand, have public affairs specialists who are employed in PAO work as a full-time career specialty. The different approaches to PAO work seem stark, but one point should be clear from the outset: The youngest, greenest PAO has had at least several months of intense preparation for media handling, and is usually assigned as an assistant to a more experienced older officer. Most mid-career PAOs have already obtained a BA or MA in journalism, public relations or communications. And they have all dealt with novice military reporters aplenty, especially after Operation Desert Shield/Desert Storm.

What does Col. Smith at Fort Apache do for a living? His responsibilities are a combination of hometown publisher, corporate public relations vice president and overall crisis manager, several senior PAOs explained.

"You've got staff responsibility for community relations," explained Army Col. Bill Mulvey, who as a senior Army public affairs officer managed the Central Command's press facility in Dhahran, Saudi Arabia during the 1991 Persian Gulf War. "You're putting out the post newspaper with maybe 20,000-25,000 circulation."

The PAO of a mid- to large-size Army facility will usually be a lieutenant colonel or sometimes even full colonel — commands like an Army division will have a captain as PAO. The large bases have a staff for handling both internal and external communications. Since military services like their uniformed personnel to move on, and up, to new jobs every 2-3 years, most larger PAO shops will have a civil service deputy who is there to provide long-term management continuity. So the first data Lt. Col. Smith will know about you when you call is whether your newspaper has ever covered his post; and whether that coverage has been haphazard, adequate or comprehensive. In short, your paper or TV station will have a reputation with him, even if you don't.

Making the first contact

During your first encounter, here is what Lt. Col. Smith will most likely suggest you do:

■ E-mail or fax him your bio, and any previous stories you might have written on military subjects and a memo on any specific story ideas or goals for your new position;

■ Schedule a visit to his shop to receive a formal command briefing, to take a quick tour of the post, and to have an off-record chat in which you can size one another up and establish what I term the two-track approach to coverage: what immediate events require coverage despite your lack of preparedness, and what training/indoctrination events are forthcoming that specifically will increase your professional knowledge, with or without coverage of that specific event.

He'll offer to send you some basic background material on the base and its tenant commands and units. Much of this information is now readily available on command websites, as we will discuss in Chapter 12.

Here's what Lt. Col. Smith will do but not tell you. Once he has your bio and clips, he's not going to just file them. Lt. Col. Smith is going to get on the telephone to his contacts in the civilian community — say, a reporter at a rival media outlet — and ask all about you. He'll talk to public affairs officers at other local bases to see if they have ever dealt with you, and if so whether it was a positive experience. He'll talk to other PAOs at commands elsewhere, and perhaps even at the Pentagon itself, to see if your name rings a bell. This goes on everywhere, at all levels of the military. If you survive and prosper in this beat, you'll do the same thing when first meeting a new PAO or new local military commander — pound the drums and transmit: Who is this guy?

This is not military surveillance of the civilian press, PAOs are quick to point out. "I don't keep any file of clips to keep a psychological profile of journalists," said Mulvey, who served as

PAO for the U.S. Army Corps of Engineers before retiring several years ago. "But that's not to say there is not an institutional memory, because there is."

From his vantage point as chief media relations officer for the Army, and a temporary tour as head of the Joint Information Bureau for U.S. Central Command in Dhahran, Saudi Arabia, Mulvey painted a picture of a network of PAO professionals sensitive to every twitch in their sensor system — such as a new military reporter coming on-line.

"Hey, if you want to know what this guy has written before, it's all on Nexis. If I want to know, the computer gives it to me instantly," Mulvey said. Then there's the telephone, Mulvey says: "I can't tell you how many calls I would get a day from field PAOs saying, 'Who is this guy?' Journalists continue to be amazed how much we communicate with each other, and even how much we communicate with other military services."

Still, the local PAO does not automatically have a chip on his or her shoulder, former chief Pentagon spokesman Pete Williams said. "Most public affairs people genuinely like the press, and like reporters, and really want to be helpful to reporters," said Williams.

A word of warning to the novice reporter from Mulvey: "If you screw one PAO for whatever reason, or get off to a bad start with him, you've got a lot to overcome, because he's going to be talking to other PAOs informally."

The visit

It's time to meet the commander. Make sure you have a notebook, and all of your car papers, including insurance forms (or a duty-struck MP at the gate may not let you in).

Regardless of your level of expertise or ignorance, the PAO is probably going to make an assessment of your credibility based on this first encounter. As his assistant shovels the overhead-projector slides through the machine, or while you're driving from the financial assistance office to the heavy machine gun range, he's going to be studying you to see if you are really serious about covering his base and his commanding general. Setting aside the fact that reporters and the institutions they cover inevitably clash over the particulars of coverage, what he is trying to figure out is whether you are worth the time and effort. Because if you are a novice military writer, and do not know the first thing about the infantry/armor/special forces, this officer is the key to your self-organized education on his base, his command and service branch. And if he thinks you're not serious, he won't freeze you out, but he likely will decline to go the extra mile for you on stories that require extra effort on his part.

Again, the successful strategy for a reporter to follow in this most important encounter is simple: honesty and courtesy.

Background materials you should request

Contact information: Get all of his telephone numbers: Office, cellular, beeper, fax, duty office, home, weekend cabin; also the same of all of his subordinates authorized to comment in the PAO's absence. It doesn't hurt to assure the man that you will only call him at 3 a.m. in a genuine emergency.

Background information: Each base publishes a welcome aboard booklet given to newly arriving military personnel, which usually includes a description and history of the base and its units and a base telephone directory. Also, most large bases publish an annual economic impact statement that provides an overview of the personnel, salaries and contract dollars distributed in the local economy. Occasionally an unclassified training calendar is available which will pinpoint upcoming training events that merit coverage.

Biographies: Narrative biographical profiles and service chronologies (dates of assignments and promotions) and formal mug photos are available for the base commander, vice commander/chief of staff and unit commanders.

Wiring diagrams: Many bases publish an unclassified table or organization poster showing commanders, subordinates, all military organizations and tenant units (military outfits on post that report to another headquarters command elsewhere). They are useful not only for quick reference to command organization, but usually list key officials and work numbers. Also, military commands have a service instruction, usually a 1/2-to-1-inch thick "organization manual" that provides a fuller description of each office and unit in the base or headquarters. If the PAO won't give you one, show him you mean business and send him a FOIA request for this unclassified document (See Chapter 11).

Advice: Don't be afraid to ask the PAO for his views on how you can best initiate your ongoing coverage. No two bases, commands or military leaders are the same, and the variety of local issues is infinite. Remember, you are exchanging professional courtesies at this point. Routine coverage does you no harm while giving the PAO and his bosses a small payback for their effort to help you; and most important of all, this transactional phase of your relationship sets you up for the single most important reality of the military beat: You cannot break important news stories, detect significant policy decisions or impacts, or unearth wrongdoing if you don't have the first idea of what they are!

How to....

Cover intelligence intelligently

It is a multibillion-dollar enterprise that is apart from, yet completely intertwined with, the military.

Orbiting satellites watch for nuclear detonations, pluck faint electronic emissions from radio car phones out of space, photograph through clouds using radar technology. Submarines on covert reconnaissance missions record acoustic signatures and blade counts of other submarines. Aircraft and fixed-base listening posts, underwater sonar networks and paid snitches work in all nations and in all possible scenarios, gathering information for processing, analysis and — often enough — military use.

The military reporter cannot but touch the fringes of this highly classified world, since it permeates the entire military infrastructure. But a reporter new to military coverage will quickly learn that this is veritably the hardest part of all to crack, a "wilderness of mirrors" where truth, as one analyst told me, is one of about 18 tactics commonly employed.

It can be done.

But it requires more of the qualities that a military reporter must cultivate to succeed in covering the military itself: more patience, a thicker skin, and especially, more basic knowledge of history, organization, procedure and folklore.

It is helpful that the principal civilian intelligence agency — the Central Intelligence Agency — in early 1992 announced the beginning of a fundamental shift in its relationship with the public and news media, putting a new focus on openness where openness could benefit both the agency and the taxpayers and citizens it is charged to protect. Doubtless, the traditional issues deemed most newsworthy by reporters — covert action, clandestine intelligence gathering, sources and methods — will remain cloaked, but overall, the promise was that some more overt relationships between intelligence services and reporters could be possible.

It is now — for those reporters willing, patient and creative enough to cultivate sources within the community. And careful enough to separate journalistic fact-gathering from the clear, but hidden, agendas of those who would offer data from behind opaque walls.

The novice military reporter will probably have enough on his or her plate to keep from immediately delving into this other universe, but that needn't stop one from preparing for source cultivation and issue exploitation.

The basics remain the same: Study your eyes out. Identify your interest, either by specific organization or topic, and maneuver on the flanks. Find academic or think-tank experts on intelligence agencies and functions, take the back bearings from newly published intelligence histories or studies. Go straight to the agencies involved, if you have a topic pertinent to their charter, and request interviews or a briefing. Sometimes, you'll get in.

The ironclad advice offered here is uncomplicated: Get as much of your story reported and triple-sourced before you ever pick up the telephone to request an interview. At best, you may anticipate a deeply backgrounded confirmation or "waveoff" of your article's details.

With the end of the Cold War and the current easing of superpower military tensions, the history of intelligence operations is a rich vein of journalism that few reporters have mined.

The four decades of the Cold War were full of near-collisions between the United States and the Soviet Union, and many of them specifically originated with intelligence-collecting efforts themselves. Even today, a decade after the collapse of the Soviet Union, stories regularly appear revealing new allegations of the Cold War:

■ Dozens of U.S. military aircraft were attacked, and many shot down, performing intelligence-gathering "ferret" flights on behalf of agencies such as the CIA and National Security Agency, and many incidents went totally unreported.

■ The Navy's nuclear submarine fleet has a long, distinguished, and highly classified history of hairy intelligence missions.

■ Major bloody military incidents, ranging from the 1967 Israeli attack on the *USS Liberty* and the North Korean seizure of the *USS Pueblo* a year later to the 1983 shoot-down of Korean Airlines Flight 007 and the EP-3 Incident on China's Hainan Island in 2001, all stemmed from, or were indirectly connected with, intelligence flights.

■ Soviet and U.S. spy-vs.-spy campaigns have produced major scandals touching both the military and intelligence agencies.

The spy scandal that erupted in 1985 with the arrest of retired Navy warrant officer John Walker, two relatives and a Navy buddy provided a door that led into a major intelligence story. It is summarized here as a useful model of how a journalist can breach the closed world of intelligence in pursuit of a major issue.

When Walker was arrested, I was working in his hometown of Norfolk, Va., as an editorial writer specializing in naval and defense issues, so the scandal demanded immediate in-depth analysis. I followed the reporting disclosures from one pace behind, attempting, in an admittedly limited fashion, to provide the newspaper's readers with perspective and context.

In short, I devoted weeks to reading, interviews and brainstorming with colleagues to put the scandal into context.

Some months later, I moved 3,000 miles away to take a similar editorial-page job in Seattle, and continued to monitor the Walker spy scandal as the stories moved from FBI arrest disclosures into the murky world of the Navy-Pentagon-CIA "damage control" effort. I persuaded my editorial page superiors that it would be worthwhile to cover the San Francisco-based federal espionage trial of Walker's associate, Jerry Whitworth, since Walker himself had agreed to a plea bargain without trial, and since one of his agreements was to testify in detail, publicly, for the first time about his nearly 20 years as a KGB agent. I attended the 1986 trial.

Next, I made my first brush with the intelligence community itself in a front-door approach to the Navy: I contacted several senior officials with whom I had worked, and requested a background session on their efforts to repair the damage from the espionage ring. Since many of the details were now a matter of public record, and since they didn't have to answer a single question that they didn't want to, the Navy team agreed to talk.

Pragmatic journalism: It was quickly clear to me that Navy officials wanted something out, more details on how nefarious Walker had been, and — presumably — to let people know that they had things in hand; I wanted to press them, for what it was worth, on whether the Navy really knew the extent of the damage to secure military communications critical for warfighting success, or whether, as some Navy people had privately told me, the Navy intelligence crowd was still whistling in the dark over the true extent of the espionage implications.

Can't hurt to ask.

I asked.

The message from the Navy was that Walker & Co. probably had real American blood on their hands: They provided information alleging a direct connection between Soviet intelligence gains from the Walker spy ring and several bloody military incidents during the late 1960s. I tested the allegations against my own growing set of facts and judged the allegations supported enough by outside inference and data to be credible.

The analysis article ran.

A year went by, and I had put the entire matter, and a bulging file box, aside. Then, within weeks of taking up a full-time military reporting slot, a stranger walked in.

Stirred by a completely different article I'd written, the man — call him Joe — called in cold. "I'd like to talk about a serious issue. Something is wrong and no one in command realizes what has come down."

We met. Joe was a retired naval intelligence official, and had an angry story to tell about KGB espionage, damage to the U.S. Navy, and what he termed as daydreaming at the top over the impact.

John Walker again.

Joe did not want to give me details at first. In fact, there were many areas that he flatly refused to discuss at all. But when he heard my recitation of my own self-education in John Walker's espionage, Joe decided to bend a little.

And he provided — tersely, carefully, and selectively — enough information to enable me to confront the Navy with a story on just how far the impact of the spy ring had rippled out from the tightly compartmented realm of military communications to the worldwide arena of ship movements and nuclear missile submarines.

In short, Soviet submarines had learned of the blind spots in the U.S. Navy's underwater submarine sensor system, and thus informed were able to sneak closer inshore on reconnaissance missions than the Pentagon ever realized. I was able to report that in Washington state, Soviet subs had sneaked into the Strait of Juan de Fuca (separating the Olympic Peninsula and Canada's Vancouver Island) presumably to find potential hiding spots and minefield locations.

What made this possible were three elements: Through circumstance, I saw the Walker story as it broke; through previous underpinnings in military coverage, I immediately realized the significance of the issue; and through a conscious effort to master the hard technical nuances of the story, I created enough professional credibility that key sources were willing to test their own consciences in the attempt to provide information to the public about a disaster in their ranks.

Chapter 5

Going to Meet the Man
Good relations with the commander pay off

Your first encounter with a senior local military commander marks a major milestone in the creation of your military beat. The relationship you establish with him, his senior staff and the PAO will determine in great part whether or not your coverage of that base and its units will succeed. As with any other journalism beat, your relationship with the top commander will echo down the chain of command, determining cooperation, access and special consideration for non-routine requests.

You should schedule that get-together session at the earliest mutual opportunity. For you, "earliest" means as soon as you are comfortable with the bare-bones outline you've gotten about the base he commands, and how that facility and its units will fit into your coverage strategy. For him, "earliest" means whenever he has an hour to kill.

Afterwards, you will most likely recall a 45-to-60 minute conversation in a spacious office adorned with plaques, flags, quirky military souvenirs and group photos. There, you, the general and his PAO will sit around discussing a variety of subjects in a very relaxed, almost informal tone. The general, of course, will ask you about yourself, where you've worked and your interests. He'll obviously be interested in hearing what prompted you to assume or initiate a military beat at your organization. At some point, he'll express interest in whether you ever served a hitch in the military yourself, or if any close family members have done so. With the prompting of the PAO, you might ask the general's impression of local press coverage, receive a civil if not too accurate reply, and then he will move on to tell you what themes and local issues he considers important. Maybe he'll suggest a thing or two for you to consider. Write them down.

What you won't know for a while — weeks or days — is whether the general has decided it is in his best interest to really work with you or not. But you'll find out as you begin covering events, writing stories and receiving feedback from the PAO and the military people you've encountered.

Let's back up to the beginning and look at the encounter from the point of view of the other two parties: the general and the PAO.

The general's perspective

Like death, taxes and Pentagon duty, reporters are an inevitable consequence for the military officer who survives the intense competition to make flag rank. He has probably had several encounters with the press since he was a colonel. He has received formal instruction on media issues as part of his professional background preparation for senior command, conducted by special cadres of his service's national PAO staff who have taught him how to behave in TV interviews, the different deadlines and needs of print vs. broadcasting, among other things. He has risen through a system which uses the press, as any government organization does, to protect its resources and safeguard its mission and budget. Yet he is also a product of a professional officer corps which — rightly or wrongly — assigns the press much of the blame for its woes, ranging from the collapse of public opinion supporting the Vietnam War to the ongoing struggle over defense dollars in Congress.

So it is very important that you can look at this officer as more than an older guy with stars on his shoulders and grey hair who saw the 'Nam or Persian Gulf first-hand. Your professional self-education must start by gleaning this man's experience within the context of his own military service culture. Did he attend West Point, like Persian Gulf commander Gen. H. Norman Schwarzkopf, or receive his commission through the ROTC program, as did former JCS Chairman Gen. Colin Powell? Or did he start as an enlisted soldier, as did former JCS Chairman Gen. John Shalikashvili? What are those ribbons on his chest and in his bio? Is that the Good Conduct Medal or a Purple Heart next to a Silver Star? Does his master's degree — it is almost an exception for a flag-rank officer not to have at least one — signify a sub-specialty such as financial management or operational analysis? Do his ribbons signify significant combat experience or staff duty? The handouts and bios will readily assist you in determining such an understanding — if you have been doing your homework.

The sensor eye of an Army laser-guided Copperhead shell seems to be staring back at this Army technician as a Fort Lewis artillery unit prepares to fire the precision-guided weapon during a field training mission. Military commands actively encourage the press to come and watch them at practice, not only for publicity, but to educate the press in the high-tech realities of modern combat. (Photo: Ed Offley)

"New reporters have to know who they are dealing with," warned Stewart Powell, the White House correspondent and former national security reporter with the Hearst Newspapers. "They have to know how the officers got to their current rank and job. You meet a major who is a public affairs officer, you had better know that he's been in the service about 10 years and has done a lot of things — he's experienced." By transfer, a general or admiral is one of only several hundred senior executives responsible for anywhere from several thousand to several tens of thousands of men and women under his command. They don't just walk in the door and sit down, either.

And they have an idea of who you are as well.

The generals and admirals of today have directly or indirectly witnessed how well the military and its PAO infrastructure controlled the press in Grenada, Panama and the Persian Gulf War, and they are well aware of the current budget constraints and resource shortages in journalism that impede in-depth coverage, experienced reporters warn. So don't think that glibness or a chip on your shoulder will impress someone who flew 80 combat sorties over Hanoi before you were even born. Regardless of his initial impression of you as a journalist, and the assumed rave review he has received in advance from his PAO about your innate journalism ability and open-minded desire to learn your specialty, the blunt fact is, to the general and his peers you are one of them: the raving mob at the gate when a helicopter has gone down, the people who stubbornly pronounced the M1A1 tank a "lemon" up until the hour Abrams tank crews whipped the Iraqi Army on the sands of Kuwait.

So despite his awareness of military PAO guidelines, and his love for the Bill of Rights, the general in all probability has serious private doubts about dealing above minimum with you and your media outlet. The simple fact is that his own gut feelings tell him that you may be more trouble than you are worth.

One important point: The general cannot and will not freeze you from his base; he legally cannot do that — although in times of crisis, security threat alert or operation he can temporarily ban all reporters and non-essential civilians from entering the facility — nor can he refuse to deal with you, unless you have committed some major crime on post. What we are talking about here, and what you are negotiating with the general for here as well, is to win his confidence to go beyond the minimum of returned phone calls, faxed releases and set-up photo opportunities. You are trying to persuade this man to open some real doors to you for hard-to-get news access, enterprise stories, and crisis response.

That level of access, cooperation and interaction is going to happen only if the general wants it to happen, and it is up to you — novice though you are — to convince the general, his chief of staff and his PAO that it is in their interests to do that. Good luck.

The PAO's perspective

He has lost little face or risked his general's wrath by bringing you in for a chat — that's his job. But within minutes of your departure the commander, chief of staff and PAO are likely to discuss their impressions of you, your seriousness of purpose, the credibility of your interest, and whether any specific coverage ideas you discussed are worth doing. The PAO's neck isn't on the chopping block here — that occurs if and when you or some other reporter start using him as a go-between on a story that may threaten the general's community reputation or career (more later).

Some words of advice for the meeting:

■ Play it straight.

■ Study the general's biography in advance, and if necessary, go over it with someone who can translate some of the acronyms. If this guy has the DSC for LAMSON 749, find out what that means so that you can let him know that you found the Laotian Invasion fascinating as military history — it will impress the fellow more than the trivia aspect, simply because no one ever reads those bios anyway.

■ Don't surprise the PAO in that get-together, e.g., don't tell the general you were a 4-F draft deferment if you had earlier told the PAO you fought the North Vietnamese 320C Division at Khe Sanh.

■ Do admit things that are self-evident: You're new on the beat, you have a lot to learn, you want to get up to speed, you are open to ideas. Sure, he may try to have a slice of you later, but there's plenty of time for stiff-necked journalistic independence after you've successfully established yourself. This is humble time.

■ Try for the general's approval of one specific proposal you'd like to tackle for a story — join an upcoming maneuver, take a low-level night-vision-goggle flight in a Blackhawk, spend a weekend in the mountains with Alpha Company. If the general turns to his chief of staff and says, "I don't see any problem with that," you're on your way.

■ It won't hurt to drop the old soldier a note once back at your desk, thanking him for his time, effort, etc. He has probably never gotten one of them from a reporter before and it will help knock away some of his stereotypes of what reporters are.

Some true encounters (I swear it)

■ The rear admiral commanded a naval aviation wing of over 100 combat aircraft assigned to squadrons that deploy for six months at a time aboard the Pacific Fleet's aircraft carriers. His word would open or slam doors shut. The reporter walked into his office for an initial cup of coffee and chat. "Reporter, huh," the fellow said with a smirk. "What the f*** do you want?" The reporter answered quietly, "If I ever have to come up here and cut your throat, I'd like it to be at least the 15th time we've met and talked that year." The two went on to develop a very successful and professional relationship.

■ When a local reporter asked for a get-together conversation with the new submarine group commander, the officer's PAO representative responded that the admiral had decided the only way he wanted to deal with reporters was through the fax machine. "Just fax a question, I'll walk it into him and we'll fax you the answer." The reporter ran into this admiral a month later at another base's reception and told him, "There is a war of ideas going on about your service, and you have deserted the battle-field." Later, thanks to the intercession of one of the admiral's superiors, they developed an acceptable relationship that did include face-to-face talks.

■ After the Air Force base got a new wing commander, his PAO called a reporter first. "The colonel would like to meet you." The reporter nearly fainted dead away. So it can happen.

■ The National Guard general, recently promoted, and the reporter decided to get re-acquainted and discuss the general's wider responsibilities. The reporter had three specific topics in mind, and the hour ended all too soon. As he left with the PAO, the reporter saw the general still glancing glumly at his crib card with a long list of topics that had not been mentioned. The reporter felt a pang that was not guilt — compassion, maybe? He went back for another chat later.

■ The general's chief of staff, a full colonel, dusted off the blue-ribbon command briefing for the new beat reporter, and he and the base PAO went at it for 90 minutes — taped narrative, multi-screen slide show, written handouts and a four-color brochure with dozens of fact sheets, pamphlets and the like — all you wanted to know but were afraid to ask. "Any questions?" the senior PAO asked at the end. "Er, yes. Are you a colonel? Or a corporal?" They still talked about that reporter, years later.

How to...

Find extraordinary stories in routine events

It comes in by e-mail, fax, snail mail, telephone, messenger, parcel service — everything but a bottle with a cork in it: The avalanche of the routine.

You groan. Yawn. Pitch the envelope — unread and unseen — on the unstable mound of paper at the side of your desk, and turn back to that unpolished lead to the story you promised your editor three days ago.

The tidal patterns of the slush pile are readily discerned. Monday is Blue Monday, for that's when the bale of indigo-colored General Accounting Office reports arrive fresh from the Friday press conference where the report's news value sparked an overnight wire report. The thick letter-sized envelope from the Army Directorate of Used Landmine Recycling will have a p.r. news release and muddy 5 x 7 photograph of the latest Mark 77 Glorck-buster — of no use to anyone but the project manager. The handsome tabloid newspaper is from the Taiwanese non-embassy (you got on the mailing list God knows why and your paper will receive three copies a day for perpetuity even after you go under a bus). The blizzard of paper — single sheet folded thrice, stapled and labeled — is from the Navy or Air Force hometown news center containing the latest names of enlistees, etc. An invitation to a reserve unit change of command arrives by fax. In!

Out! You snarl, hoping to pry open a sealed newsroom window and send the stuff ticker-taping to the parking lot below.

For the novice, a word of advice: Don't.

Out of the slush piles, some wondrous stories appear.

Exhibit One: Flipper goes nuclear

Anyone wanting to dredge a channel, drop a piling or otherwise develop property on navigable waters has to receive permit approval from the U.S. Army Corps of Engineers.

In Washington state, where the Puget Sound coastline meanders for hundreds of miles from Whidbey Island to Olympia, and where dozens of rivers and lakes fall under federal environmental laws, the permit applications flow into the Corps of Engineers office like water over a precipice.

And the Corps, as a matter of PAO routine, mails out copies of each application to the local news media, including a project description, blueprint sketches and other details. The city desk and military beat mail slots turn white with these stapled news releases every morning, and on many days they fly unread into the nearest trash bin.

A bored assistant city editor one morning retrieved his pile of Army Corps of Engineers releases and instead of tossing them into the round-file, decided to read each one. And in between proposed pier renovations and marina pilings appeared a story that Tom Clancy never dreamed up:

"Proposal: Marine Mammal Holding Facility," the application began.

"Address: Naval Submarine Base, Bangor."

In the dry bureaucratic language of forms, the Navy's high-security submarine base on Hood Canal, homeport to eight Trident missile subs, wanted to build a floating condo for as many as 16 "marine mammals."

When I arrived at work that morning I found the ripped-open news release with the editor's scrawl on top: "What the hell is this?"

The first call, to Bangor, alerted me to the fact that something weird was afoot:

Reporter: "What's this about putting marine mammals in Hood Canal?"

PAO: "WHO TOLD YOU THAT?"

Reporter: "Gee, Keith, it's on an Army Corps of Engineers press release."

PAO: (long pause) "Oh shit."

Six hours and several dozen phone calls later, I had a solid story on how the Navy was planning in great secrecy to station a platoon of bottle-nosed dolphins at the submarine base to serve as sentries against saboteurs and other intruders.

Revelation of the project opened up a labyrinth of other issues stemming from the Navy's top-secret marine mammal project then run by the Naval Ocean Systems Center in San Diego, including: accusations by former Navy dolphin and sea lion trainers that the mammals were being abused and poorly cared for in captivity; disclosure of a spate of dolphin deaths in captivity, including one being trained at another base in Puget Sound; an environmental and legal challenge to the project by civilian animal-rights organizations; explanation by two experts — a former U.S. intelligence official and a Soviet military intelligence defector to the West — that the dolphins were aimed at preventing attack by a special cadre of Soviet commandos whose prime strategic target in wartime would be the Bangor base; and, finally, more than a year later, an announcement by the Navy that it had called off the dolphin deployments.

Not bad for one humdrum little press release.

Exhibit Two: Eyes in the sky

Another Bangor tale. This one started with a printer's error. The Oct. 8, 1990 issue of the trade journal *Aviation Week & Space Technology* landed in the in-tray with the normal diversity of stories about commercial airlines, military systems and space topics, but one story about a Soviet effort to commercially market space imagery in the West using a radar-imaging satellite called Almaz caught my eye. What was interesting was a small cigarette-pack-sized photo on one page captioned as showing Puget Sound from space. The photograph, however, resembled an ashtray with two cigar butts in it more than the landforms of Washington.

I was about to toss the magazine away when a memory surfaced: Hadn't the U.S. Navy been experimenting with radar satellites to attempt to track submerged submarines? A computer library search found several articles in which the "wake detection" idea was discussed and in which Pentagon officials had worried aloud that Almaz had been devised as a tool to hunt U.S. submarines.

Out of curiosity, I called an acquaintance at *Aviation Week* and asked about the murky Puget Sound photograph.

"Oh yeah," my colleague said. "That was an error. They used a photograph of a burning oil rig in the Persian Gulf instead of the Puget Sound shot." The next issue included the correct photo. It showed a narrow band of water surrounded by the east and west land boundaries of the sound — as well as details of the underwater canyons and landscape of the bottom of Puget Sound.

I got hold of the U.S. marketing company representing the Soviet space consortium and received by overnight delivery a glossy brochure containing the Almaz marketing information, and a copy of the original satellite photograph.

There not only were the coastal boundaries and underwater landforms of Puget Sound clearly visible — but so were the missile bunkers, mooring pier and explosive-handling wharf at the Bangor Trident sub base! Not to mention the entire maneuvering route that the nuclear missile subs must take to get to the Pacific Ocean.

When *Aviation Week* had published the story of Almaz and

the residual concerns that Pentagon officials held concerning its military potential, they failed to realize that the sample photo confirmed their story far more than its clarity and detail indicated. In consolation, the Soviets' American marketing firm didn't realize it either.

Conclusion: When you're about to toss that release or article away and something in mind says "hold it," let your intuition and innate curiosity have their way.

Exhibit Three: The submarine that wasn't there

For five years in the mid-to-late 1980s, the Pentagon published an annual "Soviet Military Power" publication enumerating in detail the military capabilities of the Soviet nuclear and conventional forces. A highlight of the publication was its double-truck color world map showing the range, extent and depiction of deployed Soviet forces. And for most of those years, the Soviet strategic submarine force was depicted in the North Atlantic and eastern Pacific Oceans by a large blue oval showing the patrol patterns for *Yankee*-class nuclear-armed submarines.

Well, one day in 1989, the Soviet Navy quietly stopped sending those older submarines to the Eastern Pacific, which was a hazardous voyage through a massive U.S. submarine detection network comprising underwater hydrophones, U.S. attack submarines and P-3C Orion anti-submarine patrol planes from Alaska, Hawaii, Midway and Guam. Why? Because the newer Soviet Delta-III nuclear missile subs have a missile whose flight range makes it unnecessary to travel that far to hit its targets.

Now, neither the U.S. Navy nor the Soviet Navy, for different reasons, had any desire to issue a press release on the sudden disappearance of Soviet missile boats from that offshore patrol corridor. The Morskoi Voennoi Flot kept its habitual silence, and the Pentagon, in its own sneaky way, decided to disclose the submarine shift and hide it at the same time: When the 1989 edition of "Soviet Military Power" came off the printing presses, the Defense Department cloaked the absence of Soviet submarines in the Eastern Pacific by editing over the change. Rather than depicting a wide swath of empty ocean, the Pentagon report contained a graphic index right where the *Yankee*-class subs had once lurked.

When confronted with the change, U.S. Pacific Command officials shrugged in confirmation and said the move represented no significant shift in military power. But having touted the Soviet threat in those close-in terms for so long, the Pentagon seems to have granted the Soviet Navy a courtesy, in allowing its retreat to distant submarine bastions to occur with little trumpeting for our side.

Chapter 6

Going Into the Field
Your knowledge grows on the road

You've been on the military beat for several weeks now, your desktop is beginning to fill with publications and reference books, and your PAO contacts are beginning to call you with routine story ideas. Hopefully, you've gotten into print with local spot stories, release pickups, and wire chases, and are feeling that — so far — you are successfully transitioning into the military specialty. Your colleagues are beginning to salute and call you "General" as you enter the newsroom.

You've met both the PAOs and the local military commanders in your primary coverage area, and believe that it's now time for some hands-on work. It's time to spread your wings a little. You decide to organize an assignment in the field with a local military unit. If your local contact is a competent PAO, he or she wants you there, too. Most field visits require only routine approval from the local commander. Others, such as indoctrination ship or aircraft rides or participation in distant or overseas military exercises, must be negotiated by the local PAO with his superiors in the military chain of command.

More ambitious coverage, such as coverage of multinational military exercises overseas, may require special Pentagon and foreign host nation approval and visas. The good news is that, in these latter cases, the military unit "sponsoring" you will do a lot, if not most, of that groundwork.

The bad news is that this bureaucratic process constitutes an effective veto power by the military over your participation. However, in my 20 years of military coverage I have only heard of a handful of cases where reporters were tossed off such a trip. Once a Scandinavian government participating in a major allied military exercise in the Norwegian Sea suddenly announced that it wanted no foreign coverage of activities close to the Soviet Union, and weeks of U.S. Navy PAO planning went out the window. Note that this was a political, rather than military, attack of chickenshit-itis. But military variants can happen too.

It is in field coverage that the novice military reporter will hasten his knowledge of technical issues, develop a feel for military people both as soldiers/sailors/airmen and as individual citizens, and begin to expand beyond calendar and budget-driven stories to discuss issues driven by training, tactics and strategy.

Routine training

Here is a sample of local and regional peacetime "field exercises" that colleagues and I have covered in recent years:

Army/Marines/Army National Guard

■ Small-unit infantry maneuvers in local training areas using military "laser-tag" gear for simulated live-fire drills;

■ Mass airborne parachute drops of the elite Rangers or other specialized Army units, witnessed from the drop zone, followed by field maneuvers against OPFOR (opposition force) training units;

■ Tank and mechanized infantry tactical exercises, including overnight visits with the units;

■ Squad practice on a specialized "urban combat range" where live ammunition fire is permitted inside closed structures, as well as live fire on rifle, missile and hand grenade ranges;

■ Helicopter unit operations covered through flights in a combat training regime;

■ Battalion- and brigade-strength "force on force" desert warfare pitting M-1A1 tanks against simulated Soviet armored formations;

■ Amphibious landing maneuvers involving Navy high-speed hovercraft and Marine helicopters.

Navy

■ Routine "embarks" (embarkations) to ships at sea for several hours to interview officers and crewmen of ships returning from overseas deployment;

■ Longer trips aboard Navy warships for naval exercises that can last several days and offer the gamut of naval warfare, including carrier air operations, naval gunfire, missile shoots and shipboard drills;

In the jump seat: The author used a super-wide angle lens and cable release to catch this group portrait during an orientation flight in a B-52H.

■ Day trips on attack and missile submarines;
■ Jet flights in tactical Navy aircraft (F-14, A-6E, F-5E) (after successful completion of a water survival and aviation physiology course and a flight physical medical exam).

Air Force
■ Orientation flights in practically all types of aircraft (B-52H, KC-135, KC-10, C-141, C-130 and F-15). (Flights on tactical aircraft and bombers require passing a flight physical medical exam and an aviation physiology course);
■ Paratroop and cargo airdrop exercises observed from aircraft;
■ Specialized ground command/control operations such as activation of a combat airfield in a remote location.

Overseas
■ NATO "Reforger" exercises, including military flights to and from the United States;
■ U.S.-South Korea "Team Spirit" wargames, including precise military movement from the United States to Korea simulating response to a crisis;

- Navy port visits to the Soviet Union;
- U.S. Air Force cargo airdrop mission to the South Pole;
- Navy amphibious landing exercises in the Caribbean.

As you can see, the opportunities for field coverage span from a morning on the local Army post to a two-week overseas trip to the South Pole. What all of them require, apart from soliciting permission to attend through the local base PAO, is a corresponding degree of advance planning on both sides. Successfully integrating field coverage into your desk calendar requires a long-term approach that can begin many months before the event actually occurs.

One word of caution: A professional PAO will work very hard to get you approved for field trips if in his opinion you are ready for it; this is not political or ideological screening as much as it is a determination on his part that you are capable of handling the physical challenge and are competent enough on the particular subject to grasp it and write capably of what you have seen. A good PAO will also candidly tell you if he thinks you are not ready for such an ambitious trip, and a good PAO will also work with you to get you to the point where his superiors agree that it is not a waste of time for you to do so.

Once you and the PAO have identified a notional coverage idea, you should open a file and start organizing. I find it handy to use a single legal pad with separate sheets for paperwork planning, logistics and research.

Here is how one complex field coverage assignment — involving three separate military services and a foreign government — was carried out.

Field coverage — Exercise 'Team Spirit 88'

Until they were suspended for political reasons in the mid-1990s, the "Team Spirit" exercises were held every two years in South Korea to test the U.S. military ability to rush military reinforcements to the Korean peninsula in event of attack from North Korea. The maneuvers covered the spectrum of conventional combat from naval exercises to infantry war-games and Air Force live-fire drills. Today, similar exercises are still regularly held in the Western Pacific (Cobra Gold), Central Pacific (RIMPAC) and

Egypt (Bright Star).

Print media participation in the 1988 "Team Spirit" exercise, held six months before the Olympics Games in Seoul, is profiled here as a model for coverage planning.

Paperwork planning

Most field coverage involving more than a day-trip visit for interviews and watching units will require formal requests for participation, often to more than one level of the local unit's chain of command. The local base, its immediate headquarters, and possibly the Pentagon headquarters branch of that service will all have to pass on and approve your request to travel with, or meet up with, a local unit involved in distant training. For example, when the *Seattle Post-Intelligencer* decided that I would travel to South Korea for two weeks to observe local Army, Navy and Air Force units participating in this biennial, multi-service war game, it was necessary to obtain the following approvals:

South Korea — visa;

Japan — transit visa;

Air Force — formal approval, in the form of special travel orders, to permit me to fly from McChord Air Force Base, Wash., to Osan, South Korea, onboard a C-141B taking paratroopers for an airborne assault exercise;

Army — approval by I Corps headquarters and the 9th Infantry Division, with concurrent approval by the 8th U.S. Army headquarters command in Seoul, to join up with Fort Lewis infantry units on the ground in the maneuvers;

Navy — approval by the Chief of Naval Information office, U.S. Pacific Fleet public affairs office, and the aircraft carrier *USS Midway*, to travel from Korea to the ship, then operating in the Sea of Japan.

There was nothing exotic or mysterious about any of these requests.

Having learned the general nature, time-frame and unit participation in the Team Spirit exercise from military spokesmen, I began contacting the appropriate consulates and military public affairs offices about 45 days before my intended departure date. In this case, the Military Airlift Command's suggestion that I apply for approval to cover their ambitious airlift mission from the U.S. West Coast directly to South Korea provided me with my own coverage start date. A telephone call to Army officials at Fort Lewis confirmed that a major portion of the ground maneuver exercises would be taking place within a two-week period after the scheduled airdrop. Also at this point, I made a request to Navy public affairs officials to obtain access to 7th Fleet warships in the exercise at a mutually convenient time during my trip, with the proviso that I would inform a Navy PAO representative in Seoul of those dates as soon as I had learned them.

In all cases, what the PAOs wanted was a formal letterhead memorandum or note that:

■ Constituted the formal request;

■ Provided the PAO offices with sufficient schedule and coverage information to allow them to confer with their operational commanders and exercise schedulers to see how and when I could be fitted into the maneuver;

■ Formally confirmed that I would be entering South Korea legally and would have the funds to provide for my own stay and return commercial flight to the United States after covering the events.

There were three reasons why this request received prompt approval from the 10 separate PAO offices involved. First, as someone who had been writing about the military for nearly eight years at that time, I already knew and had worked with many of the senior PAOs whom I contacted. Second, through informal conversations and research, I had been able to determine within a tight focus the events and units that I wanted to cover, so that my request was not wildly unrealistic or a nightmare for the "operators" to consider. Third — and most important — I gave the PAOs enough lead time to massage the request through their own internal chain of command and to receive the necessary review by senior officers.

Simultaneously, of course, I was preparing for my editors a travel budget, story outline and communications links.

Logistical planning

Given that in war games, soldiers don't really die, tanks don't always shoot live cannon shells, and warplanes often feign missile fire, I initially decided to avoid daily spot coverage. At the time I was the only local reporter on the manifest so the initial plan (this exercise took place long before the emergence of the internet and real-time e-mail correspondence) was to take notes and upon return to the United States write a chaptered special report on the war game. That decision would allow me to leave my laptop computer at home, since I was already going into the field with a heavy camera bag in addition to a rucksack.

Planning flexibility required

Less than a week before my scheduled departure aboard a McChord-based C-141 for South Korea, I learned that two other local reporters, one from a newspaper and one from a TV station, at the last minute had applied and received permission to cover the war game. My editors and I decided that instead of a chaptered saga written weeks later, we would now have to file daily by phone and fax.

So the coverage that followed was modeled after what a reporter would reasonably try to file in event of a genuine military emergency. My article list included:

■ A spot "mission briefing" story based on the actual Air Force briefing, 24 hours before departure, where the senior Air Force officer leading the flight of six C-141s to South Korea explained to his aircrews what procedures they would employ in a complex operation that included radio silence from the moment engines were turned on in Washington state until the time, about nine hours later, when Army and Air Force paratroopers leaped out of the side doors for the 15-second plunge onto a Korean drop zone.

■ A stage-setting story, filed from I Corps headquarters in the mountains of South Korea, explaining the exercise battle scenario: The Korea-based U.S. 2nd Infantry Division and several South Korean Army units would play the "Orange," or enemy forces, while the Fort Lewis troops and other South Koreans would play the U.S. and its allies.

■ A long narrative file, based on several days in the field with an infantry company from the Fort Lewis-based 9th Infantry Division, detailing what combat skills were being tested; what exercise artificialities were necessary because of safety concerns, money limits or host-nation sensitivities; and how the young American soldiers coped with pressures common to war games and actual combat — physical fatigue, loneliness, filth and hunger.

■ A Navy report, datelined from the carrier *USS Midway*, that underscored the "real world" component of Team Spirit 1988. During a two-day visit to the carrier, Soviet warships and aircraft were frequently observed approaching the U.S. battle group, and combat aircraft were scrambled on numerous times to approach, observe and identify the Soviet units playing arm's-length tag on behalf of their North Korean allies. This was my first encounter with the EP-3 Aries reconnaissance aircraft, exactly 13 years before the Hainan Island incident in April 2001 involving the fatal collision between an EP-3 and a Chinese fighter.

■ A follow-up analysis piece, structured on interviews with United Nations Command officials, on the prospects for war or political accommodation between the two Koreas.

Lessons learned for a reporter

Given that this coverage occurred in a friendly allied nation actually at peace, it is unlikely this coverage strategy would work in a real war. In fact, few of the tactics that served me well in Korea in 1988 were relevant to the situation in Operation Desert Storm three years later. But these pointers, gleaned on the mock battlefield, should be useful for journalists venturing into field coverage:

Research before you leave: Don't expect to find ready access to basic information (units, weapons, commanders' biographies) once you arrive in the exercise area. The commanders and even PAOs I knew from home were overworked, exhausted, and almost too busy grappling with their own logistical and communications problems — not to mention the war game itself — to provide the materials and routine help one quickly comes to expect at the local base. Weeks prior to departure, I scrounged from local PAOs and my own files a cross-section of reference material that would be essential in filling out any story on those organizations. Similarly, veterans from Asia coverage advised me to compile in advance a ready abstract on South Korean history and politics, the Korean War, and other subjects indirectly relevant to the assignment.

Travel light: I missed my laptop computer, but excellent fax, telex and telephone service provided transmission backups. The rule of thumb for military travel is to drag one large bag and a shoulder bag/grip, and keep the large bag half-empty on the outbound leg of your trip (you'll want space for souvenirs). There's no baggage check-in service in the Air Mobility Command missions I've flown. You pick it up yourself off the cargo pallet on the tarmac — period.

Cultivate the exercise-area PAOs: At one point in the Korea trip, I was advised by a Fort Lewis PAO that it was up to me to rendezvous with his colleague, the 9th Division PAO, in order to join the infantry company for several days in the field. The "where" and "when" were TBD. The next day, back in my Seoul hotel room, the PAO, now 120 miles away, informed me that I was supposed to meet his colleague at 9 a.m. the next day at the intersections of Highways A and B — another 70 miles to the east of where the Fort Lewis officer was then situated. How to get there? I panicked as I threw gear into a pack and raced by cab across the Korean capitol to the U.S. military headquarters at Yongsan. Take a cab? Too far and expensive. Rent a car? Impossible. I couldn't abandon it in a war zone, simulated or otherwise. Fly? There were no commercial airfields close by and even so they were probably secured for the exercise.

I found the local public affairs office at Yongsan and poured out my tale of woe. "No sweat," said an Air Force senior master sergeant. He picked up a phone and called an Army friend at a base near the exercise area, then issued instructions: I was to take a Korean bus to the city adjoining his friend's base. I would take a room at the such-and-such hotel ($24 per night, no cable TV). At 9 a.m., his friend, Sergeant Smith, would meet me in the lobby and take me to the 9th Infantry Division. I did, and he did. Sergeant Smith, on his second tour in Korea, knew every back roadway from Pusan to China, it seemed. The following morning he and I drove about 60 miles to the east, doglegged south, stopped for a coffee break, asked some U.S. soldiers where the 1st Brigade was hiding out, crossed a ribbon bridge, reached Yong-In, and there saw my infantry company settling in for an ambush. I thanked Sgt. Smith profusely as I slung my gear into a 9th Division Humvee. I never saw the division PAO again (maybe he's still waiting under the yum-yum tree.) I know a PAO miracle when I see it.

Chapter 7

Surviving the Pentagon
The 'Puzzle Palace' is an essential stop

It is the seat of power for the U.S. military, the headquarters building for the armed services and their political superiors. It is the physical manifestation for the vast, multiple military chains of command — not a single chain, but many — that define the roles, missions and very existence of the local bases and units you cover. And on Sept. 11, 2001, it became a battlefield in the ongoing war against terrorism. It is an inevitable duty station for many, if not most, military officers in the course of their careers. It has an underground subway stop, five sides, insufficient parking, its own shopping mall, leaky roofs, fast food and over 20,000 inhabitants who can enrich your coverage or stifle your most earnest attempts as a reporter to document the activities of the U.S. military.

Installed within its dreary stone facade are the office of the secretary of defense and his staff; the office of the chairman of the Joint Chiefs of Staff and the Joint Staff, his warfighting planners; and the headquarters of the Army, Navy, Air Force and Marine Corps. Elsewhere throughout the Washington, D.C., area are several dozen autonomous Pentagon agencies, ranging from the super-secret National Reconnaissance Office, which controls overhead satellite reconnaissance, to the local motor pool.

Even if your coverage focuses on a mere handful of local military bases, and the units and military functions they carry out, your path as a military reporter will inexorably draw you to this former garbage dump on the bank of the Potomac River. For the supreme civilian and military leaders there make the decisions that define what your local base and its units will do, and therefore what you will do.

Assuming that your position is that of a regional or statewide military writer, and your turf is farther away than a day trip from Washington, D.C., the brute reality is that you will mostly have to grapple with this five-sided beast by telephone and e-mail. One of the more common patterns you will find in your local or regional military coverage is monitoring the wires from Washington for any defense-related story, and scanning those stories for local angles or clues ignored by the Pentagon reporters who by necessity must embrace the wider perspective.

Dropping a bombshell

On Friday, Sept. 27, 1991, at 5 p.m. PST, President George H.W. Bush in a televised nationwide address dropped the journalistic equivalent of an atomic bomb. He announced major, unilateral nuclear-weapon cuts in the U.S. armed forces, including a decision to strip the Navy of most of its tactical nuclear weapons, to retire older land-based ICBMs scheduled for retirement under the START I Treaty, and to consolidate nuclear command and control under one headquarters. Hours before Bush spoke, I and my editors knew that the Bush speech would be extraordinarily significant in Washington state, which at that time had, unofficially, one of the largest concentrations of deployed nuclear weapons in the nation. We began planning for a significant "take-out" story explaining what impact, if any, the president's announcement would have on our bases and commands. There were challenges from the outset.

It being 8 p.m. on a Friday night in the "other Washington," there was little access to either governmental or even outside experts, who were long gone from their offices. And homes, too, I learned as I burned through my Rolodex. So as the hours ticked away, my coverage approach to this breaking story devolved to a combination of previously excavated nuclear facts, some hasty phone calls to local military PAOs, and one defense-oriented congressman with whom a late-night telephone connection was made. The story fell together in a straightforward manner. As we monitored the TV broadcast, three immediate local impacts emerged:

■ The president's "uncocking" of the Strategic Air Command bomber and missile force would have a historic impact at Fairchild Air Force Base near Spokane, Wash., where for decades, at least six B-52H bombers — loaded with 20 ALCM nuclear cruise missiles, B61 nuclear gravity bombs and SRAM short-range nuclear missiles — had stood ground waiting for the klaxon sound to send their crews aloft toward nuclear Armageddon. (Three years later the Air Force would transform Fairchild to an aerial refueling tanker base after the nuclear reductions first announced that night prompted the air service to shrink the bomber fleet to only two B-52 bases.)

■ The president's announced decision not to change the current number of multiple-warhead Trident missiles aboard *Ohio*-class missile submarines based at the Bangor Submarine Base on Hood Canal near Puget Sound meant that the strategic importance of the Bangor Submarine Base and Submarine Squadron 17's eight submarines would grow as the other components of the nuclear arsenal shrank. (Indeed, the next year Pentagon figures showed that the "sea-based" leg of the strategic nuclear forces would inevitably grow to half of all deployed weapons.)

■ The announced creation of a new multiservice U.S. Strategic Command to manage and control both Air Force and Navy nuclear weapons would have significant technical and bureaucratic impacts of an unknown nature for both the Air Force and Navy bases in the state.

The unofficial nuclear weapon count for Washington state military bases — derived by outside nuclear experts from snatches of unclassified Pentagon data — was already on file, from a major enterprise series in 1990; local PAOs, though caught by surprise like the rest of the country, were able to confirm and update several key, time-sensitive facts about their facilities; the congressman put an informed spin on the significance of the Bush speech; the wires provided backup confirmation that what I had heard with my own ears was no hallucination — and the *Seattle Post-Intelligencer* had a Page 1 exclusive "what it all means" article about what was then one of the most significant nuclear arms reduction announcements of the entire Cold War era.

The art of late Friday bombshells

The Bush I administration's major nuclear announcement was unusual in itself because, in contrast to other policy shifts, few details had been leaked in advance of the speech. But the Friday afternoon squeeze is a time-honored tradition at the Pentagon. What better way to jettison a major news announcement than late in the day on Friday where, even if reporters can seize the topic, they are forced to consign it into the black hole of Friday night's news broadcast or Saturday's newspaper edition? Every military reporter quickly learns to keep his or her schedule open and desk bare every Friday afternoon simply because the chances are good for a Pentagon bombshell around quitting time inside the Beltway.

A senior Pentagon PAO once had the nerve to complain to me that the congressional General Accounting Office was unfair because it frequently released reports critical of the Pentagon late in the day on Friday, giving Pentagon PAOs little or no chance to put their own "spin" on the story. Hmmmm.

So add this to your list of things to be ready for — the sudden Pentagon announcement which directly or by implication opens up an entire story or line of stories pertinent to your coverage. You must not only be sensitive to the military issues and topics that exist in your area, and have the ability to respond to disclosures like this promptly, but you must also have a beachhead inside the Pentagon itself to wring whatever data, confirmation, backgrounding or quotes you need.

For that to be possible, you at earliest opportunity should plan a pilgrimage to the Pentagon to lay some groundwork for all of those crash long-distance calls. If you are getting the management support you require for a full-time military beat, this should be a regular part of your annual activities.

Your Pentagon visit also should set the stage for getting your significant stories published in the *Early Bird* news summary (see the end of this chapter).

Think of it as a bureaucratic field trip.

Destination Pentagon

For your initial Pentagon visit, plan on at least 7-10 days for obtaining the bare minimum contacts and backgrounding essential to your beat. You should try for a minimum of one full day with each military service, as well as several days to work local congressmen on Capitol Hill and other source experts in

Washington, D.C., such as think tanks and military associations. My own initial Pentagon trek, involving three of the major services — Air Force, Navy and Army — took a full two weeks.

Here are some goals you should shoot for in your Pentagon visit:

■ Visit the assistant secretary of defense/public affairs and the Directorate for Defense Information (DDI).

This is the main public affairs organization for the secretary of defense and DoD civilian leadership as a whole, the controlling authority for media relations in major military operations and decisions from top Pentagon leaders. For instance, generic information about a Navy Aegis missile destroyer can be obtained through the Navy's PAO network, but all information about the 2000 terrorist bombing of the *USS Cole* was controlled by the ASD/PA and DDI staff.

I learned this early in my military reporting career when the Navy Reserve unit Mine Group 1 in Seattle was activated suddenly for service in the Persian Gulf. For years this had been a backwater training command whose six vintage wooden minesweepers and shore facilities attracted scant publicity, and whose public affairs contact was the local Navy base. Within hours in 1988, however, the local unit became the focus of worldwide media interest — and all information and media queries were abruptly shifted from Seattle to the Pentagon.

How do you as a reporter learn that the Navy story has been hijacked? Ask. When your good buddy the local Navy spokesman in a monotone refers all questions about the ships to the Pentagon press number (703) 697-5131, or when he locks you and a dozen others inside a wire fence compound outside of

---

Pentagon PAO Numbers

Assistant Secretary of Defense/Public Affairs ....(703) 697-9312

Directorate of Defense Information ....(703) 697-5131

Air Force Media Relations (Pentagon) ....(703) 695-0640

Army Media Relations (Pentagon) ....(703) 697-2564

Marine Corps Public Affairs (Navy Annex) ....(703) 614-4309

Office of Navy Information (Pentagon) ....(703) 697-5342

---

earshot of the busy pier when you show up to cover the minesweepers' departure, consider both as good hints that the topic has been yanked up to the E-Ring of the Pentagon.

Once you get to the spacious office of the DDI in Room 2E765 of the Pentagon, which resembles a large newsroom staffed by mid-level and senior military officers, you should make an effort to meet the specific "action officers" there who handle the PAO "accounts" (institutions and long-term issues) that crop up on your beat. Your bottom line is to turn that exhausted voice at the other end of the line into someone you know personally. A current breakdown of the DDI structure and its current press officers is available on request from DDI.

■ Visit the appropriate service headquarters public affairs offices.

The senior public affairs officer, or media relations branch officer, for the Army, Navy, Air Force or Marines, is not someone you will work with on a daily basis. But he is a most important person to know, given the speed by which your initiation as a military reporter and your ongoing performance will flash down the PAO communications pipeline. Try to schedule a 20- to 30-minute coffee session with him and his assistant, and go prepared to answer their questions on what you want to accomplish on your beat, your conception of media relations with that service, and other ideas.

While you are in that PAO shop, also try to meet any action officers or spokesmen who deal with specific areas pertinent to your local commands. This is something you will have identified while arranging your visit by telephone. For example, within the office of the Chief of Navy Information (CHINFO), there are several spokesmen who specialize in queries about naval aviation and aircraft carriers, while others deal with the submarine force and surface warship communities. Current staffing, PAO "accounts" and telephone numbers for the Pentagon public affairs offices of the armed services are also available.

■ Request specific-subject background sessions.

With advance planning and foresight, you can successfully request background interviews with senior military officials on topics or trends you have identified as essential to your beat.

What will vary is the rank and seniority of the briefer, the time allowed you and the quality of material you receive. As a beginner to the beat, harbor no illusions that on this initial visit the Pentagon is going to bestow upon you the secrets of the realm. You will obtain useful material in great quantities, though, and as you gain experience, good clips and Pentagon feedback, you will find backgrounders more available and more productive, for the simple reason that your Pentagon contacts will have decided that you are worth the effort they have to make to set up the sessions.

■ Prepare to scrounge.

Throughout your visit, ask for and take one of everything — but go there with a detailed shopping list. If an Air Mobility Command base is in your primary coverage area, go to the Air Force PAO desk and ask for everything pertinent to that area: AMC budget, reports, background information papers, etc.

■ If it's not free, buy it.

If you haven't gotten one already, get a Department of Defense telephone book, available through the Government Printing Office. Although new editions appear quarterly to reflect the inevitable personnel turnover, most office numbers remain the same year in and year out. Query your Pentagon contacts for any reports or books published either privately or through the Government Printing Office that may be worth obtaining. Visit the Pentagon shopping mall for book sales.

■ Have fun while there.

Enjoy the Puzzle Palace and either rejoice in your location far from the building or begin planning for an assignment with the Pentagon press corps, whichever applies.

Attend at least one Pentagon press briefing (normally held on Tuesday and Thursday afternoons at 1:30 p.m. — check the DefenseLink website news page for daily Pentagon activities). Introduce yourself to Pentagon spokespeople and the small but talented mob of full-time Pentagon reporters who attend. In particular, attempt to meet any of the Pentagon regulars whose bylines appear frequently in your newspaper. Take a guided tour of the building if you have time and comfortable shoes.

■ Service your investment wisely.

When you get back home, start talking to these new contacts frequently. Their days are a mirror-image of yours — quiet moments, hours of sudden crisis, days of slogging through the budget — and the more you talk with them, the more they will remember and make that extra effort for you. Human nature will do more than Pentagon regulations to ensure success.

How to...

Use the *Early Bird*

" ... *one of Washington's best read and most influential newspapers.*" — Hedrick Smith in his treatise on capitol politics, The Power Game: How Washington Works, (Random House, 1988)

"In Washington, people do not always have time to read the papers, at least not all the papers. To assist those in government service to see what the press is saying about things is an in-house daily press-summary sheet called The Early Bird ... relating to all manner of government operations." — The Sum of All Fears, by Tom Clancy, (Putnam, 1991)

If you want your article to be read by the secretary of defense, all six members of the Joint Chiefs of Staff and senior Pentagon aides before breakfast — and if you want your telephone calls and requests to the Pentagon to be taken seriously — there is one easy way to reach both goals: Submit your stories to the Pentagon's in-house news summary, known as the *Early Bird*.

Previously assembled by hand using fax machines, scissors and glue, the daily news summary now is a self-contained web document complete with index that is available through numerous Defense Department web sites, or as an e-mailed file you receive each working day. It comes in three versions: *Early Bird*, which contains between 40-50 news articles per edition; *The Early Bird Supplement*, which runs about the same size with additional stories, columns and editorials, and the *Radio-TV Defense Dialogue*, a text synopsis of television and radio stories and inter-

EARLY BIRD

THURSDAY, August 20, 1992

NEWS HIGHLIGHTS

U.S. OFFICIALS HEAD TO SOMALIA: U.S. officials visited Somalia on Wednesday to prepare for a massive relief airlift. On Tuesday, Marine Brig. Gen. Frank Libbuti, to command the military airlift from Mombasa, Kenya, said U.S. soldiers will be responsible only for getting the food into Somalia, but not for getting it from airstrips to the needy. U.S. officials are to arrange for humanitarian agencies to unload, store and distribute the food on the ground. (AP)

NEWS...Pg. 16

WASHINGTON POST   Aug. 20, 1992   Pg. 1/21

Delivery Questions Delay Airlift of Food to Somalia

By Keith B. Richburg
Washington Post Foreign Service

NAIROBI, Kenya, Aug. 19—A planned U.S. airlift of food to starving Somalia faced delays today as military and relief officials looked for ways to protect the supplies from thieves and ensure their delivery to the people in most desperate need.

Leaders of the joint public-private effort said in

AIRLIFT...Pg. 9

WASHINGTON POST   Aug. 20, 1992   Pg. 1

Plan to Bar Iraqi Flights Contains Risks for Allies

Fragmentation, Stronger Iran Role Cited

By Caryle Murphy
Washington Post Foreign Service

MANAMA, Bahrain, Aug. 19—The U.S.-led move to ban Iraqi aircraft from flying in southern Iraq is a significant shift in Western strategy for undermining Iraqi President Saddam Hussein, but it **NEWS** courts a danger that **ANALYSIS** Washington and its allies have sought to avert the pos-

sible fragmentation of Iraq.

The official reason for the so-called "no-fly zone", in which Iraqi aircraft would be barred from flying south of the 32nd Parallel, is to shield the predominantly Shiite population there from government bombings and strafings carried out in the name of quelling a persistent, but low-level Shiite insurgency.

PLAN...Pg. 10

NEW YORK TIMES   Aug. 20, 1992   Pg. 1

A New Resolve on Iraq

Plan to Use Air Power in Southern Region Recognizes Shiites' Plight and U.S. Politics

By MICHAEL R. GORDON
Special to The New York Times

WASHINGTON, Aug. 19 — The decision by the United States and its allies to place a protective military umbrella over the southern third of Iraq is a complete reversal of a policy adopted and aggressively defended just after the gulf war.

News In March 1991, the Bush
Analysis Administration concluded that shooting down Iraqi helicopters to thwart a crackdown on the Shiite Muslims in southern Iraq

would be the first step toward a Vietnam-style military quagmire. Today some of the same officials who once urged caution are sounding the alarms, building the case for combat patrols to protect the Shiites.

The dramatic turnabout reflects a shift in tactics for undermining President Saddam Hussein and what Administration officials describe as a better understanding of who the Shiites in southern Iraq really are: a persecuted people, and not necessarily the precursors of a radical Islamic state that would align itself with Iran.

What About Ground Attacks?

It is also a way for the Republican White House to demonstrate its resolve in the face of Democratic criticism that Washington ended the Persian Gulf war prematurely and that its policy toward Baghdad has been indecisive.

Though Administration officials insist that the patrols, which will be carried out with British and French forces, are not motivated by election-year politics, they acknowledge that taking a sterner stance toward Iraq is likely to be politically popular.

RESOLVE...Pg. 4

SEATTLE POST-INTELLIGENCER   Aug. 20, 1992   Pg. 1

Largest movement of nuclear weapons since Cold War began

By Ed Offley
P-I Military Reporter

In what experts describe as the largest movement of nuclear weapons since the Cold War began, tens of thousands of missile warheads, bombs and artillery shells are being transferred to a small number of military depots

in anticipation of the final trip to a Texas bomb factory for disassembly.

Thanks to several arms control agreements, the collapse of the Soviet Union and shifts in Pentagon policy, the U.S. nuclear arsenal has shrunk from 24,000 to 19,000 weapons since 1985. It will decline to about 5,400 by the year

2000, analysts Bill Arkin and Stan Norris say in a comprehensive review of U.S. nuclear forces.

The report, "Taking Stock," confirms that Washington state will become the largest repository for nuclear weapons later in the decade. The study was issued by

WEAPONS...Pg. 2

This publication is prepared by American Forces Information Service (AFIS/OASD-PA) to bring to the attention of key personnel news items of interest to them in their official capacities. It is not intended to substitute for newspapers and periodicals as a means of keeping informed about the meaning and impact of news developments. Use of these articles does not reflect official endorsement. Further reproduction for private use or gain is subject to original copyright restrictions. Please pass this copy on to someone else who needs current news information, then...

PLEASE RECYCLE

---

views on current military topics.

The media and military have long had a tacit agreement to suspend the normal rules of copyright restrictions for mutual benefit: The Pentagon is able to benefit from this daily "one-stop shopping" of current news, and the media participants enjoy the benefit of guaranteed readership by senior officials not only in the Pentagon but the White House, Executive Branch and Congress as well.

The summary is managed by the American Forces

Information Service (AFIS), a subordinate agency reporting to the assistant secretary of defense/public affairs. Establishing a professional relationship is easy: Telephone the staff at their Alexandria office, (703) 428-0023, or email them at cnars@hq.afis.osd.mil.

Once your flow of stories begins appearing regularly in the summary, you will immediately notice that your physical location and size of news operation mean little: You are being read and are a player in the defense reporting environment.

Chapter 8

The Defense Industry
No uniforms, lots of stories

Covering the defense industry is a vital and important subset of military reporting, and it can be just as frustrating and challenging as monitoring the uniformed services.

Defense contractors, like the Pentagon client they serve, can be secretive, manipulative and hardnosed toward reporters — and they can also be proactive, willing to help and significantly informative. As we will point out in this chapter, there are several key differences in policy and culture that will affect how a reporter can effectively report on industry.

There are three overriding issues that will dominate news about the defense industry for the foreseeable future. They are:

The contraction of defense industry

The American defense industry has been undergoing a profound transformation that rivals any change affecting its customers in the Department of Defense and armed services. During 1993-2000 alone, more than 40 separate defense manufacturers merged or were acquired by other firms, resulting in a dramatic contraction in the industry that left six military industrial giants to dominate the field. They are Boeing, Lockheed Martin, Raytheon, General Dynamics, Northrop Grumman and Litton. This trend has sharply colored much of the press coverage of defense industry given the implications of production line shutdowns, layoffs and major changes to the size and structure of the surviving firms.

The DoD procurement crisis

Many observers warn that the U.S. military today confronts a serious resource crisis that has been steadily growing over the past decade, and argue only over the severity of the situation. Then-Pentagon acquisition chief Dr. Jacques Gansler in 1998 described the situation as a "death spiral" resulting from the annual migration of $10 to $15 billion from the department's procurement accounts to pay for unplanned maintenance and repairs on aging and obsolescent military equipment. It has been further exacerbated, Gansler and other experts say, by the Pentagon's reprogramming of modernization funds to pay for unanticipated current costs of humanitarian and peacekeeping operations. Some defense analysts have warned that a much more severe crisis — a defense "train wreck" — is looming within the next few years because of the aggregate impact of a 40 percent cut in the size of the military, a 70 percent cut in procurement, and the sustained high operational tempo.

The revolution in business affairs

Since the mid-1980s no less than 18 major commissions, panels and other study teams have specified the negative impact of inefficient Pentagon bureaucracy and obsolete acquisition regulations on both the armed services and the defense industry. Former Pentagon officials and outside experts say that the two-thirds of the Pentagon budget currently allocated to infrastructure and support functions, about $200 billion per year, constitutes a prime target for deep reforms — and reprogramming into procurement accounts — given the Bush administration's surprising disclosure in early 2001 that it did not intend to seek major increases in the overall defense budget.

That is the controversial and potentially bitter environment in which U.S. defense contractors are now competing to build the next generation of combat aircraft, warships and other weapons for the U.S. military. Reporters assigned to cover the institutions or specific procurement programs will find a rich harvest of stories once they have succeeded in building professional relationships with their counterparts in industry.

Corporate public relations professionals and veteran military reporters agree that — like the military — there is no common stereotype of the defense complex. Rather, each corporation, and to a significant degree, differing production centers within each defense firm, approach media relations differently, often as a result of previous experience and management preference.

"This is an entirely different game from covering the Pentagon," said veteran reporter Bill Richards, who has specialized in coverage of aerospace corporations and the Defense Department itself. While it is possible for a diligent reporter to cultivate military sources on a philosophical basis — a mutual respect for the underpinnings of good strategy, for example, that impels the source to provide reasoned criticism of his own service branch — that is extremely rare with a corporate public relations professional because of his relationship with the company.

"In covering a private corporation, you are dealing with a person whose first loyalty is to the company and he is not going to do you any favors at the expense of the company," Richards warned.

"The military public affairs officer's responsibility is clear

---

Then and now: A decade of defense contraction

As the two charts attest, most of the leading defense contractors in 1990 have now merged with former competitors.

The Top 10 Defense Contractors in 1990*

1.	McDonnell Douglas Corp.	$8,211,427
2.	General Dynamics Corp.	6,306,093
3.	General Electric Co.	5,588,964
4.	General Motors Corp.	4,106,570
5.	Raytheon Co.	4,070,955
6.	Lockheed Corp.	3,552,628
7.	Martin Marietta Corp.	3,491,992
8.	United Technologies Corp.	2,855,766
9.	Grumman Corp.	2,696,966
10.	Tenneco Inc.	2,409,935

The Top 10 Defense Contractors in 2000

1.	Lockheed Martin	15,125,846
2.	Boeing	12,041,420
3.	Raytheon	6,330,613
4.	General Dynamics	4,195,923
5.	Northrop Grumman	3,079,615
6.	Litton Industries	2,737.284
7.	United Technologies	2,071,536
8.	TRW	2,004.857
9.	General Electric	1,609,329
10.	SAIC	1,522.077

*Contract values in thousands. Source — Department of Defense

when it comes to whether or not you have to respond to a reporter's request," said Tom Burgess, a public relations executive who previously worked both as a military reporter for several newspapers and later as corporate media relations manager for General Dynamics Corp. "But the private sector is not driven by requirements codified in law." (One exception: Publicly owned corporations are required to file quarterly earnings reports, annual reports and other documents with the Security and Exchange Commission.)

Those two realities will govern your strategy for reporting on defense industry. Other factors you should consider:

■ A story involving a defense contract will probably require both military and corporate sourcing, although it is not uncommon for the military to maintain sole control over information release. You'll find out if that is the case when you make your initial query.

■ Despite their interconnection, the Pentagon and its contractors rarely cooperate or jointly manage information release. In fact, by policy if not by custom, it is rare for military public affairs officers and corporate press managers to communicate with each other at all. Therefore, it is folly to assume that if one inquiry path is a dead end all roads are closed.

Still, if the information you seek can be released, corporate public relations staffs can usually respond quicker, and with more detailed data, than their military counterparts, said David J. Shea, who joined the Hughes Aircraft Corp. as communications manager following his military PAO service, including a stint as director of defense information in the Pentagon.

"Industry guys are well stocked with information that the average (military) public affairs officer won't have," Shea said. "We try to dig up a reservoir of previously cleared material on a defense program." Industry is also a good source of stock still photographs and video imagery on weapons systems and other major procurement items.

But all in all, the defense industry itself — despite a decade of major contraction — is too big a landscape to offer neat generalizations.

A company's information policy may "often be the result of the personality of the program manager" and not reflect a formal company policy, one spokesman admitted.

Defense industry coverage strategy

If you have a sizable defense industry presence in your primary coverage area, you should employ the same start-up program for coverage that you have designed around the military commands in your region: identification, initial PAO contact, key official meeting, story identification and field visits.

Other sources of information and education include your local or state Chamber of Commerce, defense industry labor unions, local university business schools, and think tanks that specialize in defense procurement issues. Also monitor:

Stock brokers: If you have a particularly large industrial base, seek out prominent local stock brokerages for in-house analysts who monitor defense industry stocks, particularly your local firms and their competitors. If none are found locally, contact Wall Street firms.

Lawyers: Attorneys who practice corporate or trial work involving defense firms and employees can be invaluable sources as well, particularly if a local defense company is involved in litigation over procurement issues, employee health or job claims, or federal False Claims Act allegations. Network your local legal community.

Congress: Your state's congressional delegation will play an important role in obtaining background information not directly accessible through either industry or military sources. Also, cultivate staffers on the House and Senate Armed Services and Appropriations defense subcommittees; Government Operations committees; and committees involved with employment and tax issues.

Pentagon reports: The office of the secretary of defense publishes numerous annual and biennial reports on prime defense contractors, including a breakdown by state and labor market; a roster of educational and nonprofit organizations that receive research contracts; nationwide roster of all contractors receiving over $10,000 in work; and list of subcontractors. For details, contact the Defense News Division, office of the assistant secretary of defense/public affairs. Telephone: (703) 695-0192

Other federal agencies: The Securities and Exchange Commission receives quarterly 10-K earnings reports from publicly owned corporations. You should arrange to obtain at least an index of those reports, if not the documents themselves. Often, a submerged procurement issue will first materialize in the financial reports. The Internal Revenue Service will provide Form 990 federal income tax records on nonprofit organizations registered with the IRS, such as think tanks.

Trade journals: The defense industry is covered in depth by a profusion of trade magazines, newspapers and newsletters whose reporters speak the language and understand the nuances of obscure policy decisions. Military association groups also track industry through their journals. Once you have identified the range and tier of industry within your primary coverage area, you will be able to identify the journals that most closely serve your needs as an "inside" monitor of the industrial sector you are chasing.

Defense associations and groups: Trade organizations have representatives who can be useful in providing comment and suggestions when the specific firm itself cannot respond. You should establish connections with the trade associations to which your local defense firms belong.

How to...

Decipher the defense budget

This really happened: One day in the early 1980s, one daily newspaper hit the stands with a headline on Page A-4 that read, "MX missile is killed," while on Page A-5 of the same issue a headline stated, "MX missile wins approval."

Both stories were accurate, and their juxtaposition — while embarrassing to the newspaper — accurately depicted one day's skirmish in the ongoing Pentagon budget war. Two committees in Congress had come to different conclusions on the controversial new land-based ICBM, and — alas, two different editors treated each story without realizing the other was in production.

Think of a pile of money — a huge pile, some $300 billion — and think of what that money buys. Warships, nuclear weapons, fighter planes, trucks, desks and swivel chairs, MRE rations, hammers and nails, paychecks and retirement checks, ball-caps and Trident missiles. Dwell for a moment on the military service prestige, civilian jobs, political careers and, oh yes, national security interests, at stake and you will realize: You cannot escape the Pentagon budget if your beat is the military.

Defense spending underpins everything, from the economic impact of a military base on your city or state, to the success or failure of the U.S. military in a major-theater war. It is the centerpiece of a major debate on how the U.S. military will transform itself to meet the new emerging threats while protecting long-standing security interests.

Even the military beat organizer's question, "Where to begin?" is indeterminate, for the Pentagon budget process frequently appears as a Mobius strip, an endless loop with no beginning or end. The first stealth bomber was built by Northrop — in the late 1940s. The YB-49 was cancelled after less than a dozen planes were built. It came back as the B-2 in the late 1980s. We will have 21 B-2 bombers — for a slightly higher unit cost. In the 1950s we had the Nike missile system to shoot down enemy bombers. In the 1960s we had the ABM (Sprint) missile to shoot down enemy missiles. Ronald Reagan's Strategic Defense Initiative has reincarnated as the Bush II administration's National Missile Defense system.

History twists and turns, but that old defense budget just keeps flowing along. And it is the military reporter who must attempt to provide factual presentation, translation into English, and perspective to a topic that often defies logic.

Think positive: You as a reporter will be chasing bits and pieces of the current or planned Pentagon budget, e.g., local base expansion, Army unit deactivation, etc. The poor inmates at the Pentagon are, at any one moment, grappling with five budgets: The current spending plan, the proposed next-year budget, and the "out-year" draft budgets that comprise the rest of the legally required Pentagon defense plan.

The Pentagon budget process is so vast, complicated, bureaucratically muddled and politically charged that books continuously churn out of the publishing industry's loading docks with the newest system failure, boondoggle or prescription for sanity. Since there isn't enough space in this manual to delve into the budget details that a career military reporter should master, this chapter offers instead an initial guide map for self-education on the various elements of the defense budget most likely to impact the local newspaper or TV station.

On paper, the Department of Defense budget appears as the product of a relatively straightforward process. (On paper, we won the war in Vietnam.) Like the rest of the federal budget, its roots lie in the United States Constitution: The Executive Branch is responsible for the conduct of foreign policy and the defense of the nation. Congress is responsible for writing the checks.

For the local reporter just beginning the military beat, a coverage strategy for budget issues — paralleling the general blueprint that he or she has crafted to organize and carry out that specialty — will allow a quick run up to speed on pressing local budget issues while avoiding stress and burnout.

The plan recommended here will enable the reporter to compile information and maintain watch on dozens of budget items, trends and accounts directly affecting his or her primary beat coverage area. It is a straightforward, three-step procedure.

Set up a filing system

Open in your file system a set of indexed budget files in which you can place the raw inputs, such as clips, releases, interview transcripts, etc. Although the "budget season" is in high gear from late winter through autumn, budget decisions and events occur continuously, so issue monitoring and filing should be an ongoing effort as well. Files may be arranged as follows:

Defense budget (national): A file on general Defense Department budget events, trends, reports and studies that examine the Pentagon as an entity. If you have a large military presence, add separate files by military service or command.

Defense (personnel): A separate file on military personnel issues, including pay, benefits, layoffs, promotions. Many of these policies are set from the Pentagon as a whole for all services; others are service-specific.

Defense (state): A file of each major base or command in your primary coverage area with an index of budget issues pertinent to that base, compiled from PAO briefings, interviews, and previous stories. For example, a budget file on the local Air Mobility Command base should include data on aircraft procurement issues affecting the aircraft types that operate there, as well as any specific budget trends affecting the base, parent command or Air Force as a service.

Military construction: Depending on the project, money total or controversy, this can be indexed either by base or specific project. A $500,000 addition to the Army barracks is one thing, but a $253 million missile retrofit is another. Use common sense.

Defense contractor: If your coverage includes one or more major defense firms, create a file on the defense companies and weapons that are involved.

Build PAO contacts

The Pentagon and local military commanders are not the only sources for budget stories. Other players who should be contacted and cultivated include:

Congressional delegation: Find the defense expert member(s) in your state delegation and signal your interest in coverage of military budget issues. Identify and get to know not only their administrative assistants and press spokesmen, but any staffers responsible for handling military budget affairs. Build up your own off-hours phone list for these key Capitol Hill staffers, inasmuch as they are useful as an "early warning system" for Pentagon budget surprises, and also are useful for explaining budget technicalities and obtaining both Pentagon and congressional studies that otherwise might be hard to obtain.

House and Senate defense committees: Even if your state has no representation on the four key defense committees (House and Senate Armed Services, House and Senate Appropriation defense subcommittees), it is critical for you to establish a working relationship with members and their staffs who work military budget issues critical to your coverage area. For example, if your newspaper focuses on Navy issues, search for a friendly congressman on the seapower subcommittees of the House or Senate Armed Services Committees. You will find, as in the local delegation, a commonality of interests even if the congressman himself is from a distant state.

Budget experts: Build your own budget maven file, with contacts not only in Washington, D.C., but in your own state and region as well. State governments, large localities and regional chambers of commerce often have planning staffers with an expertise on military budget issues and economic impact of defense funds, and they can be of great help in advancing your personal knowledge as well as serving as an "explainer" on technical issues. Similarly, local universities and colleges will often have faculty experts — teaching government, political science, economics, etc. — who can translate things into English.

Labor and industry: Assemble a chart of the biggest defense contractors in your state or coverage area, and work with their press relations departments to identify the procurement issues relevant to them. Also, network through their professional groups to find other useful business/industry contacts pertinent to the detailed issues on your local beat. Local chambers of commerce will also be helpful for identifying less-visible subcontractors who are involved in specific defense programs. Local labor councils or unions will round out your active contact list for employees who affect and are affected by the defense programs up for annual review in the budget process.

Draft a budget agenda

Having identified the players, the overall set of issues, and the myriad of story opportunities, you should sit down with your editor no later than November or early December of each year and identify any hot issues that are likely to erupt when the Pentagon budget is released in January or February.

Obviously, you will want to write an advance overview based on current budgets, previous debates, etc., that local commanders, congressional sources and other experts will help you weave. There will likely be a handful of obvious controversies — a base slated for closure, hazardous materials cleanup funding at a military site, etc. — that go on from year to year.

Your year-end planning for the budget is an opportunity to get creative, and avoid burial in an avalanche of wire copy two months down the road. Use it to pick a theme, a less-traveled topic (benefits cuts affecting local personnel, how local civilian shipyards fear the future of contracts) to choose some representative slices of that massive spending plan that (a) offer useful examples of the whole and (b) serve to highlight the specific impacts of defense budget decisions on your community and state. Merely a day of phone checks with your PAO contacts, industry spokesmen, congressional offices and an outside expert or two will give you the raw list from which your priorities will come.

Such planning will also demonstrate whether the opportunity exists for a "process" story, in which you use a specific and local budget item to examine the tug-of-war itself throughout the 9- to 10-month span between Pentagon proposal and presidential signature. Strictly enterprise, stories of how the base was funded, the aircraft upgrade cancelled, the Army unit deactivated, and the like, require months of collection and shoveling but reward the reporter and reader/viewer alike with real knowledge gained.

Chapter 9

Beware of Ambushes
The floating coffin and
other horror stories

As you navigate your way from initial beat planning toward full military coverage, you will discover some unpleasant realities. Your road is full of potholes, and you will quickly become aware that they are the result of landmines which have exploded under the feet of those reporters who have gone before you. Here are some of the traps, ambushes and other nasty surprises awaiting you:

The myth of PAO knowledge: One of the more common errors a novice military reporter will make is to assume that his PAO contacts always have the answer to all of the questions. While the PAO may be fully in the know on one occasion, on another he or she may be the last to know — even after you and your readers.

The myth of the commander's omniscience: Another easy way for the military reporter to drive off a cliff is to assume that the local commander, above and beyond that official's PAO, is fully possessed of the facts. Even in a formally structured military hierarchy, the commander himself may be shorted out of the loop for a number of reasons.

The hidden saboteur: You are negotiating with higher authority for a logistically or bureaucratically ambitious assignment. You are informed that the senior commander is enamored of your proposal. Does that ensure success? Don't hold your breath.

Betrayal and counter-betrayal: You've pulsed the system, your sources have delivered and your story is ready to go. But suddenly, a rival media outlet comes up with your hard-earned scoop. Congratulations! After months of beat planning, source cultivation and playing it straight, you've just been stabbed in the back! The counter-point: Your telephone rings and a distant military contact is on the line offering you an exclusive, the rare leak on a silver platter that only *The New York Times* is supposed to get. Why this fortune? Somebody else is being stabbed in the back, and you're the blade.

Omerta: You are fully engaged with a monthly pattern of beat checks, story proposals, base visits and other routine milestones. Suddenly, nothing works. Your calls go unreturned, the most routine requests are denied, commanders are unavailable for any reason and you begin to doubt your sanity. Why? The answer is simple.

Let's look at these categories, in order:

1. The myth of PAO knowledge: Jack Dorsey and the floating coffin

Jack Dorsey had been on the military beat for *The Ledger-Star* in Norfolk, Va., for only a few short weeks in 1980 when a major lesson about the military-media relationship got rammed down his throat.

"I got a call," the veteran journalist said. A sailor was calling him cold. "I'm on the (destroyer) *Farragut*," the sailor said. "We were just off the coast of Virginia and we had a burial at sea. And it was atrocious. The casket wouldn't sink, so the Marine honor guard that had dropped the casket overboard was told to go back in their fatigues and bring out their M-16s and to fire into the casket to make it sink."

The sailor went on, "We stopped the ship, and that's exactly what they did. They fired and fired and fired."

The sailor pressed Dorsey to check it out.

Dorsey started out at the Navy's front door. He approached the PAO for the commander, surface forces, U.S. Atlantic Fleet, a lieutenant commander. "I told Mike (the PAO) what I knew and he said he'd check it out and he called me back in a few hours and said, 'Bullshit, it didn't happen.'"

"There was a burial at sea," the PAO went on. "It was proper, routine, nothing happened."

Knowing the PAO to be "an honorable man," Dorsey said his initial reaction was that the sailor was "a crazy kid" trying to peddle a sea story. At this point, Dorsey was inclined to treat the allegation as one of those one-source concoctions that never get past a reporter's notebook.

"But he (the sailor) called me back and I told him what I had learned, and he said, 'Would you come out to my house tonight? I'll have some other sailors there and they will tell you their version of the same story.'"

Perplexed, Dorsey drove out to the sailor's house late that evening, grumbling. "You don't want to do it but you do it," he said of the evening rendezvous.

"Lo and behold, not only did he have three sailors from the ship ... in addition they gave me photographs that one of them had taken of the incident. They gave me details. I had the story. I didn't even need the Navy's confirmation. But I said to myself, Naaah, I'll give the Navy one more chance, so I called Mike and said, 'Mike, I've got some additional information on this thing, would you let me talk to the admiral?' He said — it's now 10 minutes after 4 p.m. — 'If you can make it out here by 4:30 the admiral will see you.' So I'm fighting rush hour traffic out there."

Ushered into the admiral's inner sanctum, Dorsey listened patiently as the PAO and his admiral explained in great detail why the allegations of Marines firing bullets into the unsinkable coffin were so much hogwash. The admiral said, "I've talked with the commodore (ship's squadron commander), who was aboard the ship that day, I've talked with the commanding officer. Jack, these boys (the sailors) were pulling your leg."

"What about these?" Dorsey said as he slowly pulled the photos out of his jacket pocket and spread them on the admiral's desk. Both the admiral and PAO gaped.

The admiral recovered his composure. "By God," he said, "You write what you write. I've been lied to."

So Dorsey did. And shortly thereafter he had a front-page follow-up story about how the admiral relieved the destroyer captain of command, and issued a career-killing letter of reprimand to the commodore. And military reporter Dorsey never forgot the very important lesson he had learned: Before an organization as large as the Navy can lie to the press, it usually has to lie to itself first.

"This information (denying the incident) came from honorable men," Dorsey said in retrospect of the admiral and his PAO.

"You don't get dummies in that business."

What you do get from time to time, Dorsey warned, is a hard lesson in the myth of PAO omniscience. Your query to the PAO will prompt him or his commander to pulse their organization for the facts. Never assume that they automatically get those facts.

2. The myth of the commander's omniscience: three vignettes

A. Need to know: The Fort Lewis-based 2nd Ranger battalion air-dropped on Point Salines airfield in Grenada on Oct. 25, 1983, so reporters in Washington state flooded the Fort Lewis authorities with requests for information. (Note: The Rangers are a "tenant" organization at Fort Lewis, answering to a different operational chain of command than the corps headquarters based there.) The commanding officer at Fort Lewis, a three-star Army general, was asked about the operation the following morning.

"No comment," the general said in a statement issued by his PAO.

Translation: The base commander, like everyone else, learned about the Rangers' combat mission when his morning newspaper arrived.

This is a technical dilemma that will confound the lazy or unprepared reporter. High-security military operations, particularly involving classified equipment or special operations units, are conducted under a rigorous "operational security" regime where a minimum of people — inside the military or out — know what is going on. Mastering the operational chain of command for a particular organization will not guarantee that you can learn all of the facts in time for deadline, but it will prevent you from wasting your time seeking answers from the wrong commanders.

B. We are pleased to announce: The fax machine lit up and a news release whirred into the newsroom tray.

Two Aegis cruisers (the Navy's newest, $1 billion missile ships) will be home-ported in Seward, Alaska, according to the announcement by Sen. Ted Stevens, R-Alaska. The release was made in conjunction with a deputy assistant secretary of the

Navy.

"I hope they get there," a veteran Alaska reporter said in between cigar puffs when apprised of the news release.

Why?

"Because," he said, holding out his wrists and flipping them quickly, "those ships will look great when they roll over on their sides twice a day when the tide goes out."

Next the reporter called up the PAO of the three-star admiral in charge of all cruisers in the U.S. Pacific Fleet (a "type" command responsible for maintenance, training, personnel and other down-to-earth details, like where the ships will be home-ported).

"I'd like a comment from the admiral," the reporter asked.

"He's not here, he's out at sea right now," the PAO groaned. "I guess he'll have a comment when he learns about this decision."

Lesson: The "seam" in the chain of command from senior military commanders to the civilian leaders of each service, and the secretary of defense at the top, is in reality a gaping chasm from which many controversies, backstage deals and other interesting news issues gestate.

(The cruisers never did get to Seward.)

C. The Navy-Navy game: The base closure announcement landed in the city like a nuclear warhead. After more than 30 years of continuous active service, and hundreds of millions of dollars in Pentagon construction during the 1980s, the Navy was recommending that Whidbey Island Naval Air Station be closed.

Local civilian officials and retired Navy people scrambled to respond to the recommendation, which came out in a list of several dozen military bases throughout the country. Faced with the loss of their largest employer, as well as their very identity as a close-knit Navy town, the people of Oak Harbor, Wash. were savvy enough in the ways of the military to know that such a recommendation did not make economic or military sense. (The Navy's recommendation, in fact, was not a proposal to shut down Whidbey Island's naval aircraft wing, but instead, would have transferred the unit lock-stock-and-barrel to a base in California.)

For nearly three months, the "Save NAS Whidbey" committee poked, prodded, researched and responded at a series of commission hearings, and — having demolished the Navy economic assessment — persuaded the independent base closure panel to remove the base from the hit list. Whidbey Island remains open.

It was an uphill battle primarily because most of the bases targeted for closure were indeed obsolete or no longer needed in a military sense. Those other bases, too, generated a firestorm of congressional and local political effort to save them from closure. So in addition to fighting the Navy bureaucracy, the city organizers also had to fight against a common perception that they were in it simply for survival — which played a great part, to be true. Most regional newspapers, TV stations and other media outlets, after skimming the broad outlines of the issue, immediately concluded that Whidbey was a nice base but, too bad, the Cold War is over and hard decisions have to be made. And after a flurry of initial stories, most media stopped covering the issue.

Those who stayed on the story would learn some surprising facts: (1) The base had been tossed on the Navy closure list — that is, the roster of recommended base closures forwarded by a civilian assistant secretary of the Navy to the office of then-Defense Secretary Dick Cheney — long *after* the Navy's own formal, in-house review process had been conducted. (2) The Navy (e.g., this top-level bureaucratic committee) assembled a rationale for the closure that defied facts, dollars and common sense. And (3) clear evidence emerged of a bureaucratic sleight-of-hand in which the "uniformed" Navy was told one thing and another thing was done *vis a vis* base closing recommendations: The three-star admiral in charge of naval aviation programs had told a friend in the city that the base was not on the closure recommendation list. He spoke truthfully: Whidbey Island was not added until after that senior admiral had forwarded the uniformed Navy's recommendations to his civilian superiors and conversed in confidence with his friend.

To the consternation of those media pundits who had already buried and eulogized the Whidbey Island base, the independent Base Realignment and Closure Commission voted unanimously to take the naval air station off the list.

Lessons: Don't ever assume the military — whether a service or even component of a service — to be a monolith. Starting with the units and bases you cover, learn the identity, traditions and goals of the various tribes. They go to war with one another more times than you would ever suspect.

3. The hidden saboteur

After two decades of military coverage, this is one encounter that can still bite. It helps if the senior officer (through his PAO staff) knows and approves of an embark request, complicated assignment or tricky interview schedule, particularly if the topic is controversial. A word from the top will cut like a knife through butter, whereas a lieutenant advocating your request to an admiral is — like you — trying to swim up a waterfall.

But an admiral's OK doesn't always work, either.

The reporter wanted to cover a local aircraft carrier that was deploying to the Persian Gulf. But instead of a routine deployment story, he had a better idea: Fly out to the ship on one of the air wing jets once it had left port; interview the pilot, ship's officers, sailors etc.; and hang around a few hours to capture the tension and bustle as more than 5,000 men and women began to acclimate themselves to a six-month foreign cruise — to a war zone, in fact.

The local PAO loved the proposal. The reporter's Navy contacts in the Pentagon loved the concept. Most importantly, the fleet commander's PAO thought it a positive idea (from his institutional needs) and forwarded the idea to his boss, the fleet commander. And the admiral loved the proposed story.

But the story did not happen. Why?

As the days before the ship departure dwindled to a handful, the project suddenly had "problems." The reporter faxed more memos to everyone he had contacted, and received mumbles in return. More phone calls — silence. Finally, he was told that it wouldn't happen — something had come up.

What? The apoplectic reporter demanded.

I can't tell you — complications, the PAO said.

Later, the reporter found out that a staff aide somewhere in the vast chain of command had decided that he didn't like the idea, and it took very little to kill the request.

Lesson: No admiral will go against his own tribe for a reporter. Or, don't assume anything. Finally, shit happens.

4. Betrayal and counter-betrayal

Why would your military contacts screw you out of a story,

and why in another case could that leak on a silver platter be someone else screwing someone else?

Answer: Because they think the result will be more favorable to the interests of their services.

Many veteran reporters interviewed for this manual said there had been cases where they were pursuing a story, had a good hold on it, and were begged by their military contacts to hold off — "We're checking this out."

"So you hold off a day, sometimes a week, then you see the goddamn thing broken in *The Washington Post* or *The New York Times*," one reporter said. Then he chuckled. "That has happened to me, but I've benefited from it, too."

A variation of this is a pre-emptive leak in which you are given material that on surface appears to be a good story, but in the end turns out to be a selective leak aimed at minimizing the impact of some other reporter's bombshell.

Another variation of this theme is when you get an anxious call from a PAO or commander who has something very urgent to tell you, and what he ends up telling you is a straight "spin" story aimed at undercutting someone else's scoop that just made Page One of the *Early Bird*.

5. Omerta: When the system totally shuts down.

If you are doing real well with a military service, local base or particular commander, and suddenly nothing works anymore — he won't return your calls or faxes, and even the most routine event is not advanced for your coverage, and you're beginning to wonder if something isn't terribly wrong with you, do this: Stop, take a deep breath, and look at your calendar, then when you determine you can divide the year by four and end up with a whole number, relax. Because the entire Department of Defense goes underground during presidential election years!

How to...

Cover a serviceman's death

There is no easy way to cover the death of a military serviceman or woman.

A reporter must balance the need for aggressive fact-finding with sensitivity for the grieving family members who will be the primary source of biographical information in the story.

The story can break with little or no warning, giving the journalist mere hours to assemble the minimum facts for a spot news story. The military PAO network must balance in its own cumbersome way the privacy rights of military families with the service's policy goal of openness and candor.

But even with those forces in harmony, the nature of the event itself will often preclude easy reporting. Facts are often unavailable, given the nature of the mishap, the ongoing investigation, as well as time and space constraints.

Such an incident might otherwise be only a news brief in the world news page, or it might come as part of a story that leads off the network TV news. No matter what, the reporter thrust into this time-intensive race for facts must approach the story with care and discretion.

The Defense Department has an ironclad information policy regarding death or serious injury to military personnel: No information will be released on a specific individual until the primary next of kin have been formally notified by CACO (casualty assistance calls officers) and that notification has been confirmed back through the administrative chain of command.

Standard PAO policy within the military services is to make an initial news release of an accident or mass casualty within one hour of its being reported within military communications channels. It may, on the other hand, take several days for next of kin to be located and informed of the specific fatality affecting them.

Thus the most common complication encountered in a death or casualty event is the time lag between news disclosure of a fatality — including sufficient details to identify the individual or unit as pertinent to your newspaper or TV station — and the official identification of the victim.

If you notice a wire story of a military accident or death that might affect your local readership, here's a five-step strategy for getting the facts with all deliberate speed:

1) Initial contact: Call the senior PAO from the base you think might be affected and request help in getting the story. At this point you don't know whether the soldier was stationed locally or not, but you're covering your bets. Specify that you respect the privacy rights of the family members but you want to write a factual, accurate account of what has happened.

Offer to bring the PAO up to speed on the story if he or she is missing information. Many smaller PAO offices do not have ready access to the wires and he will appreciate your effort to help him stay informed.

2) CACO involvement: Ask the PAO outright if his base is involved in sending a casualty assistance calls officer to the family, and if so, request that the PAO or CACO representative serve as the intermediary for your newspaper or TV station. If this is not known yet, ask the PAO to let you know if a CACO has been appointed from his base, or to inform you if another facility is handling the situation.

Meanwhile, contact the headquarters-level PAO office in the Pentagon for the service involved, and make the same pitch.

3) Initial information needs: Tell the PAO what your minimum needs are for a hard news story:
■ Victim's full name (verify)
■ Age
■ Home of record
■ Military rank
■ Date of entry in service
■ Current military specialty and unit assignment
■ Brief explanation of unit function
■ Primary relatives (spouse, children, parents), their home towns
■ Other relatives (siblings, grandparents), their home towns
  Reiterate that your desire is for accuracy and completeness.

4) A message to family members: Ask the PAO/CACO to pass along the following message to the family:

"Realizing that the death of your relative is a major shock, we (the media outlet) have no wish to intrude at this time of sorrow. But we seek your help with minimum disruption in assembling a full and accurate account concerning the death of your loved one. Essentially, we need to verify basic biographical data about your relative, and at the same time invite you to make any remarks about his military service and life that you feel pertinent. We request that you contact our reporter (name and telephone number). If you prefer, (the PAO) can serve as a go-between. Also, we would request any information on planned funeral services, as this is part of the normal coverage of an event like this."

Also request, at their discretion, to borrow a photograph that might be used with a story.

Also signal your interest in covering the funeral or any memorial services, by requesting the name of the funeral home that will handle those arrangements, and asking for the family's guidance on whether they accept coverage or prefer privacy.

If the family grants an interview, or relays the data to you through a PAO, fine: You'll meet deadline with a spot story of relevance to your readership or market. If they decline contact, drop it and move on. The only thing worse than going to press with an incomplete account is to add to the stress and sorrow of an already grief-stricken family.

5) Consider a local pool: During the Persian Gulf War, many local TV stations and newspapers voluntarily pooled coverage of stories dealing with those killed in action or taken prisoner. You and your editor should always have this idea ready if it appears that the family is apprehensive about a media invasion.

If you follow up on the mishap that claimed the serviceman's life, e.g., an investigation into the cause of the incident, be sure to advise the family in advance of your forthcoming story so that they aren't blindsided by it. What appears to you to be a routine investigative or analytic story will, to the families, be a strong aftershock to the trauma they have already experienced.

Chapter 10

TV Broadcasting Challenges
Tech issues make the job tougher

Once you've got all forces moving and everything's being taken care of by the commanders, turn your attention to television because you can win the battle or lose the war if you don't handle the story right.
— Gen. Colin L. Powell, then chairman of the Joint Chiefs of Staff, address to the National Defense University, Dec. 13, 1989

Military coverage is particularly difficult for the local television journalist in ways that his or her print media counterparts never experience: Not only must the TV reporter master the same range of difficult military topics and attempt to neutralize the institutional mistrust of the military, but he or she must also overcome some difficult technical burdens inherent in television broadcasting. In addition, he or she will probably never be able to commit the time and investment needed to fully prepare for covering military subjects.

Military coverage in most TV markets, said author and veteran military TV journalist Mark Sauter, "is mainly not a beat at all."

Even on the network level, said veteran NBC reporter Fred Francis, who covered military operations in the 1980s and early 1990s, the only group harder to find than full-time print reporters specializing in defense are their counterparts from radio and television broadcasting.

But two trends in journalism underscored by the 1991 Persian Gulf War and subsequent incidents underscore the need to invest in military coverage capability at the local TV station level, veteran broadcast journalists and other observers say:

First, future conflicts, whether small-scale military operations like Kosovo or larger interventions like Operation Desert Storm, will again be dominated not just by TV news, but by the growing demand for live, global transmission of TV news. Even if the Pentagon attempts to reverse its post-Desert Storm PAO guidelines and re-impose restrictions on access and mobility by journalists, the public itself will demand no less than the saturation coverage experienced in Dhahran, Washington, D.C. and local TV markets in early 1991 and the wall-to-wall coverage following the terrorist attacks on Sept. 11, 2001.

"Absent any willingness by the news media to exercise self-restraint," then-Navy chief of information Rear Adm. Brent Baker wrote following the 1991 Persian Gulf War, "media competition and numbers will likely continue to grow in future crisis and war operations."

Obscured in the raw power of live coverage from Baghdad, Dhahran and Washington, D.C. was a journalistic sea change, one TV military reporter told a Center for Defense Journalism seminar analyzing the Gulf conflict: "During the seven months of the Desert Shield/Desert Storm crisis," NBC's Francis observed, "television journalism broke most of the major stories, from (disclosure) of the first troop movements to the outbreak of war itself. You got all of that on television and you got it first."

A second trend is that the TV networks — as a result of continued budget constraints and the growth of satellite transmitting capability by most local stations — will in event of future conflicts be inclined to throw a good deal of that coverage responsibility back to large- and medium-sized TV markets that include major military commands in their coverage areas. When the crew of a U.S. Navy EP-3 surveillance aircraft returned to Whidbey Island Naval Air Station in April 2001 after being detained in China, NBC carried live images of the emotional homecoming ceremony, but it was the local Seattle affiliate that provided the reporters, producers and transmitting gear. The Pentagon, too, is aware of this trend, and in recent operations such as Somalia and Bosnia/Kosovo established organized "visit the troops" trips for local and regional broadcast reporters (as well as print) to gain coverage that the cash-strapped networks would probably ignore. In short, a unique challenge and opportunity exists for the local TV reporter willing to organize his or her basic education in the military arts.

In *Live From Baghdad, Gathering News at Ground Zero* (Doubleday, 1991), his memoir of the Persian Gulf War, CNN producer Robert Wiener noted, "Television news has only two things going for it that beat the written press. It's the best medium in the world for capturing emotion, and it's immediate."

A reporter-photographer team from KING-TV in Seattle interviews Army Col. Mark Hertling atop his M3 Bradley armored personnel vehicle during a brigade field exercise at the Yakima Training Center. (Photo: Ed Offley, *Seattle Post-Intelligencer*)

That's accurate but incomplete, this print journalist concludes.

Television journalism during the pre-war crisis and 43-day conflict also demonstrated the potential capabilities of broadcast journalists in informing Americans about their military and the harsh realities of modern combat.

For the TV military reporter attempting to break in as a military specialist, there are two distinct challenges:

1. Preparation: The TV reporter must organize and carry out a self-education plan and a coverage strategy beginning with the immediate local market and expanding outward as his or her capabilities and confidence grow.

The tools for that are the same for print and broadcast journalists as described in the opening chapters of this manual: Identifying the primary coverage area in terms of bases, commands, issues and priorities; connecting with the local commanders and their PAOs; scheduling backgrounders, visits and initial story ideas; moving forward with steady intensification of both the reporter's preparation and actual coverage.

2. Technical issues: The second challenge is TV-specific: Organizing the necessary technical preparations, mapping out broadcast tactics, compiling videotape archive footage, negotiating live feed points, and identifying security concerns and restrictions at local bases that could impede live broadcast capability.

Veteran TV journalists say the technical issues are less thorny than the basic steps of self-education about military-specific topics. Basic study is essential, they say.

"Read," said Charles Jaco, a Cable News Network veteran of both the 1989 Panama invasion and Operation Desert Shield/Desert Storm less than nine months later. "People (in the military) will generally speak to you if you take the time to know a little about what they do. The fact remains that most journalists were never in the military and have no idea of what the military does." That's identical advice long-term print reporters tell their novice counterparts.

Veteran TV reporters urge the basic, step-by-step identification and collection of knowledge that every beat reporter — print or broadcast — must undertake to become literate about his or her specialty.

A positive (but not fawning) attitude is essential to win sufficient trust to establish a working relationship with the military commanders and organizations you want to cover.

"If you come onto a military base acting uninterested, they (military personnel) will pick that up easy," Jaco said. "But they will respect an adversary if you are well-armed with a body of knowledge." And they will laugh at you if you act dumb.

Former Air Force PAO Capt. John Litten told one howler of a story from the early days of the Desert Shield military buildup in Saudi Arabia: A local TV crew decided to air a live report on airlift operations at McChord Air Force Base near Tacoma, Wash., for the early evening broadcast. The TV team made no effort to contact either the Air Force or local base officials, Litten said. Rather, they opted to cover this military story by setting up a live feed point outside the base and improvising.

"They went down to the road near the end of the runway

(outside the base) and set up for a live shot," Litten recalled. "I'm sitting in my office and watching the whole thing on TV."

"Another C-141 has just taken off from McChord Air Force Base as the United States continues its buildup of troops and equipment in the Arabian desert," the reporter breathlessly intoned into the microphone. Five minutes later, the four-engine transport took off a second time: It was engaged in a routine touch-and-go training flight.

"I watched it all on TV then got in my car and drove out there," Litten said. "I told them, 'What are you doing?' "

Litten said he handed out his business card and encouraged the TV station to call McChord's PAO staff the next time they wanted to do a military story. Litten shook his head and sighed. "It's too late once a war starts, or a conflict begins, to ask, 'How do I get access?' " he said.

TV reporters must cultivate local military officials for the same reason as print journalists, Litten and other PAOs say. Not only is it self-evident that the reporter know his topic, but in the gritty, day-to-day world, reporter-PAO relationships do count.

"If an airplane crashes here today," Litten says, "Who is going to get access? Who is going to get that extra time (with officials)?"

Not the bozos at the end of the runway.

How do military PAOs (and their commanders) view the television media? The short description is — the most useful, yet most dangerous element of journalism.

The PAOs you will meet are particularly sensitive to and aware of the emotional power of your medium. Their responses to your queries and story proposals will hinge on that raw power as much as the journalistic content of the story itself.

A military aircraft crashes and the local TV station races to throw together a spot news file. What's the first thing that usually happens? The local PAO involved will provide whatever information he is authorized to release. He will probably refuse to go on-camera.

"Nobody will do that on camera for the (local) TV station," said Sauter, who has covered a number of such mishaps. His corollary: To succeed in getting that basic (for a TV report) element, the reporter will have to have earned unusual respect and trust with his or her military counterparts. And even then, don't count on it.

As noted in Chapter 4, the PAO has been formally trained in the tactics and impact of journalism on his or her service, while the reporter probably is uninformed of the role and mission the local military command carries. Television is a major subject in PAO training programs, as it should be.

This is one military service's perception of the power of TV journalism:

"Television interviews are 'show and tell' performances — no more, no less," Rear Adm. Baker cautioned in a concise "skills handbook" of PAO topics published for new Navy commanding officers a decade ago. "TV tends, in short segments, to accent 'style' over 'substance.' During the televised Iran-Contra scandal hearings in 1987, one reporter noted that (White House aide Lt. Col. Oliver) North 'was, quite simply, a TV star. And his sheer ability to project sheer force of personality into America's living rooms — to 55 million viewers a day — once again raised serious questions about television's blinding power to elevate style over substance to influence hearts and minds and, perhaps more important, to change both the nature of public discourse and the course of policy.' "

"The point is that television is an important channel to be used in educating the public," Baker concluded. (Educating the public on the Navy's terms, that is.)

Rather than automatically stiff-arming TV reporters as their instincts would normally dictate, the Navy during the 1990s embraced a new and pro-active approach toward the news media. This was the consequence of several difficult episodes — including the failed closed-door approach toward the press in the 1991 Persian Gulf War, and a prolonged scandal following the 1991 Tailhook Association convention where several dozen aviators allegedly fondled females during the group's annual convention in Las Vegas — that resulted in searing negative press coverage. In response, senior Navy officers, led by then-Chief of Naval Information Rear Adm. Kendall Pease, organized a "revolution in public affairs" to deal with the press in a more open and engaged fashion, particularly with broadcast media.

The Navy today stresses pro-active media training — no different really from the short courses large civilian corporations run for their executives — with the help of the service's PAO infrastructure. This is how the Navy PAO recommends that a ship captain, squadron or wing commander or base commander prepare for your interview (my comments added in italics):

"To control the course and content of an interview, a person must prepare for the interview and go into it determined to repeatedly deliver set positive 'commercial' messages. No matter what the interviewer asks, the interviewee should steer his answers to the 'commercial' messages. Be positive in attitude, don't be passive. Answer questions with your 'commercial' in mind."

Be prepared for the Navy's line by thoroughly researching the issue or topic that forms the basis of your interview, lest you lose the battle for spin control.

"What is meant by 'commercials' is the point or theme you want to get across to the (TV) audience. One should also remember that positive themes result in positive public views or images of the naval service. To dwell on negative themes will normally result in a negative overall image."

The Navy (like other military services) is now showing awareness that the televised image is as important as the news content itself. This may be basic journalism or PAO strategy, but for the military — particularly the Navy — to be positively embracing it is a development as revolutionary as the invention of gunpowder.

"Cosmetics: This means, simply, to look your best in dress and grooming."

This is another sign of respect for the power of TV imagery.

Three commandments conclude the TV strategy. All are logical and understandable, given the Navy's goal of preserving its institutional reputation, delivering a corporate "line" on a key issue, and attracting and maintaining public support.

"1. Thou shalt not lie or knowingly mislead a reporter. If you can't answer the question, don't say 'No comment.' Instead, give the reason, 'I don't know,' or 'I can't answer that because of security.' To many reporters, 'No comment,' means, 'There must be some truth to the issue which is tied up in the question.' "

This is a positive step, rather than a hindrance, for it will make officials say nothing at least in complete declarative sentences, which make better sound bites than a mere "No comment" ever did.

"2. Thou shalt not comment upon matters beyond your command responsibilities. For example, recently a fleet commander was interviewed by a newspaper reporter, who noticed that in a previous assignment he had been in the Navy's Pentagon budget planning and programming office. The reporter pointed to the fleet commander's budget experience and then asked, 'What do you think the Navy's top three budget priorities should be?' The fleet commander stated that he was no longer a Navy budget expert and could only speak from a fleet commander's point of view. The admiral then said, 'As a fleet commander, I need funds for ... ' "

This is a poor example of what is actually a very firm and usually sensible military PAO guideline. If a local plane goes down overseas, this is why the local Navy recruiter isn't going to tell you anything about the safety record of that aircraft. He probably doesn't know and on-air guessing isn't exactly a career-enhancer. Unfortunately, this can lead (not only for TV but print reporters, too) to what I term the chain of command squeeze. That's when you find a succession of officials who chant variations of, "That (answer to a question) is above my pay grade," until you do find a senior enough official, but by then it's 11 p.m., the Pentagon's closed and he doesn't take calls at home.

"3. Thou shalt always keep cool and professional even in the face of hostile questions. Generally, when a reporter becomes abusive, rude or overly hostile in his/her questioning, the public empathy will go to the underdog or person being interviewed. Also in a crisis situation, the calm appearance of a person in charge goes a long way to provide a positive image of our military people."

The late Lt. Gen. Tom Kelly, who served as a Pentagon briefer dur-

ing Operation Desert Storm, knew that reality and used it brilliantly when the normal Pentagon press corps deployed en masse to Saudi Arabia, leaving the Pentagon briefings to inexperienced stand-ins. Then-Secretary of State Al Haig failed to remember that point following the 1981 shooting of President Reagan. Haig's attempt to reassure a jittery public ("I'm in charge here") instead frayed nerves everywhere.

Technical preparation for military coverage

Live feedpoints — The new military reporter and an experienced cameraman or studio technician should consult with every military base within the station's primary market for a pre-approved live feedpoint. In fact, if the base is a large facility, several locations should be identified and tested using station gear to ensure direct access in event of a story requiring break-in feeds or prolonged on-scene live reports. Similarly, the station should identify and inform the local base of a feedpoint location just outside either the base's main gate or in front of a recognizable military landmark for live remote transmissions if security concerns prompt commanders to close the base to reporters. Another important area of pre-negotiation is for the station's legal staff to attempt standing overflight agreements and possibly even landing rights in event a story justifies traveling to the base via station or leased helicopter or fixed-wing aircraft.

B-roll — Your station should have lengthy, varied and compelling B-roll tapes of every major aircraft, weapon system, unique military unit (e.g. paratroopers, military police dog teams), and local commanders from every base in your primary market. If there is one thing the TV reporter and producer can safely assume, it is that the local base will not have that material available for instant release in event of a crash or other breaking story.

An integral element of the military reporter's initial military contact visits should be the hunt for B-roll. The base and military service PAOs will understand your request for either military tapes or the opportunity to shoot the footage yourself. And you should program each visit or story as a parallel opportunity for shooting updates on that library. If your local station is a network affiliate, ensure that network file videotapes are stored and filed so that you can employ them as B-roll sources in event of a breaking story.

If your station employs a full-time or contract stringer in Washington, D.C., contact him or her to arrange B-roll shots of senior military officials, locales (Pentagon, congressional hearings, etc.) and the like. Each military service and base has at least one annual open house (either Armed Forces Day or July 4) which will provide you with an all-day opportunity to videotape static equipment displays, aerial demonstrations and the like.

Other sources for B-roll include: the Defense Department public affairs office and its website, www.defenselink.mil; manufacturers and subcontractors of the military equipment; National Archives (for historical footage, e.g., World War II).

Still photos — In preparation for times when Pentagon officials refuse to go on-camera for interviews, contact the Directorate for Defense Information (703-697-5131) and request a current roster of media action officers, their "account" listings of commands and issues, and current still photographs. That will enable you to use a still photo with voice-over of a recorded telephone interview as a last-ditch defense. Obtain and file both local PAOs and commanders as well. Still photos can be retrieved and downloaded at the images page on defenselink: www.defenselink .mil/multimedia/.

How to...

Cover the nuclear story

It has been a full decade since the leaders of the United States and Soviet Union significantly relaxed the long Cold War nuclear standoff between the two superpowers.

But that doesn't mean nuclear weapons have ceased to be an important subcategory of defense reporting — far from it. They still play a leading role in U.S. foreign policy and military strategy, and provide Russia with its last handhold onto the world stage as a major power.

As with the rest of the U.S. military, the topic of nuclear weapons has become obscure due to a combination of force reduction and realignment (fewer nuclear bases and commands at a smaller number of sites), while all but a handful of specialist reporters have long abandoned coverage of the subject.

But nuclear weapons are still in the news. Consider these current issues:

■ An ongoing Pentagon review of the entire U.S. nuclear force structure;

■ Unresolved START Treaty issues between the United States and Russia over future maximum force levels (warheads and launching platforms);

■ A Navy proposal to convert between two and four Trident ballistic missile submarines into conventionally-armed Tomahawk cruise missile platforms and SEAL commando vehicles;

■ The impact of proposed National Missile Defenses on existing nuclear arsenals;

■ The breakdown in global non-proliferation agreements, and the threat of a nuclear war between India and Pakistan;

■ Pentagon consideration of developing low-yield earth-penetrating nuclear weapons for use against hardened underground sites;

■ Ongoing safety and environmental concerns over the cleanup of the Cold War nuclear weapons complexes, and disposal of hundreds of tons of weapons-grade uranium and plutonium.

This is a technically complex subject to report on and write about, but with the Cold War a decade over, what was once nearly impossible to research and cover due to strict secrecy has now become somewhat more accessible.

Academics and independent nuclear researchers offer a wide range of expertise and archival background material for the reporter willing to invest the effort to master this arcane subject.

Three research institutions based in Washington, D.C., are very helpful to reporters in this subject area:

Natural Resources Defense Council (www.nrdc.org): An independent science and policy research institution that devotes a sizeable amount of its effort on monitoring nuclear weapon issues. Published the encyclopedic six-volume "Nuclear Weapons Databook" in the 1980s.

Federation of American Scientists (www.fas.org): This public policy organization's web site is a multi-layered and comprehensive portal gateway to information and news about nuclear weapon issues (as well as other arms treaties and chemical and biological weapons), with links to dozens of other useful organizations and sites. It is also based in Washington D.C.

Center for Defense Information (www.cdi.org): The nonprofit military-oriented think-tank has an excellent institutional knowledge and data library on nuclear weapon issues.

For unclassified Pentagon data, access the U.S. Strategic Command website at www.stratcom.mil.

Case history: 'When the bomb breaks'

This is a profile of how one nuclear weapons project was planned and executed.

What would happen in the event a nuclear weapon were destroyed in a major accident? Would innocent civilians be at risk? Would the U.S. government be able to cope with the different responsibilities thrust upon its emergency response teams? To what degree can the odds of such an accident be predicted? What can civilians expect of their federal government in terms of

Four B61 nuclear bombs on display: Two days before I took this photo, Air Force officials at Fairchild AFB told me they could neither confirm nor deny the presence of nuclear weapons at the base. However, tourists and visiting reporters could photograph simulated nuclear weapons during an open house celebration. (Photo: Ed Offley)

honesty and candor if a nuclear weapon accident were to happen?

That was the goal of an 18-month investigation by the *Seattle Post-Intelligencer* during 1989-90 into the Pentagon's nuclear weapon accident response capability: To define the threat, assess the institutional capability to deal with a nuclear weapon accident, and to review in the government's own words how it had performed in a series of realistic field and command-post drills over a 12-year period from 1977 through 1989.

The final product was a three-day package of seven investigative stories, augmented by several sidebar articles and a wide range of graphic art and photography that revealed the following:

■ The federal government's emergency-response network responsible for handling a nuclear weapon accident would probably fail to protect the unwary public from lethal radiation in event of an accident serious enough to cause the release of plutonium, enriched uranium or tritium gas from a broken warhead;

■ The Pentagon and U.S. Energy Department-led teams, in annual exercises since 1977, consistently failed to warn the public (in tightly orchestrated scenarios) that a wind-borne radioactive plume from a weapon accident threatened them;

■ Even though the end of the Cold War had reduced military tensions and the likelihood of nuclear conflict, new arms reduction treaties and budget-driven nuclear reductions — ironically — increased the odds of an accident, since the weapons ultimately had to be taken to an Energy Department weapons factory in northern Texas for disassembly. Experts say an accident during movement of the weapons — particularly by aircraft — is the most likely scenario that would result in the physical destruction of the warheads or bombs and the dispersal of volatile nuclear material into the environment;

■ A central reason for experts' private predictions of collapse after a nuclear accident stems from the government's dedicated attempts to be ready for such an accident — another irony. More than three dozen military and civilian federal agencies, state and local organizations would likely converge on an accident site, plunging the evacuation, weapon recovery, decontamination and site restoration efforts into chaos;

■ Nuclear radiation scientists revisiting earlier dosage studies from Hiroshima and Nagasaki had recently determined that low-level radiation is nearly twice as much a health hazard as initially computed, thus — in effect — the inherent dangers from a nuclear weapon accident's fallout have been doubled as well;

■ On the local and state level, emergency response officials reported continuing frustration in their attempts to coordinate planning and training with their military neighbors. The cause of that poor communication is also bureaucratic: Some military commands generally known to house nuclear weapons were prohibited from preparing for nuclear weapon accidents with their civilian counterparts because to do so would violate Pentagon policy rules by confirming the presence of nuclear weapons;

■ A significant number of outside nuclear experts and both former and current government officials interviewed for the project agreed that the Pentagon and Energy Department could — and should — design an "early warning" system to alert civilian rescue and police agencies in event of a nuclear weapon accident;

■ Evidence of past U.S. governmental deceit on nuclear weapons safety appeared as well. In the guise of national security, the Pentagon has carefully dissembled and when necessary, directly lied, to conceal the magnitude of earlier nuclear weapon accidents. In a 1950 mishap, an Air Force B-50 bomber jettisoned an unarmed Mark IV atomic bomb into the St. Lawrence River northeast of Quebec when the aircraft lost an engine. Although the nuclear warhead material was absent, the device that exploded in the river was a 4,000-lb. bomb with critical nuclear weapon design information inherent in its components. The Canadian government was never told.

Launching the project

The idea for this series dropped on my desk one afternoon in early 1989 in the form of two unrelated documents. The first was a wire-service story from the *Exxon Valdez* oil spill in Alaska, in which a local environmentalist derided the state's 28-volume emergency response plan for oil spills as "the best piece of maritime fiction since *Moby Dick*."

The second item was an updated survey of the U.S. nuclear arsenal by the nonprofit Natural Resources Defense Council, which indicated that because of programmed Navy missile submarine retirements, the number of nuclear weapons likely stored in South Carolina had significantly declined. (Turning to a 1985 reference volume on nuclear weapons, I confirmed my hunch. This change meant that the known nuclear inventory at Washington state's two known nuclear weapon installations, the Navy's Trident submarine base at Bangor and the B-52H wing at Fairchild Air Force Base near Spokane, would place the state at the top of all 50 states in terms of the number of nuclear weapons within their jurisdiction.)

I wondered how the federal response plan for a nuclear weapon would compare to Alaska's oil-spill plan?

How to find out? My editor and I identified six basic steps.

First, I set an initial priority (time and storage space) to the effort. My first step was to obtain four large file storage cartons and to carve out a large area in the corner of my desk. The facts were certainly out there but if experience prevailed, they would come buried in cubic feet of government papers and manuals.

Second, I went looking for what had been done before on this specific topic. Through the newspaper library, several computer-archive systems, and one or two research groups and think tanks that focus on nuclear weapon issues, I discovered to my surprise that the answer was: Not much.

Among the documents I was able to find were two that provided initial concepts for the investigation. The congressional General Accounting Office in 1987 had inquired (at the request of local congressmen) about the adequacy of Navy nuclear accident response planning. The report concluded that things were okay but could be better. The second blueprint document was a 1981 report by the nonprofit Center for Defense Information summarizing and updating the 32 known nuclear weapon accidents that the Pentagon confirmed had occurred since 1950.

From the GAO document I was able to identify some basic federal government documents and manuals utilized in planning and training for an accident, and the broad outlines of a multi-agency approach to nuclear weapon accident response. From the CDI report I had a pinpoint chronology of known weapon accidents that in several instances would highlight what could be anticipated if the real thing were to occur in 1989.

The third step was to compile a "to get" list of nuclear weapon accident after-action reports, governmental reports, organizational manuals, Army, Navy and Air Force nuclear surety (safety and security) rules, and the unclassified working documents issued by the Defense Nuclear Agency.

Fourth, I began to work the delicate task of confirming what was already known about the number, quantity and movement patterns of nuclear weapons at the two bases in Washington state that provided the focus of my probe.

Fifth, I began to carve time out of my schedule to read the trickle of incoming material that would — by the midpoint of my investigation — be a full-fledged torrent.

Sixth, I began to stream a number of requests for the documents I was identifying as basic to my research. I ended up filing about three dozen separate Freedom of Information Act Requests (See Chapter 11), purchasing another dozen reports through the U.S. Commerce Department's technical information center, and cadging others on a friendly source-journalist basis from outsiders and a few government folks.

Early progress

After about three months of preliminary work (in which I had spent maybe 15 hours on the project), the open corner on the desk was now an unsteady mountain of documents. But the generic outline I had assembled at the outset of the project was falling into focus.

Through my study, and some preliminary background interviews, I had identified several topic areas that would form the backbone of the project as well as some unexpected trends and roadblocks:

■ The government's own reports — particularly after-action reports from annual Defense Nuclear Agency exercises — identified many recurring shortcomings and flaws in the joint DoD-Energy Department emergency response plan. Thus, my midterm research would continue to focus on securing governmental documents and reports before I set out to conduct on-record interviews or background sessions with current officials;

■ Because of tight information-security rules governing all aspects of nuclear weapons, the tension between local and state officials and Pentagon-Energy Department officials over access to training and response plans was shaping up to be a more significant issue than initially thought. So I set a higher priority toward canvassing local and state officials on their work with local military bases;

■ Outside experts and former government officials who could comment authoritatively on the issue of nuclear weapon safety were much harder to identify, locate and entice into interviews. At one point, I halted all other phases of my research and interviews to focus on this element of the story alone;

■ The issue of identifying and explaining nuclear radiation factors proved less difficult than initially feared, given access to unclassified Defense Nuclear Agency and Federal Emergency

Management Agency resource materials on the subject. Thus, an identification search for outside experts here proved necessary only to find an authoritative source or sources to comment on the government's material.

Organizing the data

The computer word processor proved a critical tool in storing, outlining and cross-referencing the mountain of different reports, subject notes, interview transcripts and other streams of data as the research phase shifted over into the interview phase of the project.

The big challenge at this point was to successfully winnow out the small bits of pertinent data from a towering column of bulky, non-indexed reports, agate-type government manuals, and transcripts from prolonged interviews. The hard way proved best: By manually entering the data into computer files, I was able to organize my own thoughts while simultaneously reviewing bulk information. Loading it in my computer made the second time around much easier.

I also found it necessary to organize separate subdirectories (by filename prefix) on my computer.

In one tabulation of files I built a matrix for summarizing flaws and successes from each Nuclear Weapon Accident Exercise after-action report, making a comparison from the dozen exercises reviewed standard and quick to carry out.

A second subdirectory contained topical working files (e.g. "radiation definitions," "nuclear weapons," "key organizations," etc.), where I would assemble information as needed to build story elements, profiles or sidebar material.

And last, a separate subdirectory contained the working drafts and final versions of the actual stories that would be written based on the raw data.

Assembling the package

A review of the final articles against the initial project memorandum reveals what any reporter knows from experience. Many of the story elements and factual disclosures were unanticipated at the beginning of research. As the raw material piled up, surprising new facts emerged. Some examples included:

■ An additional local element to the story, and one of the "anchors" to the second-day lead focusing on safe transportation of nuclear weapons, was the presence in Washington State of an Air Force special airlift squadron responsible for transporting nuclear weapons. This fact added to the direct local significance of the series to the newspaper's readers (over and above the sheer number of deployed nuclear weapons within the state);

■ A request for news clips on any incidents that might have involved nuclear weapons (there have been no certified accidents since 1980) revealed an intriguing near-mishap involving a local C-141 transport at the Barber's Point Naval Air Station in Oahu, Hawaii in 1989. As sheer luck would have it, a recent nuclear weapon accident exercise had been staged at the same facility, and the "exercise scenario" leading to catastrophe along the Honolulu waterfront was identical to the real-world emergency involving a Washington state aircraft. The juxtaposition of actual emergency and feigned accident provided the spine of a gripping description of the safety hazards inherent in air transport of nuclear weapons;

■ A background review of known nuclear accidents — for examination of the performance of emergency-response units — produced almost by chance a lead that developed into a separate investigative story of how the U.S. Air Force dropped the atomic bomb (less nuclear warhead core) on Canada, covered it up, and got away with the deed for 40 years.

The interview process

It did not take long for word to get around the Pentagon and Washington State bases that my nuclear accident project was underway: I informed them directly. The reporter who covers an institution — good news or bad — will quickly learn the value of a timely heads-up notice. I told everyone and anyone that I was doing this. Why? Because (a) The first FOIA request to a local Navy base would in any event light up the local and national PAO network — and it did, (b) I had elected to use a "front door" approach, seeking on-the-record interviews, background briefings and the like without pretense or sneakiness, and (c) given this approach — helpful if one wishes to have productive relations with the military for later stories and projects — I had determined that any request for help would require even more patience and finesse than the normal controversial stories.

In a similar issue, the novice military reporter should understand a critical aspect of the nuclear weapons subject: Even the most innocent question can be a career-killer to a military officer. I almost aborted my project in advance without knowing it when I faxed letters of intent and request to local PAOs and commanders, and in the letter noted in passing that the reason for my interest in the subject was due to the large number of nuclear weapons at Bangor and Fairchild, which I cited.

One PAO quietly told me later that his superiors were terrified that any response by them to that particular letter might be inferred by senior military officials as an improper confirmation of the existence of nuclear weapons at a particular base.

In one interview, I showed a senior officer two unclassified documents that indicated that Squadron "A" had assumed a nuclear-weapon function that until the previous year had been done by Squadron "B." The officer waved me to turn off my tape recorder and said privately, "That's true and it's probably not classified, but I can't tell you that or I'm in big trouble." So I used it without attribution.

The final product

More than a year (and a lot of other daily and enterprise stories) had passed when I finally felt I had achieved critical mass on the subject, sat down with my editor and graphics editor and began organizing the package.

The stories themselves did not take long to write, for the basic journalistic reason that the prolonged effort at research (including self-education) and fact-finding made it so. The primary editing hits were for space and length, not botched writing or poor organization, the working story outline was amended, but the presses rolled on time. The effort paid off in the published product. And none of my military contacts were fired.

Chapter 11

Using the Freedom of Information Act

It's your 'nuclear weapon'

The Freedom of Information Act is the journalist's equivalent of the nuclear weapon. It can be a powerful weapon, but used in the wrong time or place may actually be self-defeating in your attempt to obtain timely information about a military unit or subject.

Two examples will suffice:

■ An official from the U.S. Department of Energy called one day.

"I've got your Freedom of Information Act request for 'Nuclear Surety Report - 1984,' " the man said. "The Pentagon routed it over here to us for processing."

For a moment I was totally bewildered — I didn't recall a single thing about the document.

"When was the original date of the request?" I fudged. "I don't have the file right at hand."

"Nov. 24, 1989," he said.

(This was February 1992.)

I didn't tell the guy that my series on nuclear weapon accident safety had run 16 months earlier, in October 1990. The document might still have news value all its own — if I ever got it.

The fellow from DOE reiterated that I would receive a notice within 10 days that my request was being processed. "They'll send you the letter," he said. Indeed, I got a nice letter about 10 days later, but no report.

It's October 2001. I'm still waiting for the document.

■ Scanning a history of the 1962 Cuban Missile Crisis, I came upon an obscure reference to a fatal airplane crash that claimed the lives of four Strategic Air Command fliers — apart from the famous downing of a U-2 over Cuba, the only fatal incident in that tense, 13-day confrontation.

Out of curiosity and a hunch that this might make an interesting 25th anniversary news feature about the crisis, I contacted
the Air Force's historical branch and the section that holds
archival files of aircraft accident reports. I told them what I was

---

FOIA Resources

Information centers

FOI Service Center
Reporters Committee for Freedom of the Press
800 18th St. NW Suite 300
Washington DC 20006
202-466-6313
www.rcfp.org

The FOI Service Center publishes a manual, "How to use the federal FOI Act" with detailed background on the legislation, exemptions
for information release, appeal and court procedures, and the Privacy
Act. The manual costs $3.

Project Sunshine
Society of Professional Journalists
3909 Meridian St.
Indianapolis, IN 46208
317-927-8000
www.spj.org

Project Sunshine is a national network of FOI-interested individuals coordinated by the Society of Professional Journalists. The organization's website offers many resources.

FOIA requests online

The Defense Department has streamlined Freedom of Information
Act procedures by creating a FOIA website accessible through its
DefenseLink internet portal at www.defenselink.mil/pubs/foi/.

Other hyperlinks at that site will connect you to the separate FOIA
centers operated by the separate military services and nearly a dozen
separate DoD agencies. In addition, the DoD has posted .pdf files relating to electronic FOIA request procedures, Pentagon FOIA guidance
memoranda and access to online "reading rooms" where previously
released files may be located and downloaded.

---

interested in finding, and asked what procedure would best work.

I was told to submit a FOIA request for the specific records. I did so, and less than three weeks later received the documents I needed.

So it goes.

The Freedom of Information Act is a vital weapon in the hands of journalists, but those specializing in the military are advised to treat it as a weapon of last resort.

The main difference in response, as one might glean from those two examples, is that the nuclear surety material I sought was (is?) laced with still-classified national security information, while the 1962 crash of an RB-47 reconnaissance plane, while containing minor segments deleted under the Privacy Act and FOIA exemptions for internal procedure, was not.

Depending on the military agency, the subject matter, the level of classification, and the degree of controversy of the subject, your FOIA request may take weeks, months or even years to process. You must be prepared, if your request is arbitrarily denied, to launch an immediate appeal (see sample letters), and even then you may soon face the hard decision as to whether your information search is worth a court fight that could take months and (potentially) thousands or tens of thousands of dollars in legal fees.

The one piece of advice from military PAOs about the Freedom of Information Act is this: Ask verbally or in writing for the document or material from them first without triggering the machinery of a formal FOIA request. Sometimes this will get you the material. If not, then you enter into the slow pipeline.

Freedom of Information Act letters

The following are sample Freedom of Information Act request and appeal letters for use in obtaining information from the military. If you anticipate making numerous requests in the short term, it is recommended that you copy these into your computer file under a stand-alone heading. Subsequent request letters can be generated by making an electronic copy and filling in the blanks.

1. Sample FOIA request letter

(Your name)
(Address)
(Date)

(Agency FOIA Administrator)
(Address)

FREEDOM OF INFORMATION ACT REQUEST

Dear Sir:

This is a request under the Freedom of Information Act (5 U.S.C. 552).

I write to request (CONCISE BUT THOROUGH DESCRIPTION OF THE MATERIAL YOU SEEK). To assist you in this request, I attach additional information that may help you identify, locate and retrieve the material I request in this letter (ATTACH SUPPLEMENTARY INFORMATION).

This request includes any and all documents, computer tapes or transcripts, photographs, drawings or other information related to the specific document(s) in this request.

As you know, the amended Act provides that if some parts of a file are exempt from release, that "reasonably segregable" portions shall be provided. I therefore request that if you determine that some portions of this request are exempt from release, that you provide me immediately with a copy of the remainder of the material.

If you determine that some or all of the material I seek is exempt from release, I request a detailed explanation as to which exemption(s) in the amended Act you determine apply to the denial. I reserve my right to appeal any decisions on your part declaring portions of this request as exempt from release.

I am prepared to pay reasonable costs for retrieving and photocopying the material in this request, and authorize you to proceed processing this request in an amount charged on your fee schedule to me not to exceed $(AMOUNT). Please notify me immediately by telephone (TELEPHONE NUMBER) or fax (FAX NUMBER) prior to my incurring expenses in excess of that amount.

As you know, the amended Act provides that you can reduce or waive the file search and reproduction charges if that is found to be "in the public interest because furnishing the information can be seen as primarily benefiting the public." Since the purpose of this request is to obtain material for a news story to be PUBLISHED/BROADCAST by my media outlet, for the purpose of informing my READERS/VIEWERS of governmental activities, I request a full waiver of fees under that section of the Act.

As provided for under the amended Act, I expect to receive a written reply from you within 10 working days. However, if there are any questions you have about this request, please feel free to telephone me at once and I'll be happy to discuss the request with you.

Sincerely,

(Name/Title)

2. Sample FOIA appeal letter

FREEDOM OF INFORMATION ACT APPEAL

Dear Sir:

This is an appeal under the Freedom of Information Act (5 U.S.C. 552).

(IF YOUR REQUEST IS DENIED IN WHOLE OR PART, INSERT THIS PARAGRAPH NEXT):
On (DATE) I submitted an FOIA request to your agency for (CONCISE DESCRIPTION OF MATERIAL), and was assigned the following FOIA case number (FILE/CASE NUMBER, IF GIVEN). On (DATE) your agency denied my request on grounds (CITE GROUNDS FOR DENIAL). Copies of my original request and your agency denial are enclosed.

(IF NO RESPONSE TO YOUR REQUEST WITHIN 10 DAYS, USE THIS PARAGRAPH INSTEAD):
On (DATE) I made an FOIA request to your agency for

(BRIEF DESCRIPTION OF MATERIAL SOUGHT). It has been (NUMBER) business days since my request was received by your agency. Since this clearly exceeds the 10 days provided for by the amended Act, I deem my request as denied. A copy of my FOIA request letter and postal receipt by your office* are enclosed.

(CONTINUE THE LETTER):

The information I requested is clearly releasable under the FOI Act and, in my opinion, may not validly be protected by any of the Act's exemptions.**

I trust that upon reconsideration you will reverse the decision denying access to this material.

However, if you deny this appeal, I intend to initiate a lawsuit to compel disclosure.***

As I have made this request as a journalist employed by (NAME OF EMPLOYER), and this information is of timely value, I would appreciate your expediting the consideration of this appeal in every way possible. In any case, I expect to receive your decision within 20 business days as required by the amended Act.

Sincerely,

(Name/title)

* If you anticipate resistance in obtaining information through a FOIA request, it is prudent to send the request by return receipt postage to validate the delivery and time of arrival of your request.

** No legal or policy justifications are required in an appeal, but if you have any specific reasons (basis of the information, other published accounts) for believing withholding to be unjustified, it won't hurt to enclose them.

*** Use this argument only if you are serious about seeking judicial relief.

Chapter 12

The Internet, Information Technology and Military Coverage
Be sure to mine this mother lode

Even before the stunning terrorist attacks against the World Trade Center and Pentagon on Sept. 11, 2001, recent news coverage of other ongoing military operations and crises had accelerated the role of information technology and the internet in delivering the news in a rich laminate of text, still photos and graphics, audio and video imagery. While the Pentagon and a number of major military commands have scrubbed their websites to delete time-sensitive and operational information (such as the current location of deployed Navy warships), the internet remains a fertile source of current information on U.S. military and intelligence data.

The aerial collision between a U.S. Navy EP-3 Aries II reconnaissance aircraft and a Chinese F-8 fighter on Apr. 1, 2001 and the ensuing 11-day diplomatic standoff between Washington and Beijing sparked major news coverage that demonstrated how advanced information technology can bring a remote news story home to all Americans.

Part I — The EP-3 incident

When the mid-air collision occurred off Hainan Island in the South China Sea, the U.S. and Chinese governments took starkly different political positions over the incident. The Chinese insisted that the four-engine EP-3 was to blame in the mishap while the Pentagon countered — with many details withheld until after the release of the crew from Chinese detention 11 days later — that blame for the collision rested with the Chinese pilot who perished after his aircraft struck one of the EP-3's propellers.

What was striking about the incident was how information from both sides became quickly accessible to reporters in the United States and around the world.

Not long ago a similar incident would have been especially

difficult if not impossible for journalists to cover (such as the 1983 Soviet shoot-down of Korean Airlines Flight 007 or a number of Cold War encounters at sea between the U.S. and Soviet navies). Given the remote location, the short time-span involved (less than 20 minutes elapsed from the time of the collision until the EP-3 made its emergency landing at a Chinese military airbase on Hainan Island), and especially given the Cold War penchant for secrecy that dominated military coverage for most of the post-World War II era, journalists would have struggled to get the bare outlines of the story from informed military sources and official government announcements.

But thanks to the information technology revolution of the past few years — particularly the growth of the internet, the commercialization of satellite imagery services, and the proliferation of new digital transmitting capabilities — the EP-3 affair quickly became a story accessible to print and broadcast reporters from small towns across the country as well as to national and foreign correspondents in Washington, D.C., and — to a relatively open degree — in China itself. While international politics and military secrecy still drove (and limited) much of the information that emerged in the weeks after the collision, the incident was significantly more transparent to the news media and public than it would have been a decade earlier. And it stands as a portent of how reporters now and in the future can bring similar technology to bear on a complicated and controversial story.

Four broad technological capabilities played key roles in the EP-3 incident: (1) The use of internet portals and websites by both governments to disseminate and update information on the ongoing incident; (2) the widespread publishing of independent, civilian satellite photographs of the aircraft to confirm and show its location on Hainan Island; (3) the use of digital videophone images by CNN to make a covert, live broadcast of the EP-3 aircrew boarding a commercial aircraft upon release from detention; and (4) the fusion of video, audio and text into true multimedia presentations via news media internet sites.

Live via the internet from Hainan, Hawaii, Beijing, Washington

Just hours after the actual collision, a new interactive internet page appeared on DefenseLink, the Pentagon's news and information portal, www.defenselink.mil, providing a single-source location for information about the EP-3 incident and ongoing efforts to secure the release of the crew from detention. (In the summer of 2001, the EP-3 site was still accessible via DefenseLink at www.defenselink.mil/sites, and at the U.S. Pacific Command home page at www.pacom.mil).

Beginning on the day of the actual collision, the public affairs staff at Pacific Command headquarters in Hawaii — a primary focal point for coverage of the U.S. military's response — created a one-stop site providing official command news releases, transcripts of press conferences, digital photographs and other information bearing on the incident. In addition, the command created separate links to the White House, Defense Department and State Department internet sites for access to press briefings and other information released by those government departments. Between the Apr. 1 incident and the return of the disassembled aircraft to a Georgia base three months later, more than 65 separate information items were posted on the EP-3 internet page.

In turn, the Chinese government utilized its government-controlled media internet sites to issue statements and publish articles reflecting the regime's own "spin" of the story (including articles noting condemnation of the alleged U.S. intrusion by officials from Iran, Cambodia and the Sudan, among others).

Nevertheless, the incident involved two governments motivated to publish their side of the story, and a maturing internet made that process accessible worldwide.

A significant example came on Apr. 13 — just one day after the EP-3 crew flew out of Hainan — when the Pentagon released digital video images worldwide showing an earlier encounter on Jan. 24, 2001, between a Chinese fighter and an EP-3 aircraft that graphically depicted an aggressive and dangerous aerial confrontation where the Chinese aircraft came less than 20 feet from the American surveillance aircraft.

Pentagon and Navy officials say they were satisfied that the current capabilities of the internet enabled them to keep reporters fully informed throughout the 11-day ordeal, and on another level, were even more pleased that they had been able to use modern communications procedures to reach family members of the 24 crewmen much faster and more thoroughly to inform them of their loved ones' situation. Just a decade earlier, when several dozen Navy crewmen assigned to the carrier USS *Saratoga* drowned in a ferry accident in Israel, it took days before all of the victims' families had been tracked down and notified, officials recall. In contrast, the EP-3 families were all formally contacted within 24 hours of the collision, one senior official noted.

The EP-3 incident was not an exception or an isolated event in which officials could turn to the internet for putting out facts and countering misinformation. It is, rather, a model for how information on future incidents and mishaps (and larger crises) will be managed.

In the months prior to the EP-3 incident the Navy had created special internet page sites to provide information on the sinking of the Japanese fishing vessel *Ehime Maru* after colliding with the submarine USS *Greeneville* off Hawaii; on the terrorist bombing of the destroyer USS *Cole* in Aden, Yemen, in October 2000; and on its attempts to explain training requirements at the Puerto Rican island of Vieques in the face of widespread public opposition. The Army, in like vein, responding to an investigative report by the Associated Press in late 1999 that reported allegations of a massacre of South Korean civilians by American troops at the village of No Gun-ri in South Korea, created a specialized internet site to provide information on the in-depth investigation that ensued.

Live from space — the Hainan Airfield

It took only several days for U.S. reporters based in Beijing to reach Hainan Island, where they cooled their heels waiting for a breakthrough in the tense negotiations between the two governments over the fate of the detained EP-3 aircrew. In particular, Chinese military officials refused to allow the news media contingent access to either the crew or to the base where the damaged aircraft was parked.

But only three days after the mishap, print and broadcast journalists published a clear photograph of the EP-3 aircraft parked on the Lingshui airfield tarmac. The image was not released by the government in Beijing nor issued by the Pentagon. Instead, it was provided by Space Imaging Inc., a Colorado-based firm that provides commercial satellite photographic images on demand to corporate and individual customers. The photograph — with a one-meter image resolution — was captured by the company's Ikonos satellite, launched in 1999, which orbits the earth at an altitude of 423 miles.

A technological capability that for nearly 50 years had rested exclusively in the hands of national intelligence agencies of the major military powers was now available on demand to the news media. It was a major milestone in the digital revolution transforming the news media worldwide.

And like all revolutions, the satellite imagery of Hainan Island had a precursor.

More than 10 years earlier, on Jan. 6, 1991, an American reporter tried to use commercial satellite imagery to challenge the U.S. government's position on a global military incident.

Reporter Jean Heller of *The St. Petersburg Times* wrote an article ("Photos Show Buildup," Jan. 4, 1991) that questioned the U.S. government's initial contention that Iraqi Army units directly threatened Saudi Arabia shortly after the Aug. 2, 1990 invasion of Kuwait. What was the newspaper's source? Satellite photographs of southern Kuwait shot by an orbiting Soviet photoreconnaissance satellite that were analyzed on the newspaper's behalf by two experts not affiliated with the U.S. government.

"The photos are not conclusive proof that the administration overestimated Iraq's buildup along the Saudi border, a buildup that was cited as a justification for the deployment of U.S. troops," the article said. "But two American satellite imaging experts who examined the photos could find no evidence of a massive Iraqi presence in Kuwait in September (1990)." The Soviet satellite photographed Kuwait on Sept. 13, six weeks after the invasion. The newspaper sought Defense Department amplification of the discrepancy between DoD statements and the apparent lack of Iraqi troops in the overhead photographs, but a Pentagon spokesman declined to respond, Heller wrote.

The venture into independent satellite reconnaissance came subsequent to an attempt by ABC News to obtain the same evidence for broadcast. The newspaper reported ABC News decided not to air its photographs because they did not include "the strategically important area of southern Kuwait," where Iraq was thought to have laagered its army units. The newspaper alleged that the photographs it purchased from the Soviet commercial space operation constituted the missing images. The Pentagon had reported on Sept. 18, 1990 that there were 360,000 Iraqi troops and 2,800 tanks in or near Kuwait. At the time of *The St. Petersburg Times* article, the Bush administration estimated there were 500,000 soldiers in the occupied emirate.

In hindsight it is not possible to definitively resolve the contradiction raised by the newspaper's foray into satellite imagery analysis. One account of Operation Desert Shield noted that after the initial strike into Kuwait, where Iraqi units did advance toward the Saudi border, Iraqi military commanders after less than a week ordered the units back into Southern Iraq and left only a handful of conventional units within a short distance of the Saudi border. Thus, the satellite images could neither prove nor disprove the Bush administration's assertion.

But the newspaper's decision to obtain and use its own satellite imaging source marked the beginning of a new era in news coverage, where journalists could now opt to challenge the U.S. government on its single most valuable intelligence capability, its eyes in space.

The commercialization of space imagery comes as another inevitable consequence of the end of the Cold War. While it remains a relatively unexplored frontier to journalists nearly a decade after Operation Desert Storm, space satellite photography is yet another medium that the computer revolution will soon make easy to exploit by the news media.

"The rapid advancement of both communications and computational power is going to forever change the way we fight wars and disseminate information," Jeffrey Harris told a 1997 military-media conference. Harris, a former assistant secretary of the Air Force for Space, was then serving as president of Space Imaging Corporation, one of 11 civilian firms that cropped up in the 1990s to market space imagery as a business and media tool.

For reporters covering military affairs, commercial satellites whose imagery resolutions are as small as one meter — the minimum now allowed by the U.S. government — offer photographic coverage from space that rivals the capabilities of U.S. intelligence agencies just several decades ago. "The media will be a regular customer for data products and information products (from commercial satellites) — floods, earthquakes, fires, tidal waves, refugee camps," Harris told the 1997 Cantigny Conference of military officials and defense journalists convened by the Robert R. McCormick Tribune Foundation.

Harris and other experts agreed that connecting this imagery with existing computer power offers a new dimension to how television and print journalists can illustrate a breaking military story, and independently assess what their government is saying about the enemy. The impact of journalistic insertion into what has always been a strategic intelligence function — thanks to satellites and related computer processing power — sparks strong debate between the military and the media.

"The next time there's a crisis on the Korean peninsula, the media will have imagery that's almost as good as that available to the military," one military officer theorized at the 1997 Cantigny conference. "What is likely to happen is that a debate will erupt in Washington in which the President says, 'The situation is X and, therefore, I'm going to do Y.' And the media is going to go to Jeff Harris and buy imagery, either real time or archived imagery of U.S. troop deployments in South Korea and of troop deployments in North Korea, and they're going to say, 'Ah, the situation's not what the President says. It's Z.' And they're going to find some retired general who's going to say, 'That's right. I have grave concern.' And it's going to make decision-making enormously more difficult."

While that policy complication did not occur during the EP-3 incident — both the Pentagon and Beijing declined to comment or complain about the published satellite images — the availability of the image from an independent source heralded that the skies may soon be truly open to the news media in future incidents or crises.

But not just yet. Civilian satellite coverage of U.S. commando raids in Afghanistan would greatly assist the U.S. news media to observe the stealth combat that began on Oct. 19, 2001. However, the Pentagon mounted a pre-emptive strike of its own: It signed a contract with Space Imaging Inc. for exclusive rights to (and control over) Ikonos images of the conflict.

Live from a cell phone — release of the aircrew

The diplomatic resolution of the EP-3 incident, coming after days of intense negotiation between Washington and Beijing over the precise wording of a U.S. letter of "regret," led to one of the most dramatic stories of the entire standoff: The release of the aircrew and their departure for Guam and the United States via a commercial aircraft.

The moment also constituted the debut of another technological advance in live news-gathering: the videophone. A video camera that instantly transmits pictures through a telephone line, the videophone was the weapon of choice for the team of CNN reporters gathered on Hainan Island as the incident neared its climax. A *Washington Post* article noted, "Using a car battery for power, [producer Lisa Rose] Weaver's team was able to transmit footage of the return airplane landing, the detainees boarding and the plane taking off. While the footage looked rather crude and jumpy, it also put CNN nearly half an hour ahead of its competitors."

The technology promises to liberate broadcast reporters from their dependency on bulky satellite uplink transmitters that are difficult to transport, vulnerable to breakdown in harsh environments, and frequently useless because of poor connectivity with satellites.

There are at least four commercial manufacturers currently selling videophone units. A recent report by the nonprofit Poynter Institute profiled the "Talking Head 1" model produced by the British firm 7E Communications (current cost is $7,500 for the remote transmitter and $6,000 for the receiver). The "Talking Head 1" transmitter is contained inside a waterproof metal case about the size of two laptop computers that contains a "full duplex" video system, satellite telephone and control panel. It can be powered by either AC or DC batteries (the CNN videophone in the Hainan incident was powered by an adapter that fit into a rental car's cigarette lighter.)

NBC technician Adam Sharp described the videophone process in an interview with the Poynter Institute's Al Tompkins: "The crew records the story as it always did using tape-based TV camera gear. When it's time to feed the tape, there are a couple of choices, depending on where the crew is. It can edit the story in the field and send the completed story back; but in [remote locations] it usually sends the 'raw tape' back and the bureau assembles the story.

"The crew simply plugs the camera into the videophone and plays the tape. The crew dials an ISDN number in [the United States] the same way you would dial a cell phone. Instead of the call going to a cell tower, the signal bounces off a satellite. The laptop device turns the video into data. On the receiving end, a device decodes the data and turns it back into video images.

"Those at the receiving end can decide how much quality they are willing to wait for. To feed a minute of video at top quality would take between 5 and 30 minutes, depending on the quality of the connection."

In the case of the EP-3 incident, a worldwide audience, including President George W. Bush aboard Air Force One, watched the dramatic images of the U.S. crew boarding the departure aircraft as they unfolded. "We're in an era where technology has made it a lot easier to transmit images than it used to in the past; we're taking advantage of the technology," said CNN news gathering chief Eason Jordan.

Footnote: The CNN videophone was confiscated by Chinese military guards after they detected the TV crew surreptitiously filming the U.S. Navy crewmen departing. But after several weeks of haggling, Chinese officials returned the device, and CNN donated it to the Freedom Forum's Newseum in Rosslyn, Va., where it is on display with other historical news gathering artifacts.

Part II — The internet as a military reporting tool

With a specified domain (.mil), the U.S. Department of Defense, uniformed services and various defense agencies provide a stunning array of information on hundreds of websites ranging from the Defense Department's primary internet portal, DefenseLink.mil, to individual ship, unit and base websites. Both at DefenseLink and the individual armed service websites, the reporter on military assignment can quickly track down essential information for a story or research assignment.

"The World Wide Web and internet provides the Department of Defense with a powerful tool to convey information quickly and efficiently on a broad range of topics," stated a DoD press release posted at DefenseLink in September 1998. "The global reach of the internet makes information, whether a press release or a statistical chart, easily available to everyone from individual service members to the international community."

But first, two standard cautions:

First, the reporter should — and damn well ought to — realize that the information he or she can access via modem or T1 line reflects the information directives and public affairs policies of the Defense Department and/or uniformed services. Basic reference and almanac data is probably spin-neutral, but everything else, from the Pentagon spokesman's press briefing to the defense secretary's Annual Report to Congress, reflects the confluence of executive branch politics, inter-service policy debate and a host of other subjective factors. It remains the reporter's responsibility to ensure that the story derived in part from this readily-downloadable information is accurate, balanced and comprehensive.

Second, as internet expert and military analyst William M. Arkin warned in a recent monograph, *National Security Research on the Internet*, © 2000, Center for Strategic Education, The Johns Hopkins University:

> The internet is an electronic embarrassment of riches and a truly revolutionary change in the way information flows in our society. Yet as a research tool, the internet is not everything. It is not comprehensive, nor very historical, and it is by no means selective. What is on-line is there because someone has placed it there, not because it has been published or because it is deemed important by the academic or expert world. Good and bad information therefore reside comfortably together, and what is on-line is hardly a comprehensive reflection of what there is.

Bearing those warnings, it is obvious that the internet has transformed, and will continue to change, military reporting — just as every other specialty beat in journalism — because of the tremendous opening of access to information and raw data that otherwise would have been inaccessible or so difficult to obtain as to effectively be unavailable. Second, the pace of journalism (inquiries and interviews through e-mail, instantaneous world-wide publishing via posted internet sites) has transformed the news delivery process so that even a small non-daily newspaper can effectively compete with the wire services if it is utilizing standard internet services.

In less than five years, the .mil domain has become one of the fastest-growing components of the internet as a whole, particularly because Pentagon officials have quickly embraced the internet both for external communication and news, and also as a tool for its own internal communications.

(Indeed, for the very reason that this manual is being published in traditional book format, it would be a wasted effort to attempt printing out a detailed roster of specific military-related websites given the rapid pace at which even official sites are changed, redesigned and reorganized. A number of primary internet portals and other key sites — which provide user-friendly site maps, "what's new" directories and other aids — are included at the end of this chapter.) A glance at DefenseLink's multiple pages on one day — July 19, 2001 — confirmed the variety and depth of information available for journalistic use:

News: Top news stories from the internal American Forces Information Service and raw transcripts on congressional testimony and press briefings concerning a test of the national missile defense system prototype rocket and "kill" vehicle; a news briefing transcript by Secretary of Defense Donald Rumsfeld on the ongoing defense review; congressional hearing transcripts from July 18 for Deputy Defense Secretary Paul Wolfowitz; a briefing transcript from the regular Thursday Pentagon press briefing by spokesman Rear Adm. Craig Quigley; and several AFIS news articles.

Issues: Dedicated websites with "one-stop shopping" for news and information concerning the EP-3 incident, training issues on Vieques, the Pentagon's mandatory anthrax vaccination program, Gulf War illnesses, the *USS Greeneville* incident, and the proposed Joint Strike Fighter, among many others. A major issue site at DefenseLink is "Transforming the Military," a compendium of news, information and transcripts from the Pentagon and other federal agencies on the Bush administration's controversial and ambitious plan to undertake a thorough review of military force structure and missions.

Organizations: A breakdown of subsidiary websites for the Army, Navy, Air Force, Coast Guard and Marine Corps; Joint Chiefs of Staff and the nine regional multiservice combatant commands. These mini-portals contain their own news and information pages and link to subsidiary headquarters and commands. For instance, the Air Force home page at www.af.mil provides a hyperlink to every major service component command, headquarters, Air Force Base and unit that has its own web page, so a reporter looking for news or information about a specific issue — for example, aerial refueling tankers, can quickly access the Air Mobility Command website and more than a dozen subsidiary commands and bases with their own sites.

Reference: From DefenseLink to specialized organizations such as the Naval War College, Air University or Army War College, many of the .mil sites contain excellent basic information and reference materials essential for the reporter coming up to speed on military issues. Basic information including military rank and insignia, U.S. military medals and ribbons, the DoD Unified Command Plan (which formally designates the geographical areas and specified missions for the major multiservice headquarters commands) are readily available. DefenseLink also is home to the DoD Defense Almanac, a detailed compendium of statistical, financial and basic research information on current force structure, economic impact, demographics and other background data on the military. A careful self-guided tour of the DoD and service internet portals will quickly reveal these easy-to-find sites.

To fairly and comprehensively cover all sides of the story, the reporter can use the internet to obtain countervailing viewpoints, alternative analyses and critiques from Congress, independent research institutions and academic observers. These include:

Congress: Both House and Senate committees dealing with the armed services, appropriations and budget have comprehensive websites including specific sites for the posting of hearing transcripts, legislation and other information. In addition all but a tiny handful of senators and congressmen have created their own websites with an eye toward rapid posting of news releases and other information.

Industry: Major business associations, trade groups and defense companies all have multi-level internet sites including useful information on their products.

Research institutions: The "ideas industry" in Washington, D.C. and other major cities includes a large component of think tanks and institutions that focus on defense and military affairs. Their internet sites are a rich harvest of issue studies and reports, and also provide contact information for in-house staff experts who are ready and willing to assist reporters in grappling with military stories.

Veterans organizations: Personnel and benefits issues affecting military service personnel and veterans are subjects that the dozens of formal veterans organizations study as a daily tasking. They, too, are alive and well and accessible via the internet.

Part III — Data mining and the internet's long reach

Immediately prior to the Sept. 11, 2001 terrorist attacks, ongoing U.S. military operations and deployments had reached a stunning level of transparency thanks to the internet.

When the Clinton administration ordered a cruise missile attack on suspected al Qaeda terrorist sites in Afghanistan and Sudan on Aug. 21, 1998, following the terrorist bombings of two U.S. embassies in East Africa, the Pentagon imposed an information blackout on the identity and location of the military units involved. But it took only five minutes on unclassified Pentagon internet sites for the author and other journalists to learn the specific names of the Navy warships that had fired the Tomahawks.

Information continuously provided by the Navy on various websites (and available from the service's information office in the Pentagon) revealed that there were only two groups of naval warships operating in the Persian Gulf region immediately prior to the incident: the *USS Abraham Lincoln* carrier battle group, and several surface warships assigned to the Navy Middle East Task

Force (METF). The *Abraham Lincoln*, like most major Navy ships and shore commands, had created an information-packed internet home page in recent years aimed at informing the crew and their family members and the public about the carrier, its carrier air wing, the other escort and logistics ships assigned to the battle group, and even the biographies of senior commanders.

To further help family members keep track of their loved ones while at sea, the carrier's website contained one link that provided a day-by-day location map from the time the ship left on deployment from its base in Everett, Wash. (Due to security, the ship suspended precise latitude-longitude markings whenever it entered the Persian Gulf, stating only that the ship was operating in the waterway.)

A check of the *Lincoln's* locator map the day of the missile strikes turned up a tantalizing and revealing clue: The daily entries for the carrier and its battle group had abruptly ended several days before. (The dog in Sherlock Holmes' account had abruptly stopped barking). It then only required several minutes of examining the unclassified descriptions of the *Abraham Lincoln* escorts and the current METF ships through an unclassified reference manual (the U.S. Naval Institute's *The Ships and Aircraft of the U.S. Fleet*), to identify which of the ships were armed with Tomahawk cruise missiles.

The ability to scan vast amounts of unclassified information in a brief period and come up with such operationally relevant material has troubled Pentagon officials who must weigh the value of providing such information against the possibility that sensitive information may inadvertently come out.

Even as reporters were reporting on the cruise-missile strikes and the launching platforms, a Pentagon security team was making its own discovery. Two members of the Pentagon Joint Staff demonstrated how they had successfully compiled information on selected senior military commanders using commercially available internet search engines that amassed separate pieces of information that — when seen in the aggregate — "could translate into a [security] vulnerability." Taking one general officer as a text case, the two staffers were "able to extract his complete address, unlisted phone number, and using a map search engine, build a map and driving directions to his house," according to an internal Pentagon news report.

Pentagon officials ordered all military internet administrators to remove certain categories of information from their websites accessible to the public, including:

■ Plans or lessons learned which would reveal sensitive military operations;

■ Information on sensitive movements of military assets or the location of units, installations or personnel where uncertainty regarding location is an element of the security of a military plan or program;

■ Personal data such as social security account numbers, complete dates of birth, home addresses, and telephone numbers other than public telephone numbers of duty offices. In addition, names, locations and other identifying information about family members of DoD employees and military personnel should be removed.

Military journalists who have adopted the internet as their new operating arena said the Pentagon review, while sensible, would not neutralize the impact of the internet on how journalists (and ordinary citizens for that matter) use its power to rapidly collect, collate and synthesize information.

"There is a fundamental lack of understanding about the internet (at the Pentagon)," said Neff Hudson, then general manager for Military City On-line, the multi-faceted internet site for the the *Army*, *Navy* and *Air Force Times* newspapers. "Once you let information out, it's out: you can't put that genie back in the bottle." A privately-owned newspaper group that has covered the military for its members since 1948, the Army Times Publishing Co. has pioneered the use of information technology to present both conventional news accounts on defense issues, while exploring innovations such as digital video and audio segments, issue-related computer bulletin boards and "chat rooms" for those interested about military topics, Hudson said.

The company's creativity with such technology created another security dilemma for the Pentagon during Gen. John Shalikashvili's tenure as chairman of the Joint Chiefs of Staff during 1993-97. Using digital video animation techniques, MCO (as it's known on the internet) created a "virtual tour" of the chairman's private residence at Quarters 6 at Fort Myer, Va. "When (Gen. Hugh) Shelton came in as chairman, he asked us to take it down as a security risk," Hudson said. "So we took it down." The lesson from this, Hudson continued, is that "There tends to be a thought that all of this information is new out there. It's not. The difference is the speed with which we can get it."

The most dramatic confirmation of the internet's potential to transform delivery of massive amounts of information came not through a military internet site and did not directly involve the military and reporters who cover military topics. But the extraordinary demonstration of internet capacity that occurred with the release of the Office of Independent Counsel report on President Clinton and former White House intern Monica Lewinsky on Sept. 21, 1998, provided a clear indication of the information-flow dynamics that the Defense Department must contend with in the next major military crisis or war. In releasing the 453-page report directly onto the internet, Independent Counsel Kenneth Starr inadvertently gave the new media technology its most severe test since the internet exploded into popular use nearly a decade earlier.

By all accounts, the national network easily handled a historic "spike" of computer users switching to one of several sites to download or simply read the report. "The decision (to utilize the internet) prompted a digital rush hour of historic dimensions. Various web sites and internet service providers reported increases over normal usage with log-ons about 10 percent above normal," wrote syndicated computer columnists Brit Hume and T.R. Reid on Sept. 26. "And the system survived." An article in *The New York Times* called the Starr Report release, and the subsequent live broadcasting of the president's grand jury appearance via broadcast TV, cable and direct internet outlets, as a "defining moment" in the history of the internet.

It was also a bellwether for what the military can expect — both in terms of demand for raw information in real-time, and the potential for an instant mass audience clamoring for that data — as user sites continue to proliferate and new software programs go to market that offer sophisticated delivery of computer graphic animation, video and audio signals. Simply put, military crises and battle — and the underlying policy debates governing the deployment of forces to overseas hot spots — are now totally in the public domain, because the internet in just five years attained the data capacity, bandwidth and sophistication to provide information in a user-attainable array of different forms.

Some experts say a new role for military journalists will be to simply sort out the truly important issues and facts from a torrent of raw data that could overwhelm the individual internet subscriber and his or her favorite search engine. With over 1,500 internet sites currently dedicated to military topics, Bill Arkin warns that the sheer mass of information is now posing the biggest challenge to internet users seeking military and defense data. "It is no longer economical or even technically possible for the commercial search engines and mega-portals to index everything that is on-line, nor to do so in a timely and reliable manner," Arkin recently warned. "For a segment of the internet such as the .mil domain, the result is that more material goes largely un-indexed and is more difficult to find."

The bottom line is that the internet now directly involves American journalists — and citizens — as never before in the activities and operations of its armed forces, in peace and war.

But in the war against terrorism that began on Sept. 11, 2001, this trend toward transparency in reporting on military affairs has already collided with the inevitable Pentagon and intelligence agency movement to cloak ongoing deployments and other steps in order to protect operational security. As we will discuss in the next chapters, the news media and the U.S. government are struggling even harder to balance journalism's role as informer of government actions with the Pentagon's equally legitimate mission to protect the lives of servicemen and women from leaks of time-sensitive, operationally critical information.

Useful web sites

■ Department of Defense
DefenseLink: Primary web portal for DoD
http://www.defenselink.mil

■ Secretary of Defense
http://www.defenselink.mil/osd/topleaders.html

■ Joint Chiefs of Staff
http://www.dtic.mil/jcs/

■ U.S. Army
http://www.army.mil

■ U.S. Navy
http://www.navy.mil

■ U.S. Air Force
http://www.af.mil

■ U.S. Marine Corps
http://www.usmc.mil

■ U.S. Coast Guard
http://www.uscg.mil

Unified combatant commands

■ U.S. Central Command
http://www.centcom.mil

■ U.S. European Command
http://www.eucom.mil

■ U.S. Joint Forces Command
http://www.jfcom.mil

■ U.S. Pacific Command
http://www.pacom.mil

■ U.S. Southern Command
http://www.southcom.mil

■ U.S. Space Command
http://www.spacecom.af.mil

■ U.S. Special Operations Command
http://www.socom.mil

■ U.S. Strategic Command
http://www.stratcom.mil

■ U.S. Transportation Command
http://www.transcom.mil

Independent research institutions

■ Brookings Institution
http://www.brookings.org

■ Business Executives for National Security
http://www.bens.org

■ Cato Institute
http://www.cato.org

■ Center for Defense Information
http://www.cdi.org

■ Center for Strategic and Budgetary Assessment
http://www.csbaonline.org/

■ Center for Strategic and International Studies
http://www.csis.org

■ Defense and the National Interest
http://www.d-n-i.net

■ Federation of American Scientists
http://www.fas.org

■ Natural Resources Defense Council
http://www.nrdc.org

■ Project on Government Oversight
http://www.pogo.org

■ Project for the New American Century
http://www.newamericancentury.org/

■ Rand Corp.
http://www.rand.org

Military.com reference channels
This commercial web portal has a number of useful reference channels for quick access to military and veterans sites:

■ Defense industry/trade associations
http://www.military.com/UnReg/Association/1,11228,,00.html

■ Military equipment
http://www.military.com/Resources/EQG/EQGmain

■ Military installations
http://www.military.com/InstallationGuides/ChooseInstallation/1,11400,,00.html

■ Veterans associations
http://www.military.com/UnReg/Association/1,11228,,00.html

Chapter 13

Going to War I
Realtime: Covering major incidents and operations

From the U.S. Marine operation to rescue the captured crew of the freighter *S.S. Mayaguez* in 1975 to the ongoing peacekeeping missions in Bosnia and Kosovo in 2001, the National Command Authority has ordered American forces into action in small-scale incidents dozens of times over the last quarter-century. Activities have been as limited as armed "show of force" operations in the Gulf of Sidra or the aerial interception of the *Achille Lauro* cruise ship hijackers, and as complex as the ill-fated multiservice rescue mission to free 52 U.S. hostages in Iran.

This is what many reporters call "realtime" — operational incidents short of major war that still involve the use of military force against a defined foe for a specific objective.

Many "realtime" operations made banner headlines around the world when they occurred. In other instances, the true outline of U.S. military presence was not clarified until months or years later. In some cases involving special operations forces, the Defense Department still refuses to acknowledge that the operation occurred at all.

In any case, these operations — involving threatened force, self-defense maneuvers, or actual combat short of large-scale maneuver warfare — are central to U.S. military training in peacetime and the most common form of military action that the armed forces will carry out and journalists will cover. Preparing for that eventuality is a crucial goal for any military reporter.

When challenged by congressional critics for his unyielding efforts to obtain more money for defense programs under the Reagan administration's military buildup of the 1980s, then-Secretary of Defense Caspar Weinberger often touted a compelling phrase to describe the need for well-trained, highly armed and mobile forces. The military must be ready for, he said, a "come-as-you-are war."

Weinberger's comments, while succinct, underscore the nation's lack of consistency in that aim. The U.S. military has had an uneven record in recent decades with such short-fuse operations. Several applications of military force — the 1980 raid to free the hostages in Iran, the 1983 carrier bombing raid against Syrian targets in Lebanon, and even our anticipation of homeland vulnerability to terrorism, are prime examples of incidents in which we suffered major tactical failures. In others, particularly the 1985 interception of the cruise liner *Achille Lauro* hijackers, military force did its mission perfectly (although in this case politics intervened at the end to thwart the capture of the alleged terrorist ringleader).

What all incidents shared was momentous news value. A military journalist who takes his or her responsibilities seriously should gird for "come-as-you-are" coverage in response to such quick-response military operations. They will remain a fact of life in the post-Cold War world. To borrow a military concept, you should develop and maintain your own professional readiness for covering the unexpected.

Let's break that down into four components.

First, you should have the ability to quickly recognize, through analysis of wire stories or CNN bulletins, any emerging crisis that could lead to a U.S. military response, and you must instigate a daily routine of scanning the wires and other news sources for evidence of such a development.

Second, you should have mastered your primary coverage

· ·

Chronology of U.S. Military Operations, 1981-2001

Think the military just sits around during peacetime? This list shows military operations over the past two decades:

Aug. 19, 1981 — Mediterranean Sea — Two U.S. Navy F-14s from the carrier *USS Nimitz* shoot down Libyan warplanes over the Gulf of Sidra — (limited combat).

Dec. 12, 1981 — Italy — a special operations planning team from the new Joint Special Operations Command (JSOC) — now part of the multiservice U.S. Special Operations Command — deploys to Europe to assist in the search for kidnapped Army Gen. James Dozier — (counter-terrorism).

area to know which local or regional units might have a crisis response mission.

Third, you must have the street smarts, sources and informed intuition to immediately identify hints of military alert or mobilization affecting units you cover.

Fourth, you and your editors must have your own deployment contingency plan. This again is something that you should specifically include in your coverage charter: a firm mutual understanding of what type of operational crises you will be expected to cover, and a range of tactics for how you will cover it (local sources only, or a full-scaled effort for on-scene reporting). If your newspaper or TV station is limited in its budget, you should establish in advance a contingency travel fund that can be accessed immediately.

Equally important, you should have a fallback coverage plan ready in event that the operation you must cover is too far away, or events are moving too rapidly to enable you to get there on time.

By unofficial count, during 1981-2001 alone, there were more than four dozen "realtime" U.S. military operations, and that does not include Operation Desert Shield/Desert Storm. That averages out to more than two major operations each year for that period (see chronology of military operations since 1981 below).

A journeyman military reporter should be aware of the analytical "spectrum of conflict" that military planners employ. It

· ·

April 1982-present — Multinational Force and Observers (MFO) — the Sinai — Battalion-sized unit monitoring peace accord between Egypt and Israel (peacekeeping).

Summer 1982 — Central America — U.S. forces begin an aggressive series of military training exercises and infrastructure construction in Honduras (while at the same time the Central Intelligence Agency begins a covert paramili-

tary effort to raise the Contra army against Nicaragua) — (deterrence and presence missions).

Aug. 25, 1982 — Beirut, Lebanon — 800 Marines land with Italian and French troops to help evacuate PLO forces, mission ends after 16 days (peacekeeping).

September 1982 — U.S. Marine peacekeeping force redeploys to Lebanon at Beirut International ranges from routine peacetime (presence, training, humanitarian missions) to crisis response (deterrence operations, civilian evacuation) to low-intensity conflict, medium-intensity combat operations, conventional war and at the high end, nuclear war.

For not only does that changing spectrum of military activity determine which units and bases might be alerted, mobilized and dispatched, it also will determine whether the story is one handled by the national wires or a live grenade that is about to drop into your newsroom in-tray.

There is no magic formula to prepare you — only your continuous effort to decipher military structure, language and behavior, cultivate sources and report on military events. Rest assured, however, that this is the point where your routine PAO contact's verification of pending activities will no longer apply or work.

"The thing to bear in mind," said Rear Adm. Brent Baker, the Navy's chief spokesman during Operation Desert Storm, "is that as the military moves from peacetime operations to involvement in hostile action (conflict or war), the rules (for dealing with reporters) change sharply. In peacetime, there is greater media access to the military and a more open and candid dialogue. As tensions increase and we move toward a crisis and finally hostile action ... the news interest or value increases dramatically. At the same time the military becomes more 'close-mouthed' because of operational security considerations. This is the natural 'friction' in the military-media relationship during crisis and conflict."

• •

Airport following new violence.

Feb. 16, 1983 — Operation Early Call — Four U.S. Air Force E-3 Sentry AWACS aircraft and four KC-10 aerial tankers deploy to Egypt, and the aircraft carrier *USS Nimitz* rushes to the area, in a secret operation to assist the Egyptian military in a planned retaliatory assault against Libyan military targets if Libya attacks Egypt. The operation is canceled (deterrence mission).

April 1983 — Northeast Pacific — Operation Fleet-Ex 83 — the largest U.S. Navy maneuver since World War II involves three full aircraft carrier battle groups, presaging a summer of maneuvers in the region, reportedly including a deliberate overflight of Soviet-controlled Kuril islands (Cold War standoff, presence operation).

Apr. 18, 1983 — Beirut, Lebanon — U.S. Embassy blown up by ter-

Translation: The front door slams shut. (The specific impact of operational security on the ongoing Operation Enduring Freedom response to the Sept. 11, 2001 terrorist attacks is discussed in Chapter 15.)

Quite often, as a crisis erupts, the PAO himself is frozen out of the planning group, and could not tell you anything even if he wanted to. Your ability to cover the conflict — either locally or on-scene — will now depend on your own ability to read the situation hour by hour, find sources who can explain and inform, and determine whether you can get on the scene in time to provide meaningful and timely direct coverage.

Your success in this effort will hinge — in great part — not on what you do today, but what you have done over the past few months to become militarily informed, meet officials, cultivate PAOs and informal sources alike.

One trend that will not abate is the tendency by Pentagon leaders early in a significant crisis to freeze out regional and local reporters in event of U.S. military action. The formation of a DoD National Media Pool in response to the 1983 Grenada intervention (when all reporters were barred from the action) gives the Pentagon a useful tool to control the hundreds of reporters who will try to get to the scene of a military operation by taking a handful of Pentagon press corps regulars. And even then it sometimes is a farce: The DoD pool in 1989 was flown to Panama when U.S. forces invaded the Latin American country to oust dictator Manuel Noriega, but arrived too late and was kept far from

- -

rorist bomb, military forces put on alert (counter-terrorism).

Summer 1983 — The Sudan — JSOC commandos assist Sudanese military in rescue of kidnap victims (military assistance/counter-terrorism).

Sept. 1, 1983 — Sakhalin Island, RSFSR — Korean Airlines Flight 007 is shot down after intruding over Soviet airspace; U.S. military forces alerted, and U.S. Navy

assets used in search for aircraft wreckage (Cold War standoff).

Oct. 23, 1983 — Beirut, Lebanon — U.S. Marine force in Lebanon since September 1982 is attacked, barracks blown up by terrorist bomb, 241 of 350 Marines in building are killed (terrorism).

Oct. 25, 1983 — Operation Urgent Fury — Grenada — U.S. Army and Marine force of nine battalions (about 3,000 personnel), and the action. What that means is that — logistically — you as a regional or local military reporter will have to get to any operational scene on your own. For fast-moving events such as the Panamanian operation, time, space and logistical constraints act as a brake to any hasty deployment on your part. But for many other crises, such as the U.S. intervention in Somalia, the press had enough warning that reporters were on the beach to cover the amphibious landings by the 15th Marine Expeditionary Unit in December 1992.

It's the story you've been waiting for. Have a bag ready.

Logistics of coverage

In event of a future Panama or Grenada or invasion of Afghanistan you must be prepared with documents, personal supplies and communications equipment (see chapter 14).

The DoD National Media Pool members, who carry beepers when they are on the active roster, must be prepared to get from their homes or offices to Andrews Air Force Base outside of Washington, D.C. within 45 minutes of activation. If that's their time frame, it's yours as well. If trouble starts to brew in a region that you suspect could trigger crisis coverage, you and your editors must plan for a "deployment" decision within hours — not days. For one thing, since your assumption is to plan for "unilateral" coverage on-scene, you will have to rely on civil air transport to get there, and your first deadline, beyond which all others are moot, is to make the last airliner to San Suquamish before

a naval force including the carrier *USS Independence* and 12 other warships invades to rescue American students and restore law and order (originally planned as non-permissive evacuation operation, becomes medium-scale combat intervention).

Dec. 4, 1983 — Bekaa Valley, Lebanon — U.S. Navy aircraft bomb Syrian targets in Lebanon and two Syrian aircraft are shot down in retaliatory strike after

shootdown of a Navy F-14 on Dec. 3 (limited combat).

1984 — Chad — U.S. Military Airlift Command transport planes carry French soldiers to Chad in a secret operation to defeat Libyan faction in civil war (limited combat).

July 31, 1984 — Venezuelan commandos storm hijacked plane; JSOC teams provide advice (counter-terrorism).

(a) the airlines shut down or (b) CNN books the plane's entire economy section for its own use.

Another good suggestion is to make good contacts with your employer's travel agency (or your own personal connection) so that you can execute a reservation for the overseas trouble spot at 3 a.m. There have been crises that reached critical mass in hours (meaning that there were no more airline seats, or flights, available).

Scripps-Howard military reporter Peter Copeland was not on the DoD National Media Pool when U.S. military forces intervened in Panama for Operation Just Cause in December 1989. Although he operated from Washington, D.C., Copeland's experience was similar to what a regional or local reporter will face in such circumstances.

Copeland was sent down several days after the invasion itself on Dec. 20, 1989 (all combat was over, for practical purposes, by sunrise on Dec. 21), but significant obstacles to entry still remained. Since a principal military goal of the Army's 75th Ranger Regiment had been to seize Panama City's Tocumen International Airport, and since the activation of the DoD pool precluded military help for other journalists, Copeland's biggest challenge was simply to get to Panama.

"So I flew to Costa Rica instead," Copeland recalled. "I chartered a (private) plane to the border, paid a taxi to drive me to Panama, and used my Pentagon pass to sneak past the U.S. guards at the border."

• •

June 14, 1985 — Beirut, Lebanon — TWA Flight 847 is hijacked to Beirut and a Navy diver is murdered. U.S. forces including JSOC commandos are alerted and carrier *USS Nimitz* is rushed to area but crisis is resolved without use of military force (counter-terrorism).

Oct. 7, 1985 — Italian cruise ship *Achille Lauro* is hijacked and an American passenger killed, and two days later Navy aircraft from carrier *USS Saratoga* intercept airliner carrying escaped hijackers to NATO base at Sigonella, Italy. JSOC commandos attempt to apprehend them but are halted by Italian soldiers (counter-terrorism).

March 23, 1986 — Operation Prairie Fire — Gulf of Sidra, Mediterranean — U.S. Sixth Fleet conducts a series of operations in waters claimed by Libya, and attacks several Libyan patrol

Being three days late for the operation did not deter Copeland from getting excellent on-scene stories for his newspaper group, including a scoop on the first combat incident led by a female U.S. Army officer, which sparked nationwide publicity. "The story was so obvious," Copeland said. "Everyone down there talked to women soldiers, they were all over." But no one else thought to focus on Panama's role as the first "realtime" operation where women soldiers had been in combat.

Proximity and clear thought led to a first-class scoop.

But what if the crisis is too inaccessible, or too expensive to cover first-hand?

The odds are good that even if a major contingency operation is launched that involves troops from your area, you will have to cover the fast-paced, breaking story from home. It is frustrating, but still can result in excellent stories.

Remote coverage

The first thing you will have to confront is the hijacking of PAO authority from your local military bases to the Department of Defense public affairs leadership — meaning that responses to queries and requests for interviews will be handled from the Pentagon instead of your local base. If your local contacts are honest, they will tell you this without waiting for you to ask.

When the Reagan administration ordered 1950s-era Navy minesweepers to the Persian Gulf in 1988, the story had direct significance to a half-dozen media markets on the East and West

. . . .

boats and a ground missile site presence/freedom of navigation).

Apr. 14, 1986 — Libya — Operation El Dorado Canyon, Air Force and U.S. Navy strikes against Libya in response to Libyan terrorist attack in Berlin that kills one U.S. soldier (limited combat).

March 7, 1987 — Persian Gulf — Operation Earnest Will ordered, U.S. Navy warships escort

Kuwaiti oil tankers through Persian Gulf (presence).

May 17, 1987 — Persian Gulf — Navy guided missile frigate *USS Stark* is struck by two Iraqi air-to-surface missiles, 39 sailors killed and another 31 injured (presence).

May 17, 1987 — Bering Sea — Cruiser *USS Arkansas* is surrounded by Soviet Navy and Air Force units during freedom of navigation operation near

Coast, since that is where the Navy Reserve units were then based. In Puget Sound, six minesweepers from Mine Group One had been a waterfront fixture — like state ferries and grain ships — for decades. Suddenly, they were a top, breaking news story.

And equally fast, the local Navy PAOs could say nothing about the ubiquitous little ships, and were forced to refer all queries about their preparation for deployment to the Pentagon (3,000 miles and three time zones away). The Pentagon, in turn, was being tight-lipped for operational security reasons.

The normally helpful Navy PAOs on the scene were power-less to help disseminate the most routine information about the ships, and a "media availability" at pierside almost turned into a reporters' riot when local journalists were herded into a fenced compound out of earshot of anyone and prevented from obtain-ing a single quote from crewmen or PAOs.

That didn't prevent the story from being told, since wives, other relatives and friends of the soon-to-depart sailors called up newsrooms in Seattle and Tacoma to trade information with reporters. It seems the Navy shortchanged its own men on essen-tial information and they were mad and concerned enough to break security so that they could get confirmation of what they needed to know for their own families' sakes.

Pete Williams, the Pentagon spokesman during the Bush I administration, said Pentagon officials are not unsympathetic to regional and local military writers when such incidents happen. "This has to be calibrated by common sense," he said. "Call us

• •

Kamchatka Peninsula — (pres-ence).

Sept. 13, 1987 — The Mediterranean — U.S. Navy S-3 aircraft carries captured Lebanese terrorist Fawaz Younis, arrested by FBI, directly from ship to Washington, D.C. for trial — (aid to law enforcement/counter-ter-rorism).

Oct. 1987 — Operation Shooting Star — Adak, Alaska — U.S.

Navy A-6E Intruder bombers make mock attacks toward Soviet military bases from Aleutians, pulling out of "attack profile" only 90 miles from land. The secret Pacific Command opera-tion started in spring of 1986 amid increased U.S. naval maneu-vers in the Bering Sea as a response to increased Soviet mock bombing missions toward Alaska — (Cold War standoff).

Apr. 18, 1988 — Operation

when this happens." Bureaucracy and not high-handedness normally is the culprit, DoD officials admit. "Someone writes a (press) guidance and they forget about (local) reporters. They forget that not every story is written out of Washington, D.C. They are not thinking and you guys get overlooked," Williams added.

In 1994, the Pentagon again prepared to deploy the National Media Pool when the U.S. government marshaled forces for a possible invasion of Haiti. (The invasion was transformed at the very last moment into a non-combat peacekeeping intervention.) Having heard informally that several Fort Lewis Army units were poised to take part in the operation, I contacted senior Pentagon public affairs officials, who formally approved my participation in covering those units subject to the standing media pool directives.

Newsroom preparation

Preparing for crisis coverage requires work in the newsroom as well. In addition to planning your own deployment you should organize your colleagues to handle other aspects of the story should you suddenly race off to the operation.

Even an experienced military reporter can expect a real challenge in obtaining the time-sensitive background information necessary to plan his or her deployment decision.

There is no easy formula for getting this material. Your sources will know that you are asking them for extremely time-

Praying Mantis — Persian Gulf — aircraft from *USS Enterprise* attack Iranian Navy ships and speedboats after frigate *USS Samuel Roberts* hits an Iranian mine (limited combat).

July 3, 1988 — Persian Gulf — cruiser *USS Vincennes* accidentally shoots down an Iranian airliner during encounter with Iranian gunboats (limited combat/self-defense).

February 1988 — Black Sea — Soviet warships "bump" two U.S. warships conducting a freedom of navigation exercise near Sevastopol — (Cold War standoff).

September 1988 — Two aircraft carriers, the *USS Midway* and *USS Nimitz*, are stationed off Korea during the Seoul Olympics to deter North Korean aggression — (presence mission).

Jan. 4, 1989 — Two Navy F-14

sensitive information, most of which is properly classified, and they risk (from the military viewpoint) either threatening future operational security or, at least, their own organization's tight classification regulations, by telling you anything.

The crux of your success in obtaining that information will come if you have established a relationship with senior local military officers that includes a mutual respect of the fact that some of the information you require is indeed, if prematurely released, a threat to the lives of their colleagues in the field. If you have a successful relationship, it will be based in part on your own appreciation of that fact, and your willingness to segregate out the truly critical secrets from journalistically significant facts that do not imperil lives.

A tactic many reporters have used to reach common ground with their military sources is to ask for information piecemeal — that is, to acknowledge that some facts are time-sensitive, and others are not. Obviously, once the operation has been underway for a time, the fact of a local unit's involvement will no longer be a secret (although its particular location and future missions are often highly classified).

So in the initial hours of a contingency operation, when the base is sealed to reporters, rumors are rampant, and fragmentary headlines from the crisis area tell of gunfire and bombing runs, approach your sources with a pitch that goes like this:

"I don't want any information that's going to get

Tomcats shoot down two Libyan fighters in an aerial encounter over the Mediterranean Sea.

May 1989 — Panama — Pentagon orders the first of several deployments of soldiers and equipment to reinforce existing units following political unrest and growing Panamanian government hostility toward the United States.

Dec. 20, 1989 — Operation Just Cause — Panama — Invasion by

26,000 U.S. military personnel ordered in wake of killing of U.S. Marine officer and declaration of war against United States by Panamanian dictator Manuel Noriega. The objectives are to neutralize Panamanian military, apprehend Noriega, safeguard the Panama Canal and allow legitimate elected rulers to take office. U.S. casualties include 23 soldiers and 3 civilians killed and 324 wounded. About 314 Panamanian soldiers and another someone killed, but if there are men from this base in combat, there are three times as many relatives here who are frightened, worried, and just as uninformed as the rest of this community. Please tell me, to the degree that you can without breaking their operational safety, if the battalion/brigade/squadron is down there, and to the degree you can, what they are doing."

If you convince your sources of your sincerity in this regard, you will be surprised at their willingness to try and meet you somewhere on your side of a full stonewalling.

That is, if they know anything themselves. It is imperative that you look at your sources not as men or women suddenly unwilling to talk with you, but as officials — holding security clearances themselves — who may simply have been cut out of the operation.

Scan the wires and TV announcements with a fine-tooth comb as well. From the Pentagon press viewpoint, it is little news that the 1/23rd Mess Kit Repair Company (as opposed to the 2/25th Mess Kit Repair Co.) has been airdropped into combat. But if this is the unit at your local base, you are damn well interested!

It is possible in a large-scale contingency operation, such as Grenada or Panama, to infer local unit identities from remarks made on the national level. A hint or partial fact can become the lever you need to force a local or even Pentagon official to con-

• •

300 civilians reportedly died in the fighting (medium-intensity combat).

Dec. 1, 1990 — Philippines — U.S. aircraft buzz rebel positions during abortive coup, carrier *USS Midway* in area to deter Philippine military attacks — (presence/show of force).

May 1990 — January 1991 — Operation Sharp Edge — Liberia — Two Marine amphibious-ready groups patrol offshore and evacuate a total of 2,609 foreigners from civil war in several separate incursions, the largest such operation since the evacuation of Saigon in 1975 (non-permissive evacuation).

Aug. 8, 1990 — Jan. 16, 1991 — Operation Desert Shield — Saudi Arabia and Persian Gulf — The Pentagon deploys a multiservice force of over 540,000 personnel to the region following the Iraqi

Desert Shorthand: While observing Army soldiers learning to shoot their weapons through the thick lenses of a chemical warfare hood before Operation Desert Storm, this reporter discovered that even note-taking can be difficult in a contaminated area. (Photo: Robert de Giulio, *Seattle Post-Intelligencer*)

invasion of Kuwait (contingency operation).

August 1990 — Present — Maritime Intercept Operations — Persian Gulf — Enforcement of United Nations economic sanctions against Iraq (presence).

Jan. 2, 1991 — Operation Eastern Exit — Somalia — A 60-man force of U.S. Marines and Navy SEAL commandos fly from the Arabian Sea to Mogadishu and safely evacuate 281 trapped foreigners, including 12 heads of diplomatic missions, trapped in the country's raging civil war — (non-permissive evacuation).

Jan. 16 - March 2, 1991 — Operation Desert Storm — Kuwait and Iraq — U.S.-led international coalition attacks Iraqi military to force it out of Kuwait. In a five-week air campaign followed by a 100-hour ground attack, the United States suffers firm that the hometown base has gone into the fighting.

What to do then? Lots.

If a crisis continues for several days after initiation of hostilities, the local command will probably (with your loud and persistent requests) ease up on its locked-gate policy and let you and your brethren through for limited interviews and briefings. Do them, even if the comments are predictable — it's still news.

Some generic first- or second-day stories include:

Unit history (once its participation is confirmed): "From Tarawa to Tikri, the 1/23rd Infantry Battalion has long participated in the nation's wars...." Unit histories are a basic element of every command public affairs office and you will be derelict if you don't already have the history of every deployable military unit in your own files. The profusion of internet web sites dedicated to veterans' groups and specific unit associations make it easier than ever to track down former unit members for interviews.

Families: Normally, local commanders are willing to turn up members of their family support network — including chaplains, legal advisers, volunteers from other units — who serve as liaison and help to families of those sent into the operation. It's a good second-day topic with no threat to security, and the local PAOs will probably have the authority to let that one happen.

Transient personnel: One request that frequently bears a lode of journalism is to ask the local PAO to find any on-base personnel

• •

613 casualties, including 146 killed and 467 wounded. No firm number of Iraqi casualties has been determined, although early unofficial calculations that as many as 50,000 Iraqis died is now seen as an exaggeration. The Pentagon later reports that 1,082 Kuwaitis were murdered during the Iraqi occupation (major theater conflict).

January 1991 — 2001 — Operation Desert Falcon —

Ballistic missile defense of Saudi cities using Patriot missiles — approximately 800 U.S. Army personnel (ongoing deployment).

Apr. 6, 1991 - December 1996 — Operation Provide Comfort — Turkey and northern Iraq — Multinational relief operation to protect Kurdish refugees. The 20,000-strong force includes 11,000 U.S. troops at its maximum strength — Superceded by Operation Northern Watch in who might have recently trained or served temporarily in the trouble spot. They can (usually) recount their personal experiences without fear of blowing any secrets, and such first-hand accounts — from a journalistic perspective — will be informative and well received.

Casualties: You will also make great face with your military counterparts — and strike a blow for journalistic integrity — if, at the outset of the operation, you and other local media voluntarily create a "next of kin pool" to avoid alienating grief-stricken families who have just learned that a loved one has been killed or injured. (This has become quite common as a result of Operation Desert Storm).

Perspective: So we took down the Republic of San Suquamish. Is this the 23rd time since 1924 the U.S. has intervened, or the first? Is the country valuable for crude oil or kumquat exports? If you're street smart, you had a full file on San Suquamish six months before the president went on TV to confirm that Rangers were dropping out of the sky there. Why? Because most military forces targeted for interventions not only train for a particular region but make little secret of it — until they are actually in combat there. Find out from civilian experts, retired military people, congressional sources, etc. If a local academic just finished a paper on the kumquat industry, he's likely a good interview.

● ●

January 1997 (humanitarian assistance).

April-May 1991 — Operation Sea Angel — Bangladesh —— Following a typhoon that kills over 139,000 Bangladeshis and threatens several million survivors, U.S. Navy-Marine Corps team involving over 7,500 sailors and Marines conducts a major relief operation (humanitarian assistance).

June 1991 — Operation Fiery Vigil — the Philippines — The aircraft carriers USS Midway and USS Abraham Lincoln and 15 other Navy ships evacuate 19,000 Americans after the June 4 volcanic eruption of Mt. Pinatubo — (evacuation).

Feb. 11, 1992 — Barents Sea — The nuclear attack submarine USS Baton Rouge suffers minor damage in a collision with a Russian Sierra-class attack sub-

Hardware: Glean the on-scene coverage for anything identifying military hardware used, and screen it through your roster of military hardware fabricated, procured, maintained or spray-painted locally. If the M-1 tank factory happens to be two blocks from your city-room, your editor will be most pleased for any reports on how the Abrams tank fared in the mangrove swamps of San Suquamish.

After-action report: While you are chasing updates on the operation from the Pentagon briefings and whatever you can source out firsthand, it is never too early to start planning a narrative recapitulation of the actual operation from your base's or unit's viewpoint. Often, this requires negotiation with commanders for interview access, and that will normally hinge on timing — how soon the operation ends, how soon the men and women return, and whether for internal reasons the local leaders want an interlude before rehashing the mini-war. You should also assemble from wires, trade specialists and other sources an independent chronology of events onto which you can graft the narrative.

• •

marine (presence).

July 1992 — February 1996 — Operation Provide Promise — Multi-national relief operation in Bosnia-Herzegovina, including parachute airdrop of supplies (humanitarian assistance/peace-keeping).

August 1992 — present — Operation Southern Watch — Enforcement of "no-fly" zone in Southern Iraq (limited combat).

August 1992 — Operation Provide Transition — U.S. transport aircraft airlift demobilized Angolan soldiers as part of peace settlement.

September 1992 — Florida — U.S. military units assist in disaster response in the wake of Hurricane Andrew (humanitarian assistance).

Dec. 9, 1992 — March 1995 — Operation Restore Hope — 15th

Chapter 14

Going to War II
The basics: A reporter's preparations

Here are the basic steps you should take to prepare for wartime coverage. Most of them build on the basic steps to organize and maintain your military beat as related in previous chapters.

Papers and gear

Assemble your personal documents, communications gear and other equipment for the possibility that foreign coverage becomes feasible.

■ Review your passport and visas and renew any that are expired, while applying for new visas covering the geographical area of interest. If time permits, apply for visas in strategically important nations adjoining the area of conflict, for access and temporary staging if that becomes necessary.

■ Ensure that your international immunization/vaccination record is up to date and check to see if you need additional shots.

· ·

Marine Expeditionary Unit and Air Force combat controllers land at Mogadishu, Somalia, as spearhead of a 24,000-man multinational peacekeeping and humanitarian relief operation. Following withdrawal of most U.S. personnel by April 1993, a company-sized force of U.S. Army Rangers and Special Operations forces lose 18 killed and over 70 wounded in major firefight, Oct. 3-4, 1993. Two Army Delta Force personnel later posthumously receive the Medal of Honor (Humanitarian relief, low-intensity conflict).

Jan. 13, 1993 — present — Iraq — U.S. Navy and Air Force aircraft and Navy Tomahawk cruise missiles strike Iraqi air defense sites in southern Iraq, the first in what will become an unending stream of limited air strikes by U.S. and allied aircraft against the Baghdad regime (low-intensity combat).

■ Get a dozen current passport photographs and keep them with your documents for visas, press credentials or other papers you might need along the way.

■ Obtain a standard letter of support from your employer on letterhead stationery affirming that you are a staff writer on formal assignment and your employer vouches for your bona fides and logistical support.

■ If the Pentagon issues special credentials, apply for them.

■ Check through a travel agency or tourism books to ensure that your laptop computer or other gear is electronically compatible with the target area's electrical supply, and obtain voltage converters, battery packs or other accessories that will enable you to function.

■ Check through contacts, travel agents or other travel sources for the adequacy of the area's telephone, fax, telex or other communications links for backup purposes, and work out a communications plan with your editor and systems department.

■ Pack a single bag with the necessary clothing, personal items and field gear that will meet your needs for your trip, and keep it fresh and close to hand (see sidebar on opposite page).

••

March 1993 — U.S. Navy and Marine Corps units in the Pacific are placed on alert for possible deployment to South Korea following North Korea's announcement that it is leaving the Nuclear Non-Proliferation Treaty (presence).

April 1993 — December 1995 — Operation Deny Flight — Enforcement of "no-fly" zone over Bosnia-Herzegovina by Navy, Air Force and Marine aircraft, includes Navy-Marine Corps mission to rescue Capt. Scott O'Grady on June 8, 1995 after he is shot down by a Serb missile (limited combat).

June 1993 - September 1996 — Operation Sharp Guard — Enforcement of United Nations embargo against the former Yugoslavia (peacekeeping).

June 26, 1993 — Iraq — Two U.S. Navy warships launch 23

What to bring?

For one exercise I covered, my Army contact recommended a list of clothing and gear for field coverage, and I kept the stuff on hand long afterwards for subsequent assignments:

Sturdy clothing — In most cases, military commanders advise reporters to wear comfortable, rugged clothing, but NOT military uniforms such as fatigues or camouflage.

Accessory clothing — one sweater you can jettison later if necessary; thick socks; extra underwear; a wool ski cap; a waterproof poncho.

Hiking boots — ankle protection essential.

Backpack — I initially used a small daypack but later invested in an Army "Alice" pack from a local Army-Navy store. These nylon and metal-frame packs are excellent for carrying all the gear you might need, including a laptop.

Sleeping gear — Sleeping bag or less — I opted for a space blanket and used my jacket as a pillow.

Miscellaneous — I found the following essential for all field assignments: a strong flashlight equipped with red filter, which is mandatory for use with units to preserve night vision and to avoid detection; plastic drinking thermos; freeze-dried food snacks or other hiking food; sunglasses; facial wipes; a good paperback novel, as yet unread, for those 15-hour "dead time" intervals; a camping knife or utensil tool.

Tomahawk cruise missiles against Iraqi targets in Baghdad following disclosure that Iraqi agents planned to assassinate former President George H.W. Bush during a visit to Kuwait (limited combat).

July 1993 — 1997 — Operation Able Sentry — U.S. and U.N. personnel monitor the Serbian-Macedonian border (peacekeeping).

Oct. 3-4, 1993 — Somalia — Army Rangers and Special Operations forces lose 18 killed and over 70 wounded in major firefight (low-intensity conflict).

October 1993 - September 1994 — Haiti — Various operations to enforce U.N. sanctions and manage exodus of refugees (humanitarian assistance).

June 1994 — Vladivostok, Russia — More than 700 Marines con-

Research

Prepare files on the following subjects (using your own archives, trade publication articles, wire reports and PAO data):

■ All local/regional military units in your primary coverage area that are involved in the conflict or are candidates for deployment;

■ Background information on the region(s), countries involved, political and economic issues, enemy equipment and troops, forces available to the U.S. or allied coalition commander;

■ Issue files containing background sheets and your own current backgrounder notes on the vital military trends and issues that you anticipate coming into play. These might include the U.S. background in the geographic area under focus, specific problems or challenges for a U.S. military deployment to that region (airlift and sealift issues), specific weapons systems that may be brought into play and expert opinion on the adequacy of the military gear involved, and interviews with veterans of service in that particular region. Many of these documents are available through DefenseLink or other unclassified internet sites.

Your goal here should be to compile issue-particular notes that you can flesh out with on-scene interviews or briefings.

■ Write for your editors a truncated phone list of local and

• •

duct a training exercise with their Russian counterparts, the first U.S.-Russian joint exercise since 1945 (presence).

June 1994 — South Korea — The Pentagon secretly prepares to execute Operation Plan 5027, the defense of South Korea, with an Operation Desert Shield-sized military reinforcement involving hundreds of thousands of American troops. The plan is cancelled when North Korea agrees at the last moment to engage in negotiations to freeze its nuclear weapon program (deterrence).

July - October 1994 — Operation Distant Runner — Limited intervention operation in Rwanda following widespread ethnic strife in March and April including the intervention of 330 Marines during Apr. 9-12 to evacuate 142 Americans (non-permissive evacuation/humanitarian assistance).

regional public affairs officers, their commands and a paragraph or two explaining succinctly the mission and nature of the organization (whether or not you entrust them with the PAO's closely-held home number is a matter of conscience). Make copies of your issues files and leave them with the editor who will have line supervision of the G.A. reporters who will backstop you while you are gone. Meet with them before you go, answer whatever anxious questions they have, and wish them well (they'll need it more than you).

Budget

Open a running budget file to prepare your editors for the financial details they will need to assess the cost-benefit ratio of your going into the conflict.

■ Construct (your travel agent should be glad to assist) a two-week or four-week "model" deployment based on conservative cost estimates for commercial air travel, intermediate transport (e.g. ground travel from a third country into the theater of operations if civil air service shuts down to your destination), hotel and field expenses. A useful rule of thumb is to estimate "normal" lodging, per diem and ancillary costs — and triple them.

■ If you are heading into a coverage situation involving civil disorder, war or instability, don't assume that your credit cards will

....

August 1994 - March 1995 — Operation Uphold Democracy — U.S.-led multinational operation to restore democratically-elected government in Haiti (initially organized as military invasion but changed at the last minute when the Haitian regime invited the force in on Sept. 20. The only combat involved a firefight between armed Haitians and a small Marine force that left 10 Haitians dead) (peacekeeping).

September 1994 — February 1996 — Operation Able Vigil/Sea Signal — Guantanamo Bay, Cuba — A Marine Corps battalion deploys to provide security for over 40,000 Haitian and Cuban refugees temporarily detained at the U.S. Navy base (humanitarian assistance).

October — December 1994 — Operation Vigilant Warrior — Kuwait and Saudi Arabia — The Pentagon dispatches over 10,000 see you through. Take most if not all of your advance funds in cash and traveler's checks, and find at least one secure pipeline for wire transfers should you get stranded.

Coverage strategy

The best approach to covering a war is to be ready for as much as possible and to accept system breakdowns, broken promises, manipulation and disinformation as inevitabilities. The key is to get there and capitalize on your strengths. If you are "up" on your beat, current in your reading, and backed up in your files, you will be as prepared as anyone to handle not only the obvious stories, but the unexpected as well.

Here are some suggestions for what you can do to minimize the confusion:

■ Outline a half-dozen issue stories that you believe are vital to informing your readers of the nature of the crisis, and conduct background interviews at home before you leave with officials and other sources who can illuminate the specific issues.

For instance, as the Pentagon rushed thousands of tanks to Saudi Arabia to prepare for the 1991 ground war, the long debate over the reliability of the M-1A1 Abrams tank was a compelling story. Several background interviews with armor officers and other experts, conducted stateside before leaving for the Middle East, provided the spine of a long takeout of how a mass armored

• •

troops to the Persian Gulf in response to threatening military moves by Iraq (presence/deterrence).

February — March 1995 — Operation United Shield — U.S. Navy and Marine Corps support for United Nations forces withdrawing from Somalia, some units coming under fire as they depart (low-intensity combat/deterrence).

Aug. 30 — Sept. 21, 1995 — Operation Deliberate Force — U.S. and NATO forces launch 3,515 combat sorties, 13 cruise missile attacks and ground-based artillery strikes against Bosnian Serb military targets in response to Serbian shelling of Sarajevo (limited combat).

August 1995 — U.S. and Russian Marine units conduct a joint training exercise in Hawaii (presence).

battle in the desert would most likely take place, and an assessment of how the M-1A1 would fare in its first battle. A similar approach provided valuable facts on the issue of advanced night-flying and precision-guided weaponry critical to the air war.

For the ongoing war against terrorism, generic background stories on current airpower tactics using precision-guided munitions, and background stories on the structure of the U.S. Special Operations Command (units, personnel selection, equipment and previous combat operations) are relevant to you and your readers or viewers.

■ Consult with your outlet's graphic artists to construct in advance detailed maps, illustrations and photo montages that will dovetail with the outline of issue stories you plan to file. Also identify key places that can be placed on locator maps.

■ List the human-interest stories you are keen to pursue (a tickler file), and make every effort to communicate in advance through PAO channels of your desires. Is the world's oldest cruiser on patrol off the enemy coast? Is your local National Guard brigade in the thick of the deployment? Identify, ask, seek.

■ Prepare your editor for pools. If you anticipate a repetition of the Operation Desert Storm media rules where only accredited combat pool members got to go out under escort to meet with

• •

August 1995 — February 1997 — Operation Vigilant Sentinel — Show of force throughout the Persian Gulf region against Iraq following the defection of two high-ranking Iraqi officials (deterrence).

December 1995 - present — Operation Joint Endeavor — Bosnia — U.S. and NATO "Implementation Force" deploys to Bosnia following signing of peace accord. Includes support

operations by U.S. Air Force and Navy forces (peacekeeping).

February — March 1996 — The Pentagon orders two aircraft carrier battle groups with a total of 16 warships to the western Pacific near Taiwan in response to mainland Chinese ballistic missile firings viewed as a threat to Taiwan (presence).

April — August 1996 — Operation Assured Response —

U.S. units, brace your editor for one of two situations: 1) You are assigned to a pool, then vanish without a trace for up to a week before your first story arrives via corked bottle, or; 2) you do not get into a pool, the prospects are for a two- or three-week wait before your turn comes up, and you have to decide whether to pull a Bob Simon and head to the front anyway, or stick around the Joint Information Bureau and scramble for whatever stories or leads you can find there. These are the narrow options that confronted the press in Dhahran and Riyadh, and most likely are the same that you will face in a future conflict. A clear-eyed understanding between you and your editor will avoid transcontinental misunderstandings.

■ Prepare yourself as well for: Frustration, boredom, terror, angst, bad food, fax transmissions gone astray, monumental bills, excitement, good stories, lousy stories, not enough sleep, horror, death, bureaucracy, deep friendships, poor feedback, and every other journalistic sensation compressed into 22-hour working days. Keep thinking ahead about the wide range of articles — hard news and soft features — that you will encounter.

Liberia — More than 1,500 U.S. Marines deploy to Monrovia to beef up embassy security and civilian evacuation (non-permissive evacuation).

June - August 1996 — Operation Quick Response — Central African Republic — Marines involved in the Liberia operation diverted 2,000 miles away to rescue 600 refugees (non-permissive evacuation).

July 17 — mid-October, 1996 — Western Atlantic — Over 700 Navy salvage personnel deploy to recover remains and debris from TWA Flight 800 after it crashes off the coast of Long Island.

Sept. 3-4, 1996 — Operation Desert Strike — U.S. Air Force B-52s and Navy warships launch 44 cruise missiles against Iraqi targets in response to Iraqi deployment of 45,000 soldiers toward Kurdistan (limited combat).

Army Ranger Sgt. Joseph L. Herrera discusses an ongoing mass parachute drill at Fort Lewis, Wash., as the author glances up at the rest of the 2nd Ranger Battalion. (Photo: Dave Ekren, *Seattle Post-Intelligencer*)

• •

September 1996 — April 1997 — Operation Pacific Haven — Guam — Evacuation of 6,500 Kurdish refugees from northern Iraq (humanitarian).

January 1997 — present — Operation Northern Watch — Northern Iraq — Successor to Operation Provide Comfort involves a combined task force conducting aerial patrols against Iraqi forces above the 36th Parallel (limited combat).

March 1997 — Operation Silver Wake — Albania — U.S. Marines intervene to reinforce embassy security and transport civilians from city (non-permissive evacuation).

June 1998 — Operation Safe Departure — Evacuation of civilians from Eritrea (non-permissive evacuation).

June 1998 — Operation Shepherd Venture — Evacuation of civilians

Chapter 15

Going to War III

Covering the War on Terrorism:
New approaches for a new form of conflict

Not only did the four hijacked airliners, the World Trade Center towers and the Pentagon's southwest facade come crashing to earth on that black Tuesday morning. On Sept. 11, 2001, an entire nation's complacency was shattered in the deadliest terrorist attack in modern history.

So too destroyed was the complacency of a journalism profession that during the 1990s had all but abandoned serious coverage of foreign and military news.

Throughout the decade after the 1991 Persian Gulf War, both print and broadcast news organizations cut back dramatically on international news coverage. In the name of boosting stock dividends and cost-cutting, many newspapers and TV stations shed specialty news beats such as military reporting. News executives ordered to hold down costs by their corporate superiors became disinclined to invest in costly foreign coverage or even in-depth investigative projects. As the cadre of experienced military reporters who had covered the Vietnam War and brush fire incidents of the 1970s and early 1980s retired — or quit in disgust —

• •

from Guinea-Bissau (non-permissive evacuation).

August 1998 — Operation Autumn Shelter — Evacuation of civilians from Democratic Republic of Congo (non-permissive evacuation).

August 1998 — Operation Resolute Response — Response to embassy bombings in Kenya and Tanzania (security and humanitarian assistance).

August 1998 — Operation Infinite Reach — U.S. Navy cruise missile attacks against al Qaeda terrorist training camps in Afghanistan and a suspected chemical agent factory in Sudan (limited combat strikes).

November 1998 — Operation Strong Support — Hurricane disaster relief in four Central American nations (humanitarian assistance).

few were replaced. One daily newspaper in 2000 was confronted with the need to trim staff: Despite a major military presence in the newspaper's circulation area, the publisher abolished the military reporting slot but kept the features reporter who covered the love life and social scene of the local dot.com crowd. It seemed a prudent decision at the time.

With the United States now mobilizing for what is expected to be a prolonged war against international terrorism that will last for years — if not decades — publishers and broadcast managers across the nation face a daunting task of reconstituting their military reporting capability.

Such effort will be doubly hard this time around: Not only is it difficult (as explained elsewhere in this book) to attempt military reporting self-education in crisis or wartime, but the realities of this conflict create several major new obstacles to coverage that even reporters with decades of experience have not previously encountered:

Net-centric warfare: The battle against al Qaeda represents the first "net-centric" war we have ever fought — a war not against a nation-state with fixed targets and an identifiable military structure, but rather against a terrorist conspiracy designed for stealth and evasion. The U.S.-led coalition war against Iraq a decade ago — like the Normandy invasion in 1944 and the Battle of Waterloo in 1814 — pitted two conventional military forces against one another on a battlefield that the generals were able to

• •

Dec. 16-19, 1998 — Operation Desert Fox — Iraq — Following Baghdad's expulsion of United Nations weapons inspectors from Iraq, the United States and Great Britain launch air strikes against nearly 100 military targets. Over 29,900 U.S. military personnel are involved in what is the largest air campaign against Iraq since the 1991 Gulf War (limited combat).

Mar. 24 — June 3, 1999 — Operation Allied Force — In response to Serbian displacement of over 300,000 Muslims from Kosovo province, the NATO Alliance conducts a 78-day air war against Serbian targets in Kosovo and Serbia itself. Three NATO aircraft are shot down, including an F-117 stealth fighter, but all crewmen are rescued. Two Army helicopter crewmen are killed in the non-combat crash of their AH-64 Apache helicopter (medium-intensity air war).

study in advance long before the actual forces gathered to fight. This time around, the adversary is a dispersed, hidden network of dedicated terrorists who have embedded themselves in the civil societies of several dozen countries. Their hatred of the West and its modernity is matched only by their willingness and ability to use our technology against us, from encrypted e-mail to evade signals intelligence intercepts to Boeing airliners to destroy buildings.

It is a landscape of battle that resists transparency and open coverage by news organizations.

Special operations in combat: As American and British forces launched initial air and cruise missile strikes against al Qaeda and Taliban targets on Oct. 7, 2001, military officials and security experts repeated earlier warnings that much of the fight would take place out of sight, especially military raids involving an array of special operations commandos.

Speaking to reporters on Oct. 7 as the initial military attacks got underway, Joint Chiefs Chairman Gen. Richard Myers said, "I want to remind you that while today's operations are visible, many other operations may not be so visible." Not only do these elite forces depend on stealth, speed and concealment to carry out surprise attacks, but even "routine" information (e.g. coverage of a support base where supplies and replacement personnel are staged) would likely compromise their effectiveness and even jeopardize future missions.

• •

April — July 1999 — Operation Allied Harbor — Military support to Kosovar refugees (humanitarian assistance).

June 1999 — Operation Joint Guardian — U.S. Marine peacekeeping deployment of 5,400 personnel to Kosovo (peacekeeping).

August — September 1999 — Operation Avid Response — Assistance to Turkey after earthquake (humanitarian assistance).

January — March 2000 — Operation Fundamental Response — Several dozen U.S. personnel participate in United Nations observation mission to East Timor (peacekeeping).

March 2000 — Operation Atlas Response — U.S. military relief support to Mozambique (humanitarian assistance).

October 2000 — Operation Determined Response — Joint

So the fight against such an adversary will entail an equally dispersed and often covert approach employing soldiers, covert intelligence operatives, computer hackers, bankers, law enforcement officials and diplomats.

Information can kill this time: Journalists who have covered military operations over the past two decades recognize that for the first time since World War II, we are facing an adversary with sophisticated counter-intelligence skills. Osama bin Laden's terror network appears to have already exploited news media reports that disclosed information about U.S. intelligence operations against him. In particular, news reports early in 2001 disclosed that the U.S. National Security Agency had succeeded in intercepting satellite cell phone calls by bin Laden and his top lieutenants in Afghanistan. (The information was released as part of the evidence in a trial against several bin Laden accomplices accused of involvement in the 1998 embassy bombings in Kenya and Tanzania.) Several weeks later, other news reports based on U.S. intelligence sources said bin Laden and his network had stopped using the cell phones after the media disclosure of the NSA intercept capability.

Commentators in the immediate aftermath of the Sept. 11 terror attacks questioned how the United States could have suffered such a massive intelligence failure. My own uneasy question was how much of a role the news media itself may have inadvertently played in the terrorists' success.

....

Task Force deployment to Yemen to assist the *USS Cole* following al Qaeda terrorist bombing that killed 17 sailors.

February 2001 — Operation Desert Falcon/Desert Focus — Training deployments to Kuwait (deterrence).

Sept. 11, 2001 — Terrorist attacks on the World Trade Center and the Pentagon kill over 6,500 Americans (terrorism).

Sept. 12, 2001 — Operation Enduring Freedom — U.S. military deployment and force build-up in the Mediterranean, Indian Ocean and Central Asia in preparation for retaliatory strikes following the Sept. 11 al Qaeda terrorist attacks. As of Oct. 1, 2001, several dozen U.S. Navy warships, hundreds of combat aircraft and over 28,000 military personnel are involved, including an unknown number of Special Operations force units.

So a major factor in covering the war against al Qaeda may have to be something journalists have not had to confront in years: The need for self-discipline in disclosing information that could aid the terrorists. (See sidebar at the end of this chapter.)

The first battle: Sept. 11, 2001

Not only were the terror attacks on the World Trade Center and Pentagon unprecedented in their violence and savagery, but the events of Sept. 11, 2001 — described as another "Day of Infamy" like the Japanese attack on Pearl Harbor nearly 60 years earlier — were covered live on television and Internet web sites as they unfolded.

The fiery impact of a hijacked airliner and the growing pyre of the World Trade Center's north tower, followed 21 minutes later by the second airliner plunging into the south tower, the subsequent collapse of both buildings, and the live recordings of the sound of impact of a hijacked airliner striking the Pentagon, constituted a live news story whose dimensions eclipsed anything that had come before: the 1963 Kennedy assassination, the resignation of President Nixon 11 years later, the outbreak of the 1991 Persian Gulf War, or any battlefield footage anywhere else in the world. Across the United States and the rest of the world, hundreds of newspapers hit the streets with Extra editions. The major TV networks immediately went on a wartime footing with continuous news coverage for days afterwards.

But in one very real sense, it appears that Sept. 11, 2001 and Dec. 7, 1941, may ultimately stand as opposites rather than mirror images of how a war is covered.

Strict U.S. military censorship imposed in the hours after the Japanese attack prevented the American people from learning until the end of the war about the extent of the Pearl Harbor destruction (18 major warships sunk or damaged, 188 aircraft destroyed or damaged on the ground, 2,403 servicemen killed and another 1,104 injured). And while the press operated within formal rules of censorship throughout the war, there was a gradual relaxation of restrictions as the years went on. For instance in 1943 censors permitted the publication of the first photos showing dead U.S. soldiers.

The opposite pattern — transparent coverage of the initial

attack followed by a steady clamp down on information as the U.S. military responds — emerged in the first month after the attacks. For the first time since World War II, both the Pentagon and news media are grappling with the implications of operational security that governed wartime coverage six decades ago. Consider the last time we struck bin Laden:

In 1998, when the Clinton administration ordered Tomahawk cruise missiles fired against the al Qaeda terrorist network, the Navy arranged for reporters in the United States to conduct satellite telephone interviews with senior officers onboard the Navy warships even as the cruise missiles were still airborne against their targets in Afghanistan and the Sudan.

After the Sept. 11 attacks, it was still possible to "data mine" unclassified information from the U.S. Navy's websites to assemble a composite picture of the aircraft carriers and escort warships — and their weapons capabilities — operating overseas in the vicinity of southern Asia, and to indicate the potential combat power available on short notice should the president so order. If information transparency was the hallmark of post-Cold War military coverage, that era came to a screeching halt several days after the attacks when the Navy scrubbed all sensitive information out of its web pages and other military commands shut down their websites altogether.

In a similar vein, President Bush and Pentagon officials warned that many aspects of the military campaign against al Qaeda — for operational security reasons — may never be publicly acknowledged. Reports of the terrorists' counterintelligence capabilities — in particular bin Laden's shift from satellite cell phone communications to encrypted e-mail — demonstrated that unlike Panamanian dictator Manuel Noriega and Iraqi President Saddam Hussein, bin Laden is an enemy with the cunning and wiles to employ news media information to evade detection and strike again. The anticipated use of U.S. special operations commandos as the prime ground combat force against the terrorists also portended strict wartime information controls, since even the existence of many of those units is classified.

And the news media — after decades of pressing for transparency in covering military operations — began showing signs of recognition in the weeks after the terror attacks that the traditional, saturation coverage of operations might well compromise the U.S. counter-terror effort and endanger the lives of the soldiers, sailors, airmen and Marines involved. The discovery that terrorists had mailed anthrax to print and broadcast journalists did much to shape a new mood that made cooperation between the media and the Pentagon more likely.

Are you 'EWO Ready'?

Still, journalists have an obligation to cover the conflict. This chapter addresses how newcomers to military and defense reporting can best prepare themselves to carry out a difficult task in a new era where gathering information and respecting operational security claim equal importance.

Before President Bush I ended the 33-year era of strategic nuclear alert in October 1991, Strategic Air Command bomber and tanker crews stood regular ground watches in armed shelters, waiting for the signal that would send them racing across the tarmac to start their aircraft on what might be a one-way trip to nuclear Armageddon. Referring to the formal title of their presidential war messages — Emergency War Orders — a standard wall poster in those shelters asked, "Are you EWO ready?" It was a reminder for each SAC crewman not only to check his luggage, top-secret codes, next-of-kin forms and other paraphernalia. The poster asked each man on alert to check out the inside of his head as well.

So too, the military reporter ought to pose the question to himself or herself at the outset: Are you ready to participate in this war? Are you prepared, physically and mentally, to make the abrupt transition from peacetime reporter to war correspondent? Is your organization prepared to invest the time and money in enabling you and your colleagues to carry out vastly expensive wartime coverage?

Before examining a number of innovative approaches to covering the anti-terror campaign, it is useful to review some "lessons learned" from several recent military operations. These experiences offer suggestions for how the news media can operate.

Commando strikes and dispersed forces

As soon as the White House and Pentagon on Oct. 7, 2001, confirmed the launch of air and cruise missile strikes against the al Qaeda and Taliban, the obvious issue became how — if at all — journalists might be able to cover the anticipated use of special operations commandos against the terrorists. Given the classified nature of their mission and the remote locations, is it at all possible to cover such raids?

No — and yes.

Operation Just Cause, the U.S. invasion of Panama on Dec. 20, 1989, provides a classic example of a no-warning military strike spearheaded by special operations units. Even though the crisis in relations between Panamanian dictator Manuel Noriega and the Bush I administration played out over a seven-month period in 1989, beginning with Panamanian government-sparked riots against opposition political leaders, the decision to consider a military intervention and the operation itself were carried out under conditions of strict operational security.

This was dictated by the nature and design of the operation itself: a classic *coup de main* night parachute assault by U.S. Army Rangers to capture two critical airfields, a series of raids by the Army's Delta Force and Navy SEAL commandos to rescue hostages and attempt capture of Noriega, and a follow-on insertion of Army infantrymen from the 82nd Airborne Division and 7th Light Infantry Division and other units. The invasion itself was launched, executed and completed in about six hours.

As noted above, this kind of lightning-fast operation is nearly impossible to cover in "realtime" as it occurs, since the U.S. military — despite improved relations with the news media — simply will not risk operational security in a mission involving special operations forces. Such as the case when the first commando raids in Afghanistan took place on Oct. 19, 2001.

(A personal note: I had been covering the 2nd Ranger Battalion at Fort Lewis, Wash., for nearly three years when Panama went down. I had covered the Military Airlift Command's 62nd Airlift Wing at nearby McChord Air Force Base for the same period. I had expressed great interest in someday being able to cover them in combat. Local commanders told me that the only way they would even consider allowing a reporter to accompany them on a combat mission would be if that journalist had proven himself or herself as (1) physically capable of keeping up with the unit, (2) knowledgeable of the unit's personnel and mission, and (3) demonstrating respect for operational security factors that could compromise the mission and get soldiers killed. I believed I met those standards. Never mind — I was not invited to Operation Just Cause.)

Indeed, it was concern over protecting the security of the attacking force that prompted then-Secretary of Defense Dick Cheney in 1989 to delay the takeoff of the DoD National Media Pool for Panama, with the result that the hand-picked group of reporters arrived too late to witness the actual fighting.

The only plausible construct for covering special operations units in the current conflict would be for U.S. news organizations to negotiate Pentagon approval for some form of "embedded" pool to travel and live with the commandos or supporting units, operating under a formal structure of pre-publication and pre-broadcast review. There is a limited precedent for this approach.

The Pentagon opted to embed a number of journalists into Army units that deployed into Bosnia for the multinational peacekeeping operation in December 1995. Both the Pentagon and reporters who participated later agreed that the program was a success. However, to replicate such a program into Operation Enduring Freedom would require extensive negotiations and fine-tuning by both the Defense Department and the news media, particularly to address the thorny issues of operational security and the prolonged nature of the current conflict.

The Navy arranged a form of this pool in early October 2001 when it invited 17 print and broadcast journalists to fly from Washington, D.C., to the carriers USS Enterprise and USS Carl Vinson in the Arabian Sea, in advance of the naval air strikes against the Taliban, to provide coverage of the carriers and cruise missile-firing escort ships when combat operations began on Oct. 7.

As that particular pool arrangement confirmed, such opportunities are naturally limited to veteran military reporters in the Pentagon press corps and are not open to "newbies" coming into the military beat for the first time after the events of Sept. 11.

But there are other approaches local and regional military reporters may attempt. Reporters with special operations units in their local coverage area should not hesitate to request access to the units once the phase of the conflict involving their participation has ended. Such an approach would likely have to embrace pre-agreed limitations that most reporters would shun in peacetime coverage, including: An agreement to embargo publication or broadcast of the article(s) until a sufficient period of time had passed; acceptance of restrictions on using many basic facts of the operation or mission; and even pre-agreed masking of identities to protect servicemen and their families from possible terrorist retaliation. These conditions were cited and acknowledged nine years earlier when major U.S. news organizations and the Pentagon hammered out a post-Desert Storm set of combat coverage guidelines.

There is historical precedence for such secrecy: The operational archives of the U.S. Navy submarine fleet from World War II were not declassified until more than 20 years after the war ended in 1945, and the operational archives of their Cold War descendants — the nuclear attack and ballistic missile sub fleets — remain classified even today.

Limited coverage, first names only

Within hours of the terrorist strikes against the World Trade Center and the Pentagon, news organizations familiar with the Defense Department's websites were able to construct a detailed and accurate roster of naval and Marine Corps units already deployed overseas that would constitute the "first response" if a military retaliation were ordered. Similarly, even a cursory review of limited combat incidents involving Iraq, Afghanistan or al Qaeda during the 1990s provided a detailed matrix of how the Pentagon would likely respond with Air Force assets (staging B-2 stealth bombers from their base in Missouri using in-flight refueling, and positioning older B-52 or B-1B bombers to secure allied bases such as Diego Garcia, an island in the Indian Ocean).

One of the first responses by the Pentagon was to scrub its unclassified DefenseLink and related websites to remove any and all information on unit deployments and locations.

In the early days of the U.S. military air strikes against Afghanistan beginning on Oct. 7, 2001, the Pentagon denied reporters' access to deployed combat aircrews and bases, but allowed carefully restricted interviews via satellite telephone. The ground rules prohibited identifying aircrew by their full names and carefully prohibited disclosure of any operational details that might enable the adversary to glean future intentions or operational procedures. Reporters on the two aircraft carriers followed similar ground rules that withheld the aircrew identities and minimized disclosure of operational mission details.

Based on previous combat actions, it is likely that by the time this book appears in print, the Pentagon will have activated the DoD National Media Pool to report on subsequent phases of the military campaign, including Army deployments. And there were other signs that the Pentagon was preparing to selectively relax its information blackout: The U.S. Air Force on Oct. 8, 2001, permitted NBC reporter Jim Avila to fly in a two-seat F-15 Eagle mission on a combat air patrol over New York City.

Conclusion: There will probably be limited opportunities for reporters to directly observe some combat actions against the terrorists, but the odds are small and favor full-time members of the Pentagon press corps.

Going unilateral: costs and benefits

One obvious alternative to lobbying the Pentagon for access to U.S. combatant units is to travel to the area where military operations most likely will occur: Going unilateral. Such tactics were already unfolding in early October 2001 as this book went to press, with several hundred American and European journalists arriving in Tajikistan and Pakistan, where many slipped across the border into the part of northern Afghanistan controlled by the anti-Taliban Northern Alliance.

After spending thousands of dollars to get there, reporter Peter Baker of *The Washington Post* filed one dispatch on Oct. 6 that made his readers howl with laughter, while probably churning the ulcers of his newspaper's travel budget director:

> One interloper arrived by donkey over the Afghan mountains. Another sneaked into Taliban territory disguised as a woman, covered head to toe in a traditional burkha. Others convoyed for five days along bumpy roads straddling steep slopes, with both their vehicles

and their sanity breaking down along the way.

Once here, they have taken over houses, raided the bazaar and swamped the local economy with more dollars than anyone has seen in these parts since the days when the United States funded the guerrilla war against Soviet troops. They have set up ambushes to snare poor, bedraggled refugees, and enticed rebel troops at the sleepy front line into firing artillery shells at nothing in particular.

Translation: Nothing much was happening on the ground in Afghanistan.

Even early reports from Afghanistan on the initial air combat strikes were long on colorful description and short on relevant facts. Even the much-heralded videophone broadcasts (see Chapter 2) consisted of talking heads confirming they had heard explosions at a great distance.

So what is an effective coverage strategy for reporters coming into the military beat for the first time? Assuming that your time, energy and newsgathering budget does not immediately support a full-time stakeout of the Pentagon briefing room or a month in the mountains of Northern Afghanistan, there is still much you can do — and do well — as this unconventional war unfolds.

Covering the War on Terrorism

The long-term nature of the U.S. response to al Qaeda indicates that reporters have some time to organize and carry out a basic, three-layer coverage strategy that includes (1) research and identification of the focus of stories, (2) organization of coverage in depth, including "remote" coverage of local military units involved, (3) spot coverage as events unfold.

From the outset, you should at earliest opportunity sit down with your editors and determine the following:

■ A decision tree for you and your editors that will in a best-case hypothesis lead you to be prepared for on-scene coverage if the current conflict escalates to create a coherent battlefield;

■ The steps you must take to be ready for deployment, including logistics, research, communications and training of backup reporters to handle local military coverage while you are gone;

■ An early assessment (through wires, informal PAO contacts or other channels) of what you can anticipate in Pentagon press policies, restrictions, pool rules or other limits that might affect your ability to access the units you want to cover and to transmit stories to your newspaper;

■ Coordination with other members of your company (if comprised of multiple newspapers, TV stations and bureaus) to create a team coverage strategy;

■ A fallback coverage plan that assumes you either remain in your local coverage area or travel to a third location (Washington, D.C., regional military headquarters) during hostilities.

Covering the home front

Even if your publisher or station manager determines that it will not be cost-effective for you to deploy overseas in search of combat coverage, the nature of the current war against terrorism portends a number of unique "domestic" coverage strategies that merit consideration. These include:

Homeland defense coverage: Create a full-time beat that will track the ongoing efforts to deter additional terrorist actions and to respond should additional attacks occur. Reporters should establish contact with and build sources within the following federal and state agencies that have already been identified in this unprecedented domestic defense effort:

■ White House Office of Homeland Defense;
■ U.S. Senate and House of Representatives members;
■ U.S. Coast Guard local district;
■ Federal Bureau of Investigation field office;
■ U.S. Customs Service and Immigration and Naturalization Service regional offices;
■ State National Guard headquarters, including any Air

National Guard alert squadrons;

■ State, regional or municipal "first responder" agencies involved in reacting to nuclear, chemical or biological attacks;

■ State and local law enforcement agencies.

The purpose of this coordinated coverage is obvious: As the U.S. government refines and lays out the array of new laws and programs aimed at deterring future terrorist acts, the action will inevitably shift from Washington, D.C. to the states and local governments. (A harbinger of this came in late 1999 when a local U.S. Customs office in Port Angeles, Wash., captured an Algerian citizen attempting to enter the United States from Canada with enough high explosives to destroy a large office building. The terrorist, Ahmed Ressam, later confirmed he was attempting to set off a major attack against Los Angeles International Airport during the 2000 Millennium New Year's celebrations.)

It is no exaggeration to suggest that reporters will not have to travel far overseas to cover the subsequent battles of the war against terror — there may well still be plenty of stories to write right here inside the United States.

Home-based military coverage: Even while the largest newspapers, wire services and TV networks are ranging far afield to cover the ongoing battles and skirmishes against the terrorists, there is much for a local or regional reporter to do at home. As cited in earlier chapters of this book, patience and persistence with military bases and commands in your state or local coverage area will pay off with stories highlighting (1) the roles that local military units will play in domestic security or (2) possible training and pre-deployment preparations for future combat, or (3) actual operations overseas or at home.

Domestic implications of counter-terrorism: The wide array of new national security laws, relaxation of restrictions on intelligence and law enforcement operations, and use of new technology for surveillance and security create an entire subject area for the reporter covering the U.S. response to terrorism. The impact on civil liberties and due process will no doubt become a focus of debate and argument in the months and years ahead, and journalists covering this vital aspect will likely find themselves inundated as they attempt to cover the consequences — deliberate and unintended — of this unprecedented security move.

While many things remain clouded and uncertain in the immediate weeks after the Sept. 11 terrorist attacks, one thing is crystal-clear: The United States is engaged in a war on many fronts and the war will not end anytime soon. There is an urgent requirement for a new generation of reporters who can cover this conflict with knowledge, eloquence and balance.

Useful websites regarding terrorism

■ Weapons of Mass Destruction - Civil Support Teams
http://www.defenselink.mil/specials/destruction/

■ Chemical and Biological Defense Program Annual Report to Congress, March 2000
http://www.defenselink.mil/pubs/chembio02012000.pdf

■ Proliferation: Threat and Response Annual Report, 2001
http://www.defenselink.mil/pubs/ptr20010110.pdf

■ The White House
 http://www.whitehouse.gov

■ Federal Bureau of Investigation
http://www.fbi.gov

■ Centers for Disease Control and Prevention
http://www.cdc.gov

■ Central Intelligence Agency
http://www.cia.gov

■ Federal Aviation Administration
http://www.faa.gov

■ Federal Emergency Management Agency
http://www.fema.gov

■ Department of Health and Human Services
http://www.hhs.gov

■ Department of Justice
http://www.doj.gov

■ Department of Labor
http://www.dol.gov

■ Department of State
http://www.state.gov

■ Department of Transportation
http://www.dot.gov

■ General Accounting Office
http://www.gao.org

Non-governmental websites

■ Center for Strategic and International Studies
http://www.csis.org

■ Federation of American Scientists (Comprehensive portal of terrorism-related information and links to other sites)
http://www.fas.org

■ Jane's IntelWeb homesite (Subscription access to on-line sites that track terrorist organization activities)
http://www.intelweb.janes.com

■ Middle East Media Research Institute
http://www.memri.org

■ Military.com (Comprehensive independent information site on military and veterans issues)
http://www.military.com

■ The Poynter Institute (Interactive seminars and news coverage

strategies posted daily)
http://www.poynter.org

■ Soldiers For The Truth (DefenseWatch military newsletter)
http://www.sftt.org

■ STRATFOR.com
(Private open-source strategic forecasting intelligence firm)
http://www.stratfor.com

■ United States Commission on National Security/21st Century
http://www.nssg.gov/Reports/New_World_Coming/new_wo
rld_coming.htm

Rumor control and debunking sites

■ Urban Legends Reference Pages
http://www.snopes.com

■ Urbanlegends.com
http://urbanlegends.com

How to...

Know when to keep secrets

When do you publish or broadcast, and when do you hold something back?

This was a common philosophical question posed in academic seminars until Sept. 11, 2001. Today, it is a harsh reality pressing down on reporters, editors, publishers and TV executives as they scramble to cover the ongoing military campaign against the terror networks that struck the United States.

The common perception among career military people has long been that all reporters will rush into print and damn the consequences, even if the coverage is life-threatening to military people.

That is a fulcrum on which a lot of the military resentment of reporters ultimately turns, although cases abound where reporters have withheld extremely newsworthy facts because they realized that lives and operational security were at issue. Unfortunately, these instances of checked-fire by reporters are — by their nature — unpublished, and attention is inevitably drawn to cases where the press has jumped into print (or broadcast) at a critical moment in a military operation.

A reporter entering the military beat should anticipate being confronted with this dilemma.

Where has the press held its fire?

■ During the 1980 Iranian hostage crisis, many American reporters knew that the Canadian embassy in Tehran was sheltering eight American embassy staffers, and no one printed the story until they had successfully escaped from the revolution-wracked country with fabricated Canadian papers;
■ During the 1985 hijacking of TWA Flight 847 by Lebanese terrorists, several reporters were aware that a number of U.S. Navy sailors were on the aircraft, and carefully omitted any tip-off of that fact so that the hijackers (who had already killed one sailor) did not learn of them;
■ NBC television spotted the sudden departure of a U.S. Navy

aircraft carrier as it headed toward Libya in 1986 to launch air strikes against Tripoli and Benghazi, and studiously avoided any advance report to that effect (The network did, however, using word code, alert a correspondent in Tripoli who stayed on an open telephone line and was able to broadcast a live sound-track of Air Force F-111s as they raced across the city on their bombing runs.)

■ Many reporters both in Saudi Arabia and the United States knew that the Central Command's ground war operational plan in 1991 called for a massive deception effort to mask the west-ward redeployment of forces which would lead to the "Hail Mary" strike around the flank of the Iraqi defenses. No one dis-closed that critical fact.

"I'll tell you, all four broadcast networks knew about the big swing around the Iraqi right flank right before the ground war started," recalled Col. Miguel Montaverde, who was head of the Pentagon's Directorate of Defense Information in 1991. "But these folks didn't run with that information because, I'm con-vinced, good military reporters recognize that most of our rules and regulations on not revealing information have to do with the safeguarding of lives and the safeguarding of the opera-tion."

It is the reporter's dilemma to manage, particularly when scenting a major military operation, when to disclose and when to withhold facts about an operation. Experienced military reporters know that there are facts that can kill. Some categories:

■ Advance disclosure of a surprise military intervention or air strike can alert enemy defenses, complicating attack plans and increasing the odds that aircraft will be shot down.
■ Information about wartime deployment of naval forces can alert enemy submarines or aircraft to likely strike areas.
■ Counter-terror operations requiring stealth, speed and sur-prise can be blown if hostage-takers or other terrorists get even a generic warning that special operations forces are on the way.

Don't expect a medal for going against your reporter's instinct to report what you have learned. The best reward you can get is to look at your hands later and see that there is no blood on them.

There are innumerable cases in recent military history where reporters diligently covering a crisis inadvertently (or indifferently) created a potential hazard to operational security.

While the 1986 Operation El Dorado Canyon raid against Libya and the TWA 847 crisis contained examples of press caution in the face of critical secrets, both incidents also provided ammunition to military critics of the press.

While reporters refrained from fingering the captive Navy sailors, two broadcast networks did report that the Army's counter-terror Delta Force had deployed from its home base at Fort Bragg, according to David Martin and John Walcott in *Best-Laid Plans* (Harper & Row, 1988), their account of the Reagan administration's war against terrorism. "The (TV) reports were picked up by a number of other news organizations and before long the whole world knew Delta was coming," the authors noted.

(Military historians may be somewhat kinder to the press in this instance, since it later was learned that kidnapped Beirut CIA station chief William Buckley — whose job description was carefully omitted by press accounts of those hostages — had previously served as an intelligence liaison between the CIA and Delta, and had presumably delivered the Delta Force counter-terror operational plan under torture at least a year earlier.)

Or maybe not.

Leaks from the White House about impending U.S. retaliation against Libya in 1986 — which did contain specific target references — deeply angered military officials in the field responsible for planning and actually carrying out the operation.

"It really torqued me off," recalled Navy Rear Adm. Jerry Breast, commander of the carrier *USS Coral Sea* battle group, one of three flattops involved in the 1986 raid. "Some of the info I was holding above the top-secret level would repeatedly come out in the press a day or two after I received it."

Interviewed by Martin and Walcott, Navy wing commander Cmdr. Byron Duff also complained, "We would get a target list and read about it in *Time* magazine."

The motive of the leakers, who were apparently well placed

within the Reagan administration, could not have conceivably been to sabotage the plan, since it was the administration which pressed the Pentagon to carry out such an operation. Rather, the most likely reason for the leak was to put severe psychological pressure on Muammar Ghadafi. Even so, what had originally started as a simple sneak air bombing ended up involving nearly 60 Air Force and Navy aircraft because of the heightened state of alert in Libya due to the press leaks.

On the other hand, some stories cannot be held — period.

Fred Hoffman was senior Pentagon reporter for the Associated Press in 1973 when in response to the Arab-Israeli war, Soviet leader Leonid Brezhnev threatened the United States with unilateral Soviet military intervention over Israel's failure to halt its counter-attack west of the Suez Canal. The White House response was to order a worldwide military alert and to place nuclear and conventional forces on DEFCON 1 — the highest defense condition, normally reserved for preparation for immediate conflict.

Hoffman, through his AP contacts, had been able to piece together a story of bases and commands across the country going on alert, but the root cause — Brezhnev's ultimatum to the United States — remained a secret held by less than a half-dozen officials in the government.

At 5 a.m., in a Pentagon hallway, Hoffman met a senior U.S. military official (senior enough that Hoffman says he did not have to check the official's position or confirm the allegation elsewhere) who told him the reason for the alarming and mysterious alert of U.S. forces. Hoffman put the story out over the AP wire.

Implicit in Hoffman's experience was a mutual recognition between reporter and source that normal military operational security did not apply to a political and military confrontation of this magnitude between the superpowers, and that the public had a right and need to know the reason for the sudden military alert.

Military officials, when pressed, will admit that in most cases it is the timing of disclosure that poses danger, rather than the information itself. In most cases, common sense will dictate that the material is best kept secret until the operation has ended, or its execution has proceeded to a point where the time-sensitivity has passed.

In the immediate days after the terrorist attacks in New York and at the Pentagon, print and broadcast operations revealed significant operational details of the initial U.S. deployment of forces preparing to strike back.

The culture of transparency that has long defined the U.S. news media approach to military operations seemed to have survived intact in the first days after the attacks on the World Trade Center and the Pentagon.

But within weeks, different signs emerged. CNN posted a notice on its website that it was voluntarily withholding specific information on military deployments that could expose them to terrorist attack. And *The Virginian-Pilot* in Norfolk, Va., published a lengthy essay by Public Editor Marvin Lake on Oct. 2, 2001, explaining how the newspaper intended to balance its news gathering responsibilities with the need to protect operational security:

> "We're not going to put people at risk," said *Pilot* managing editor Dennis Hartig. He noted that, in past major conflicts, the paper has obtained information that would put individuals at risk but has "acted with a lot of common sense and good judgment."
>
> On Tuesday, several *Pilot* editors and reporters met with Navy public affairs officers from the Atlantic Fleet and the local base command organization to discuss restrictions on information and access in light of the country's "War on Terrorism."
>
> "The Navy has asked us for help in two areas, ship movements and base security," said Hartig. "These are reasonable requests, in keeping with our past practices. So we pledged to cooperate."
>
> The paper will not publish specific descriptions about the time, date and place of ship and troop movements, particularly when they are to occur in several days or weeks, Hartig said.
>
> And in our stories about base security, we will omit information about the specific location of extra security

or exact details about the numbers and assignments of people protecting the bases.

The Virginian-Pilot editors quickly came to realize that this new conflict, pitting American and allied forces against a murderous terror network, had resurrected a warning and slogan from a war long past: Loose lips sink ships.

It is a lesson all journalists are confronting as they prepare to cover this war.

Chapter 16

Conclusion: The Era of Volatility

Even before the stunning terror attacks in New York and Northern Virginia on Sept. 11, 2001, the United States was wrestling with a number of thorny problems as it operated as the world's solitary superpower.

While the U.S. military had been cut by about 40 percent in the ensuing decade, our political assumptions, treaty obligations and strategic premises still dictated a global span of military operations, from Kosovo to Korea and from the Persian Gulf to the Americas. Those largely remain intact despite a mind-numbing geopolitical realignment as the United States, its traditional allies and even former adversaries move to respond to the terrorists.

On the surface, the United States today should enjoy a true hegemony over potential enemies. The Pentagon currently spends more on defense than the NATO allies, Japan and South Korea combined. In 1998, the nonprofit Center for Defense Information calculated that the Pentagon budget of $281 billion represented 34 percent of defense spending worldwide, up from 30 percent of the world's total in the previous decade. The Pentagon budget in 1998 dwarfed the military spending of Russia (between $40-64 billion) and China ($37 billion).

But even before the terror strikes, the U.S. military found itself in serious trouble with a lengthening list of problems that will generate news in the decade ahead.

Despite the force reductions of the 1990s, the U.S. armed forces are still largely structured as they were during the Cold War. The unrelenting pace of overseas deployments has strained military units and personnel to the breaking point. Combat readiness, the measurement of a unit's ability to carry out its wartime mission, has been steadily declining throughout the force. The services have struggled with unanticipated personnel shortages due to a sharp decline in first-term enlistments and an exodus of experienced, mid-level career specialists. This has further strained military units that are being forced to operate with as much as a 10 percent shortage in the number of personnel required to fill the ranks.

The Pentagon itself faces a deep crisis in its attempt to modernize the force as a result of reluctance by the past two administrations and Congress to appropriate sufficient funds to purchase the next generation of warships, combat aircraft and other military hardware. The entire military infrastructure — from bases to equipment to weapons — is becoming obsolete.

As retired Adm. William A. Owens, a former Vice Chairman of the Joint Chiefs of Staff, noted in his memoir, *Lifting the Fog of War* (Farrar, Straus & Giroux, 2000):

> "Many consider the debate over the future of our military as a complex technical issue far removed from the daily concerns of the average American citizen. But the exact opposite is true: For decades we have enjoyed economic prosperity, burgeoning global trade and political stability with our major allies because of the U.S. military's success in deterring aggression and safeguarding our national interests here and overseas. We have become so accustomed to the benefits of the security umbrella our military forces have created that we fail to recognize how vulnerable we would be to aggression, instability and terrorism without it. Yet that is the precise risk we now face."

The challenges go beyond the immediate deployment of combat forces against al Qaeda and the Taliban movement in Afghanistan:

■ A possible "defense train wreck" stemming from serious under-funding of defense assets in the late 1980s through 2000;

■ The emergence of hackers and cyber terrorists attempting to damage or destroy military and civilian computer networks;

■ Protracted ethnic conflicts in the Balkans, former Soviet Union, Middle East, Africa and Asia that have the potential to escalate into regional wars;

■ The collapse of nonproliferation regimes worldwide and increased threat of regional nuclear war in South Asia (even more dangerous than before Sept. 11);

■ The increasing number of "rogue" states that are arming themselves with ballistic missiles;

■ The emergence of China as a major regional power and the potential for long-term rivalry — if not potential conflict — with the United States and its East Asian allies.

For print and broadcast journalism, the defense beat remains a vital segment of government and society that demands professional, comprehensive coverage.

What is uncertain is whether American newspapers, TV networks and other media outlets can reverse their own decade of coverage cutbacks. For those institutions who stick to it, and for reporters interested in taking on this diverse and challenging beat, there will be no shortage of front-page news from the military front.

Epilogue

Why bother? Why put up with a beat that guarantees frustration, long hours on the telephone, bureaucratic issues that even the bureaucrats don't comprehend, and an endless fight with colleagues and editors over the value of the effort and money spent?

Certainly a professional journalist can see through the tedium and gobbledygook to recognize the civic need for articulate, tough and informed coverage of military affairs. Of course, anyone studying recent journalistic history will identify the root causes of the military-media tension. But the question remains, and it is a good one:

Why put up with it all?

When I am asked that, dozens of answers come to mind.

Each is a story. Some are lengthy, some very short. A few are funny, a larger number are poignant, most are sea stories or tales from the field. I think of aircraft and helicopter rides I have taken, of overseas military exercises and conflicts I have covered. I think of what I have learned, and I think of the excitement that is a journalist's payoff when a long-hidden fact finally tumbles out of the inch-thick document, or the adrenaline excitement of chasing a breaking story on deadline. The outbreak of war and my hours of scrambling to file the biggest story of my career amid SCUD alerts is never far from mind. I remember the Ranger airdrop that went awry, sending us diving for cover as soldiers rained down on the press contingent like a bad hail, or the admiral's fury when a story made him out to be the fool that he was, or the gut-wrenching shot of the catapult as we flew off the carrier's bow, or even the dim glow of the South Pole base camp lights as the Air Force transport plane readied its cargo to drop by parachute in the midwinter twilight.

But I always come back to a story early in my career.

I was standing on the main deck of the nuclear cruiser *USS Texas* under a bright spring sky, and the Atlantic Ocean formed a jade green carpet under the bows of the ship. Three hours earlier, I had flown out from land aboard a Navy Sea Knight helicopter to cover the return of three Norfolk-based warships from long duty in the Indian Ocean. There, the *Texas*, cruiser *USS California* and aircraft carrier *USS Nimitz* had operated nonstop for nine months, patrolling the North Arabian Sea and providing potential combat power as the U.S.-backed regime in Iran collapsed, as radical extremists sacked the U.S. Embassy, and as the United States became paralyzed over the impasse of its 52 citizens held hostage. From the flight deck of the *Nimitz*, the helicopters had flown in what became the military debacle at Desert One. Now, six weeks later, and nearly 10 months after departing for distant duty, the 6,000 Norfolk sailors were coming home.

And to what? Journalists asked. Apart from the embarrassment of the failed rescue raid, the young men and women of the U.S. military seemed destined to get the same cold shoulder that their older brothers and sisters had received at the tail end of Vietnam five years earlier. Would American society, preoccupied with the issues of self and distracted by economic dislocation, coldly ignore the tremendous sacrifices and hardships that these sailors had undertaken?

What instead happened that Memorial Day weekend in 1980 was that the president of the United States flew down to personally welcome the sailors home, and tens of thousands of people from Virginia and the rest of the nation flocked to Hampton Roads to wave banners and American flags.

More than a few commentators would later say that the emotional welcome that flowed this day marked a turning point toward a post-Vietnam reconciliation between the U.S. military and civilian society.

This is what I recall: I am standing on the cruiser's main deck, interviewing a Navy senior chief petty officer. A veteran of Vietnam and of the even harder post-Vietnam aftermath when serving in the military meant not enough pay, eroding benefits, plummeting morale and six-month cruises that lasted nine months, the chief would not quit talking about how well his "kids" performed, despite the heat, the endless days without liberty ashore, despite the letters from home that bespoke personal crises, insufficient income, and family stress. But they did their job and they did it damn well, the chief said more than once. Write that down when you do your story, he said. In his gruff, no-nonsense voice, the plea came out sounding like an order.

I already grasped the message implicit in his words. What the chief really meant was that it is so easy to write about "the military" as a remote monolith, an alien culture, and a vast bureaucracy of strangers. The stereotypes are very old, and they never die. And they are as false now as they have ever been.

What this grizzled sailor, face set in stern lines, was actually telling me was something simple yet profound: *We in the military are people. We are Americans, too.*

Our conversation halted as a metallic click suddenly sounded on the 1MC loudspeaker and a short blast of the bosun's pipe sounded attention.

"Land ho! On the port quarter," the bosun's mate announced, "the United States of America."

After 213 days out.

The sailor gazed at the thin, green strip of land, ignoring the tears that streaked down his face.

Reading List: Reports

Reports of interest concerning U.S. military organization and structure:

Defense Department reports

Annual Report to the President and the Congress 2001
Current overview of DoD policies, budget and force deployment with a breakdown by services and functions.
http://www.dtic.mil/execsec/adr2001/

Defense Almanac
DoD website for organizational, personnel and budget information.
http://www.defenselink.mil/pubs/almanac/

Unified Command Plan
Detailed breakdown on the geographical and specified multi-service commands and their responsibilities.
http://www.defenselink.mil/specials/unified/

Military ranks and insignia
Details on officer and enlisted personnel ranks and insignia.
http://www.defenselink.mil/pubs/almanac/almanac/people/insignias/index.html

Military medals and decorations
Detailed breakdown on individual and unit medals and decorations.
http://www.defenselink.mil/specials/ribbons/

Weapons of Mass Destruction - Civil Support Teams
Website for information about the DoD-sponsored WMD military response teams.
http://www.defenselink.mil/specials/destruction/

Chemical and Biological Defense Program Annual Report to Congress, March 2000.
http://www.defenselink.mil/pubs/chembio02012000.pdf

Proliferation: Threat and Response Annual Report, January 2001.
Annual unclassified report on global WMD proliferation
http://www.defenselink.mil/pubs/ptr20010110.pdf

Joint Vision 2020 - Joint Chiefs of Staff
Current JCS Vision of future warfare and U.S. requirements
http://www.dtic.mil/jv2020/

Kosovo/Operation Allied Force After-action Report, 1999
http://www.defenselink.mil/pubs/kaar02072000.pdf

Report of the Commission to Assess United States National Security Space Management and Organization (Rumsfeld Commission), January 2001.
http://www.defenselink.mil/pubs/space20010111.html

Other DoD reports and publications of special interest are posted at the Pentagon's Defenselink website at www.defenselink.mil.

Defense reform — previous initiatives

United States Commission on National Security/21st Century
The Hart-Rudman Panel's website for its ongoing review of U.S. military strategy, organization and resource requirements.
http://www.nssg.gov/Reports/New_World_Coming/new_world_coming.htm

Business Executives for National Security: "Tail to Tooth Commission" Report
Independent expert panel's analysis and program recommendations for reforming DoD infrastructure, acquisition and procurement.
http://www.bens.org/tail_action.html

DoD Defense Reform Initiative Report (2000)
    Pentagon initiatives to reform DoD business practices.
http://www.defenselink.mil/dodreform/dr-broch.pdf

Quadrennial Defense Review, May 1997
    Report of congressionally-mandated report on defense organization, roles and missions.
http://www.defenselink.mil/pubs/qdr/

National Defense Panel Assessment of 1997 QDR
    Assessment of 1997 QDR by congressionally-appointed panel of experts.
http://www.defenselink.mil/topstory/ndp_assess.html

"Transforming Defense" - Report of the National Defense Panel, December 1997
http://www.dtic.mil/ndp/FullDoc2.pdf

RAND Corporation - "Taking Charge: A Bipartisan Report to the President Elect on Foreign Policy and National Security," Nov. 13, 2000.
http://www.rand.org/publications/MR/MR1306/

Center for Strategic and International Studies - "Averting the Defense Train Wreck in the New Millennium," Report by Dan Goure and Jeffrey M. Ranney, 2000.
http://www.csis.org/pubs/trainwreckexec.html

U.S. Foreign Intelligence Advisory Board - "Global Trends 2015: A Dialogue About the Future With Nongovernment Experts."
http://www.cia.gov/cia/publications/globaltrends2015/index.html

Defense Department Organization
    Basic organizational guidebook.
http://www.odam.osd.mil/omp/pubs/GuideBook/ToC.htm

Suggested reference materials

U.S. Naval Institute *Proceedings* magazine, Naval Review issue (May)
Annual almanac profile of Navy and Marine Corps including key events and issues, budget, organizational materials. Contact the Naval Institute at www.usni.org

Almanac of Seapower edition of *Seapower* magazine
Annual almanac of maritime, Navy and Marine Corps issues. Contact the Navy League of the United States at www.nlus.org

ic *Air Force* magazine annual almanac issue (May)
Annual almanac profile of Air Force key events and issues, budget, organizational materials. Contact the Air Force Association at www.afa.org

***Army* magazine "Green Book" edition (Fall)**
Annual almanac profile of Army key events and issues, budget, organizational materials. Contact the Association of the U.S. Army at www.ausa.org

***The U.S. Military Online (2nd edition)*, by William M. Arkin, Brassey's Inc., Washington and London, 1998.**
An in-depth directory for internet access to the Defense Department and other agencies, including many internal military and defense sites that are not explicitly promoted by the DoD. Contact the publisher at www.brasseys.com

CDI Military Almanac
Annual survey of Defense Department and key issues by the nonprofit Center for Defense Information. Contact the CDI at www.cdi.org.

Reading List:
Military-Media Relations

Books:

Arkin, William, *The U.S. Military Online: A Directory for Internet Access to the Department of Defense*, 2nd edition, Brassey's, London, 1998.

Fialka, John J., *Hotel Warriors: Covering the Gulf War*, Woodrow Wilson Center Press, Washington, D.C., 1991.

Halberstam, David, *The Powers That Be*, Alfred A. Knopf, New York, 1979. (U.S. news media during the Vietnam era.)

Knightly, Phillip, *The First Casualty - From the Crimea to Vietnam: The War Correspondent as Hero, Propagandist and Myth Maker*, Harcourt, New York, 1989.

Loyd, Anthony, *My War Gone By, I Miss It So*, Grove/Atlantic, New York, 2000.

Neuman, Johanna, *Lights, Camera, War*, St. Martin's Press, New York, 1996.

Sharkey, Jacqueline, *Under Fire: U.S. Military Restrictions on the Media from Grenada to the Persian Gulf War*, The Center for Public Integrity, Washington, D.C., 1991.

Stenbuck, Jack, editor, *Typewriter Battalion - Dramatic Frontline Dispatches from World War II*, William Morrow & Co., New York, 1995.

Reports and documents:

Aukofer, Frank and Lawrence, William P. Vice Adm. USN (Ret.), *America's Team: The Odd Couple — A Report on the*

Relationship between the Media and the Military, Freedom Forum First Amendment Center, Nashville, TN, September 1995.

Committee on Governmental Affairs, United States Senate, *Pentagon Rules on Media Access to the Persian Gulf War*, U.S. Government Printing Office, Feb. 20, 1991.

Dennis, Everett et. Al. Editors, *The Media at War: The Press and the Persian Gulf Conflict*, Gannett Foundation (later Freedom Forum), Rosslyn, Va., June 1991.

Ethiel, Nancy, series editor, *The Military and the Media: Facing the Future*, Cantigny Conference Series, Robert R. McCormick Tribune Foundation, Chicago, 1998.

Moskos, Charles C. with Ricks, Thomas R., *Reporting War when There is No War*, Cantigny Conference Series, Robert R. McCormick Tribune Foundation, Chicago, 1996.

Appendix 3

Reading List:
Current Military Issues

Revolution in military affairs/resource crisis

Arquilla, John and Ronfeldt, David, Editors, *In Athena's Camp - Preparing for Conflict in the Information Age*, National Defense Research Institute, RAND Corp., Santa Monica, Calif., 1997.

Bateman, Robert, editor, *Digital War - A View from the Front Lines*, Presidio Press, Novato, Calif., 1998.

Dunnigan, James F., *Digital Soldiers*, St. Martin's Press, New York, 1996.

Friedman, George and Friedman, Meredith, *The Future of War - Power, Technology & American Dominance in the 21st Century*, Crown Publishers, New York, 1996.

Goure, Daniel and Ranney, Jeffrey, *Avoiding the Defense Train Wreck in the New Millenium*, Center for Strategic and International Affairs, Washington, D.C., 2000.

Goure, Daniel, and Szarza, Christopher, editors, *Air and Space Power in the New Millenium*, Center for Strategic and International Studies, Washington, D.C., 1996.

Macgregor, Douglas A., *Breaking the Phalanx - A New Design for Landpower in the 21st Century*, Praeger Press, Westport, Conn., in cooperation with the Center for Strategic and International Studies, 1997.

Owens, William A. with Ed Offley, *Lifting the Fog of War*, Farrar, Straus & Giroux, New York, 2000.

Schwartzstein, Stuart J., Editor, *The Information Revolution and*

National Security, Center for Strategic and International Studies, Washington, D.C., 1996.

Van Creveld, Martin, *The Transformation of War*, MacMillan Inc., New York, 1991.

General military/security and strategy topics

Dunnigan, James F. and Nofi, Albert A., *Dirty Little Secrets*, William Morrow, New York, 1990.

Dunnigan, James F. and Nofi, Albert A., *Victory and Deceit: Dirty Tricks at War*, Quill/William Morrow, New York, 1995.

Fussell, Paul, editor, *The Norton Book of Modern War*, W.W. Norton & Co., New York, 1992.

Huntington, Samuel P., *The Clash of Civilizations - Remaking of World Order*, Simon & Schuster, New York, 1997.

Kaplan, Robert D., *The Coming Anarchy - Shattering the Dreams of the Post-Cold War*, Random House, New York, 2000.

Kaplan, Robert D., *The Ends of the Earth: From Togo to Turkmenistan, From Iran to Cambodia, a Journey to the Frontiers of Anarchy*, Vintage Books, New York, 1997.

Kitfield, James, *Prodigal Soldiers: How the Generation of Officers Born of Vietnam Revolutionized the American Style of War*, Simon & Schuster, New York, 1994.

Scales, Robert H., Jr., *Firepower in Limited War*, Presidio Press, Novato, Calif., 1995.

Summers, Harry G., Col., USA (Ret.), *The New World Strategy - A Military Policy for America's Future*, Simon & Schuster, New York, 1995.

Summers, Harry G., Col. USA (Ret.), *On Strategy - A Critical Analysis of the Vietnam War*, Presidio Press, Novato, Calif.

(Reissue Edition), 1995.

Summers, Harry G., Col. USA (Ret.), *On Strategy II - A Critical Analysis of the Gulf War*, Dell Publishing Co., New York, 1992.

Military history

General military history

Hastings, Max, *The Oxford Book of Military Anecdotes*, Oxford University Press, 1985.

Manchester, William, *The Glory and the Dream, a Narrative History of America*, 1932-1972, Bantam Books, New York, 1975.

Perrett, Geoffrey, *A Country Made by War: From the Revolution to Vietnam: The Story of America's Rise to Power*, Vintage Books, New York, 1990.

Civil War

Shaara, Michael, *The Killer Angels*, Ballentine Books, New York, 1974, (novel of the Battle of Gettysburg).

World War I

Coffman, Edward M., *The War to End All Wars: The American Military Experience in World War I*, University Press of Kentucky, Lexington, Ky., 1998.

Eisenhower, John S.D., and Eisenhower, Joanne T., *Yanks: The Epic Story of the American Army in World War I*, Free Press, 2001.

Tuchman, Barbara, *The Guns of August*, Ballantine Books, New York, reprinted 1994.

World War II

Allen, Thomas B. and Polmar, Norman, *Code Name Downfall, the Secret Plan to Invade Japan and Why Truman Dropped the Bomb*, Simon & Schuster, New York, 1995.

Ambrose, Stephen E., *D-Day June 6, 1944: The Climactic Battle of World War II*, Simon & Schuster, New York, 1994.

Ambrose, Stephen E., *Citizen Soldiers: The U.S. Army from the Normandy Beaches to the Bulge to the Surrender of Germany, June 7, 1944 to May 7, 1945*, Touchstone Books, New York, 1998.

Blair, Clay, *Silent Victory*, J.B. Lippincott Company, New York, 1975 (U.S. submarines in World War II).

Brokaw, Tom, *The Greatest Generation*, Random House, New York, 1998.

Bucheim, Lothar-Gunther, *Das Boot* (The Boat), R. Piper & Co., 1973.

Calvert, James F., Vice Adm. USN (Ret.), *Silent Running, My Years on a World War II Attack Submarine*, John Wiley & Sons Inc., New York, 1995.

Clausen, Henry C. with Lee, Bruce, *Pearl Harbor - Final Judgment*, Crown Publishers, New York, 1992.

Edgerton, Robert B., *Warriors of the Rising Sun - A History of the Japanese Military*, W.W. Norton & Co., New York, 1997.

Gannon, Michael, *Operation Drumbeat: The Dramatic True Story of Germany's First U-Boat Attacks Along the American Coast in World War II*, Harper & Row, New York, 1990.

Lee, Bruce, *Marching Orders — The Untold Story of World War II*, Crown Books, New York, 1995.

Morison, Samuel Eliot, *The Two-Ocean War: A Short History of the United States Navy in the Second World War*, Little, Brown & Co., Boston, 1963.

Perrett, Geoffrey, *There's a War to Be Won - The United States Army in World War II*, Ballentine Books, New York, 1997.

Perrett, Geoffrey, *Winged Victory - The Army Air Forces in World War II*, Random House, New York, 1997.

Polmar, Norman, and Allen, Thomas B., *World War II - America At War, 1941-45*, Random House, New York, 1991 (Encyclopedia).

Prange, Gordon W., *At Dawn We Slept: The Untold Story of Pearl Harbor*, Viking Penguin, New York, Reprinted 2001.

Prange, Gordon W., *Miracle at Midway*, McGraw-Hill Book Company, New York, 1982.

Stenbuck, Jack, editor, *Typewriter Battalion - Dramatic Frontline Dispatches from World War II*, William Morrow & Co., New York, 1995.

Toland, John, *Infamy - Pearl Harbor and Its Aftermath*, Berkley Publishing Group, New York, 1982.

Korea

Fehrenbach, T. R., *This Kind of War: The Classic Korean War History*, Brassey's, London, 1998.

Toland, John, *In Mortal Combat - Korea, 1950-1953*, William Morrow, New York, 1991.

Vietnam

Atkinson, Rick, *The Long Gray Line: The American Journey of West Point's Class of 1966*, Houghton Mifflin Co., Boston, 1989.

Burkett, B.G., *Stolen Valor — How the Vietnam Generation Was Robbed of Its Heroes and Its History*, Verity Press, Dallas, Tex., 1998.

Eschmann, Karl J., *Linebacker - The Untold Story of the Air Raids over North Vietnam*, Ivy Books, New York, 1989.

Grant, Zalin, *Over the Beach - The Air War in Vietnam*, Pocket

Books, New York, 1988.

Herr, Michael, *Dispatches*, Vintage Books, New York, Reprinted 1991.

Hersh, Seymour M., *The Price of Power, Kissinger in the Nixon White House*, Simon & Schuster, New York, 1983.

Karnow, Stanley, *Vietnam, a History*, Viking Press, New York, 1983.

Kitfield, James, *Prodigal Soldiers: How the Generation of Officers Born of Vietnam Revolutionized the American Style of War*, Simon & Schuster, New York, 1994.

McConnell, Malcolm, *Inside Hanoi's Secret Archives - Solving the MIA Mystery*, Simon & Schuster, New York, 1995.

McMaster, H.R., *Dereliction of Duty: Johnson, McNamara, the Joint Chiefs of Staff and the Lies That Led to Vietnam*, Harperperennial, New York, 1998.

Moore, Harold, G. and Galloway, Joseph L., *We Were Soldiers Once and Young: Ia Drang: the Battle That Changed the War in Vietnam*, Harperperennial Library, New York, 1993.

Pisor, Robert, *The End of the Line, the Siege of Khe Sanh*, Ballentine Books, New York, 1982.

Sheehan, Neil, *A Bright Shining Lie: John Paul Vann and America in Vietnam*, Random House, New York, 1988.

Snepp, Frank, *Decent Interval - An Insider's Account of Saigon's Indecent End*, Random House, New York, 1977.

Timberg, Robert, *The Nightingale's Song*, Simon & Schuster, New York, 1995 (Profile of five Naval Academy graduates from Vietnam to the Reagan era.)

Schemmer, Benjamin F., *The Raid*, Harper & Row, New York,

1976 (the 1970 Son Tay POW rescue mission).

Summers, Harry G., Col. USA (Ret.), *On Strategy - A Critical Analysis of the Vietnam War*, Presidio Press, Novato, Calif. (Reissue Edition), 1995.

Cold War

Brandt, Ed, *The Last Voyage of USS Pueblo*, W.W. Norton & Co., New York, 1969.

Brugioni, Dino A., *Eyeball to Eyeball, the Inside Story of the Cuban Missile Crisis*, Random House, New York, 1991.

Bucher, Lloyd with Mark Rascovich, *My Story*, Doubleday & Co., New York, 1970. (Account of the commander of the *USS Pueblo*.)

Cockburn, Andrew, *The Threat — Inside the Soviet Military Machine*, Random House, New York, 1983.

Coleman, Fred, *The Decline and Fall of the Soviet Empire*, St. Martin's Press, New York, 1996.

Craven, John P., *The Silent War*, Simon & Schuster, New York, 2001.

Friedman, Norman, *The Fifty Year War - Conflict and Strategy in the Cold War*, U.S. Naval Institute Pres, Annapolis, Md., 2000.

Garthoff, Raymond L., *Reflections on the Cuban Missile Crisis*, Brookings Institution Press, Washington, D.C., 1989.

Gervasi, Tom, *The Myth of Soviet Military Supremacy*, Harper & Row, New York, 1986.

Gribkov, Anatoli, Gen. (Ret. USSR) and Smith, William Y., Gen. (Ret.) USA, *Operation Anadyr: U.S. and Soviet Generals Recount the Cuban Missile Crisis*, Edition Q. Inc., Chicago, 1994.

Hersh, Seymour M., *The Target Is Destroyed - What Really Happened to Flight 007 and What America Knew About It.*, Vintage Books, New York, 1987.

Huchthausen, Peter, Kurdin, Igor, and White, R. Alan, *Hostile Waters (The Sinking of the Soviet submarine K-219 in 1986)*, St. Martin's Press, New York, 1997.

Johnson, R.W., *Shootdown: Flight 007 and the American Connection*, Viking Penguin, New York, 1986.

Kalugin, Oleg, Maj. Gen., KGB (Ret.), *The First Directorate: My 32 Years in Intelligence and Espionage against the West*, St. Martin's Press, New York, 1994.

Lewis, Flora, *One of Our H-Bombs Is Missing*, McGraw-Hill, New York, 1967.

Oberg, James E., *Uncovering Soviet Disasters*, Random House, New York, 1988.

Polmar, Norman, *Guide to the Soviet Navy*, Fourth Edition, Naval Institute Press, Annapolis, Md., 1986.

Schumacher, F. Carl and Wilson, George C., *Bridge of No Return, the Ordeal of the USS Pueblo*, Harcourt Brace Jovanovich, New York, 1971.

Other conflicts

Adkin, Mark, *Urgent Fury - The Battle for Grenada*, Lexington Books, Lexington, Mass., 1983.

Donnelly Thomas, Roth, Margaret, and Baker, Caleb, *Operation Just Cause - The Storming of Panama*, Macmillan Publishing Co., New York, 1991.

Hastings, Max and Jenkins, Simon, *The Battle for the Falklands*, W.W. Norton & Co., New York, 1983.

Martin, David C. and Walcott, John, *Best Laid Plans - The Inside Story of America's War Against Terrorism*, Harper & Row, Publishers, New York, 1988.

O'Toole, G.J.A., *The Spanish War - An American Epic 1898*, W.W. Norton & Co., New York, 1984.

Shacochis, Bob, *The Immaculate Invasion*, Viking Penguin, New York, 2000, (Haiti 1994).

Operation Desert Storm

Atkinson, Rick, *Crusade: The Untold Story of the Persian Gulf War*, Houghton Mifflin Co., Boston, 1994.

Gordon, Michael and Trainor, Bernard F., Lt. Gen., USMC (Ret.), *The Generals' War - The Inside Story of Conflict in the Gulf*, Little, Brown and Co., Boston, 1994.

Hallion, Richard, *Storm Over Iraq*, Smithsonian Institution Press, Washington, D.C., 1997.

Kitfield, James, *Prodigal Soldiers: How the Generation of Officers Born of Vietnam Revolutionized the American Style of War*, Simon & Schuster, New York, 1994.

Powell, Colin L., with Persico, Joseph E., *My American Journey*, Random House, New York, 1995.

Schwarzkopf, H. Norman, with Petre, Peter, *It Doesn't Take a Hero*, Bantam Books, New York, 1993.

Staff, U.S. News & World Report, *Triumph Without Victory - The History of the Persian Gulf War*, Random House, New York, 1992.

Summers, Harry G., Col. USA (Ret.), *On Strategy II - A Critical Analysis of the Gulf War*, Dell Publishing Co., New York, 1992.

Somalia

Bowden, Mark, *Black Hawk Down - A Story of Modern War*, Atlantic Monthly Press, Boston, 1999.

Bosnia-Kosovo

Clark, Wesley, Gen. USA (Ret.), *Waging Modern War: Bosnia, Kosovo and the Future of Combat*, PublicAffairs, New York, 2001.

Holbrooke, Richard, *To End a War*, Random House, New York, 1999.

Kaplan, Robert D., *Balkan Ghosts - A Journey Through History*, Vintage Books, New York, 1994.

Loyd, Anthony, *My War Gone By, I Miss It So*, Grove/Atlantic, New York, 2000.

Defense Department/Joint Chiefs of Staff

Crowe, William J. Jr., *The Line of Fire - From Washington to the Gulf, the Politics and Battles of the New Military*, Simon & Schuster, New York, 1993.

McMaster, H.R., *Dereliction of Duty: Johnson, McNamara, the Joint Chiefs of Staff and the Lies That Led to Vietnam*, Harperperennial, New York, 1998.

Powell, Colin L., with Persico, Joseph E., *My American Journey*, Random House, New York, 1995.

Weiner, Tim, Blank Check: *The Pentagon's Black Budget*, Warner Books, New York, 1990.

Woodward, Bob, *The Commanders*, Pocket Star Books, New York, 1991 (Military leadership in Panama and Desert Storm).

Zumwalt, Elmo R. Jr., Adm. USN (Ret.), *On Watch*, Quadrangle/The New York Times Book Co., New York, 1976.

Army

Ambrose, Stephen E., *D-Day June 6, 1944: The Climactic Battle of World War II*, Simon & Schuster, New York, 1994.

Ambrose, Stephen E., *Citizen Soldiers: The U.S. Army from the Normandy Beaches to the Bulge to the Surrender of Germany, June 7, 1944 to May 7, 1945*, Touchstone Books, New York, 1998.

Atkinson, Rick, *The Long Gray Line: The American Journey of West Point's Class of 1966*, Houghton Mifflin Co., Boston, 1989.

Bateman, Robert, editor, *Digital War - A View from the Front Lines*, Presidio Press, Novato, Calif., 1998.

Donnelly Thomas, Roth, Margaret, and Baker, Caleb, *Operation Just Cause - The Storming of Panama*, Macmillan Publishing Co., New York, 1991.

Macgregor, Douglas A., *Breaking the Phalanx - A New Design for Landpower in the 21st Century*, Praeger Press, Westport, Conn., in cooperation with the Center for Strategic and International Studies, 1997.

Meyer, John G., *Company Command: The Bottom Line*, An Institute of Land Warfare Book, Byrd Enterprises, 1992.

Moore, Harold, G. and Galloway, Joseph L., *We Were Soldiers Once and Young: Ia Drang: the Battle That Changed the War in Vietnam*, Harperperennial Library, New York, 1993.

Perrett, Geoffrey, *There's a War to Be Won - The United States Army in World War II*, Ballentine Books, New York, 1997.

Simons, A.J., *The Company They Keep - Life Inside the U.S. Army Special Forces*, Avon Books, New York, 1996.

Navy

Barron, John, *Breaking the Ring*, Houghton Mifflin Co., Boston, 1987 (the Walker spy scandal).

Crowe, William J. Jr., *The Line of Fire - From Washington to the Gulf, the Politics and Battles of the New Military*, Simon & Schuster, New York, 1993.

Earley, Pete, *Family of Spies: Inside the John Walker Spy Ring*, Bantam Books, New York, 1988.

Ennes, James M. Jr., *Assault on the Liberty*, Random House, New York, 1979.

Friedman, Norman, *Submarine Design and Development*, Naval Institute Press, Annapolis, Md., 1984.

Grant, Zalin, *Over the Beach - The Air War in Vietnam*, Pocket Books, New York, 1988.

Howarth, Stephen, *To Shining Sea, a History of the United States Navy, 1776-1991*, Random House, New York, 1991.

Hunter, Robert W., with Lynn Dean Hunter, *Spy Hunter: Inside the FBI Investigation of the Walker Espionage Case*, U.S. Naval Institute Press, New York, Annapolis, Md., 1999.

Isenberg, Michael T., *Shield of the Republic, Volume 1*, St. Martin's Press, New York, 1993.

Kaufman, Yogi and Stillwell, Paul, *Sharks of Steel*, Naval Institute Press, Annapolis, Md., 1993.

Lehman, John F. Jr., *Command of the Seas*, Scribners, New York, 1988.

Perry, Mark, *Four Stars - The Inside Story of the Forty-Year Battle Between the Joint Chiefs of Staff and America's Civilian Leaders*, Houghton Mifflin Co., Boston, 1989.

Polmar, Norman, *The American Submarine, 2nd edition*, The Nautical & Aviation Publishing Co. of America, New York, 1983.

Polmar, Norman, editor, *The Ships and Aircraft of the U.S. Fleet, 16th edition*, Naval Institute Press, Annapolis, Md.,1978.

Polmar, Norman, and Allen, Thomas B., *Rickover, a Biography*, Simon & Schuster, New York, 1982.

Schumacher, F. Carl and Wilson, George C., *Bridge of No Return, the Ordeal of the USS Pueblo*, Harcourt Brace Jovanovich, New York, 1971.

Sontag, Sherry and Drew, Christopher, *Blind Man's Bluff - The Untold Story of American Submarine Espionage*, PublicAffairs, New York, 1998.

Timberg, Robert, *The Nightingale's Song*, Simon & Schuster, New York, 1995. (Profile of five Naval Academy graduates from Vietnam to the Reagan era.)

Vistica, Gregory L., *Fall from Glory*, Simon & Schuster, New York, 1995. (U.S. Navy in the 1980s and 1990s).

Weir, Gary E., *Forged in War, the Naval-Industrial Complex and American Submarine Construction, 1940-1961*, Naval Historical Center, Washington, D.C., 1993.

Zumwalt, Elmo R. Jr., Adm. USN (Ret.), *On Watch*, Quadrangle/The New York Times Book Co., New York, 1976.

Air Force

Eschmann, Karl J., *Linebacker - The Untold Story of the Air Raids over North Vietnam*, Ivy Books, New York, 1989.

Goure, Daniel, and Szarza, Christopher, editors, *Air and Space Power in the New Millenium*, Center for Strategic and International Studies, Washington, D.C., 1996.

Hallion, Richard, *Storm Over Iraq*, Smithsonian Institution Press, Washington, D.C., 1997.

Peebles, Curtis, *Dark Eagles - A History of Top Secret U.S. Aircraft Programs*, Presidio Press, Novato, Calif., 1995.

Peebles, Curtis, *Shadow Flights - America's Secret Air War Against the Soviet Union*, Presidio Press, Novato, Calif., 2000.

Perrett, Geoffrey, *Winged Victory - The Army Air Forces in World War II*, Random House, New York, 1997.

Rich, Ben with Janos, Leo, *Skunk Works: A Personal Memoir of My Years at Lockheed*, Little, Brown & Co., Boston, 1996.

Marine Corps

Freeman, David H. and Krulak, Charles C., *Corps Business: The 30 Management Principles of the U.S. Marines*, Harperbusiness, New York, 2000.

Pisor, Robert, *The End of the Line, the Siege of Khe Sanh*, Ballentine Books, New York, 1982.

Ricks, Thomas, *Making the Corps*, Touchstone Books, New York, 1998.

Simmons, Edwin H., *The United States Marines — A History*, U.S. Naval Institute Press, Annapolis, MD , 1998.

Chemical/biological warfare

Alibek, Ken and Handelman, Stephen, *Biohazard - The Chilling True Story of the Largest Covert Biological Weapons Program in the World*, Random House, New York, 1999.

Cole, Leonard A., *The Eleventh Plague - The Politics of Chemical and Biological Warfare*, W.H. Freeman & Co., New York, 1997.

Mangold, Tom and Goldberg, Jeff, *Plague Wars - The Terrifying Reality of Biological Warfare*, St. Martin's Press, New York, 2000.

Intelligence

Andrew, Christopher, and Mitrokhin, Vasili, *The Sword and*

the Shield - The Mitrokhin Archive and Secret History of the KGB, Basic Books, New York, 1999.

Bamford, James, *The Puzzle Palace*, Houghton Mifflin Co., Boston, 1982.

Bamford, James, *Body of Secrets, Anatomy of the Ultra-Secret National Security Agency*, Doubleday, New York, 2001

Barron, John, *Breaking the Ring*, Houghton Mifflin Co., Boston, 1987,

Brandt, Ed, *The Last Voyage of USS Pueblo*, W.W. Norton & Co., New York, 1969.

Broad, William J., *The Universe Below*, Simon & Schuster, New York, 1997. (Cold War naval operations).

Brown, Anthony, *Bodyguard of Lies*, Harper & Row, New York, 1975.

Burroughs, William E., *Deep Black, the Startling Truth Behind America's Top-Secret Spy Satellites*, Berkley Books, New York, 1988.

Craven, John P., *The Silent War*, Simon & Schuster, New York, 2001.

Earley, Pete, *Family of Spies: Inside the John Walker Spy Ring*, Bantam Books, New York, 1988.

Ennes, James M. Jr., *Assault on the Liberty*, Random House, New York, 1979.

Hunter, Robert W., with Lynn Dean Hunter, *Spy Hunter: Inside the FBI Investigation of the Walker Espionage Case*, U.S. Naval Institute Press, Annapolis, Md., 1999.

Kalugin, Oleg, Maj. Gen., KGB (Ret.), *The First Directorate: My 32 Years in Intelligence and Espionage Against the West*, St. Martin's Press, New York, 1994.

Marchetti, Victor and Marks, John, *The CIA and the Cult of Intelligence*, Alfred A. Knopf, New York, 1974, with "The Consequences of 'Pre-publication Review,'" monograph on court-ordered security deletions by the Center for National Security Studies, Washington, D.C., 1983.

Ostrovsky, Victor, *The Other Side of Deception*, HarperCollins, New York, 1994.

Polmar, Norman, and Allen, Thomas B., *Spy Book, the Encyclopedia of Espionage*, Random House, New York, 1997.

Powers, Francis Gary, *Operation Overflight*, Tower Publications, New York, 1970.

Ranelagh, John, *The Agency: The Rise and Decline of the CIA*, Touchstone/Simon & Schuster, New York, 1987.

Richelson, Jeffrey, T., *American Espionage and the Soviet Target*, William Morrow and Company Inc., New York, 1987.

Richelson, Jeffrey, T., *Foreign Intelligence Organizations*, Ballinger Publishing Co., New York, 1988.

Richelson, Jeffrey, T., *Sword and Shield, Soviet Intelligence and Security Apparatus*, Ballinger Publishing Co., New York, 1986.

Richelson, Jeffrey T., *The U.S. Intelligence Community*, Ballinger Publishing Co., New York, 1985.

Sontag, Sherry and Drew, Christopher, *Blind Man's Bluff - The Untold Story of American Submarine Espionage*, PublicAffairs, New York, 1998.

Suvorov, Viktor, *Inside Soviet Military Intelligence*, MacMillan Publishing Co., New York, 1984.

Wise, David and Ross, Thomas, *The Invisible Government*, Vintage Books, New York, 1974.

Woodward, Bob, *Veil: The Secret Wars of the CIA*, Simon & Schuster, New York, 1987.

Nuclear weapons

Ackland, Len and McGuire, Steven, editors, *Assessing the Nuclear Age*, Bulletin of the Atomic Scientists/Educational Foundation for Nuclear Science, 1986.

Arkin, William M. and Fieldhouse, Richard W., *Nuclear Battlefields, Global Links in the Arms Race*, Ballinger Books, New York, 1985.

Carter, Ashton B., Steinbruner, John D. and Zraket, Charles A., editors, *Managing Nuclear Operations*, The Brookings Institution, Washington,D. C., 1987.

Cochran, Thomas B., Arkin, William M., Norris, Robert S. and Hoenig, Milton M., *Nuclear Weapons Databook*, six volumes, Ballinger Publishing Co., New York, 1986 and 1987.

Lee, Rensselaer III, *Smuggling Armageddon - The Nuclear Black Market in the Former Soviet Union and Europe*, St. Martins' Griffin, New York, 1998.

McPhee, John, *The Curve of Binding Energy*, Ballantine Books, New York, 1973.

Personnel/social issues

Simons, A.J., *The Company They Keep - Life Inside the U.S. Army Special Forces*, Avon Books, New York, 1996.

Gutmann, Stephanie, *The Kinder, Gentler Military - Can America's Gender-Neutral Fighting Force Still Win Wars?* Scribner, New York, 2000.

Mitchell, Brian, *Women in the Military - Flirting with Disaster*, Regnery Publishing, Washington, D.C., 1998.

Glossary of common military acronyms

A Army

AA Administrative Assistant

AAA Advanced Amphibious Assault; Antiaircraft Artillery

AAAM Advanced Air-to-Air Missile

AAAV Advanced Amphibious Assault Vehicle

AABNCP Advanced Airborne National Command Post

AAED Advanced Airborne Expendable Decoy

AALC Amphibious Assault Landing Craft

AAM Air-to-Air-Missile

AAR After Action Review

AARGM Advanced Anti-Radiation Guided Missile

AAV Amphibious Assault Vehicle

AAW Antiair Warfare

ABCCC Airborne Battlefield Command & Control Center

ABL Airborne Laser; Armored Box Launcher

ABM Anti-Ballistic Missile

ABN Airborne

ABNCP Airborne Command Post

ABT Air Breathing Threat

AC Aircraft; Active Component

ACC Air Combat Command (USAF)

ACDA U.S. Arms Control & Disarmament Agency

ACE Allied Command Europe

ACINT Acoustic Intelligence

ACM Advanced Cruise Missile

ACMC Assistant Commandant of the Marine Corps

ACNO Assistant Chief of Naval Operations

ACOM U.S. Atlantic Command (now Joint Forces Command)

ACR Armored Cavalry Regiment (Army)

ACS Auxiliary Crane Ship; Assistant Chief of Staff

ACTD Advanced Concept Technology Demonstration

ACTS Advanced Communications Technology Satellite

AEGIS Combat Training System

ACV Armored Combat Vehicle; Air Cushion Vehicle

AD Destroyer Tender (Ship Classification); Air Defense

ADA Air Defense Artillery (Army); DOD High Order Computer Language

AD/AS Destroyer & Submarine Tender (Ship Classification)

ADCAP Advanced Capability

ADF Automatic Detection Finder

ADI Air Defense Initiative

ADM Admiral; Atomic Demolition Munition

ADP Automatic Data Processing

AE Ammunition Ship (Ship Classification)

AECA Arms Export Control Act

AEW Airborne Early Warning

AF Air Force; Store Ship (Ship Classification)

AFDB Large Auxiliary Floating Dry Dock (Ship Classification)

AFDL Small Auxiliary Floating Dry Dock (Ship Classification)

AFDM Medium Auxiliary Floating Dry Dock (Ship Classification)

AFP Adaptive Force Packaging

AFRTS Armed Forces Radio & Television Service

AFS Combat Stores Ship (Ship Classification)

AFSATCOM Air Force Satellite Communications

AFSCF Air Force Satellite Control Facility

AFSOC Air Force Special Operations Command

AFSOD Air Force Special Operations Detachment

AFSOUTH Allied Forces Southern Europe (NATO)

AG Auxiliary General; Adjutant General; Miscellaneous Ship (Ship Classification)

AGF Miscellaneous Command Ship (Ship Classification)

AGI Intelligence Collection Ship (Ship Classification)

Glossary   295

AGM Air-to-Ground Missile

AGOR Oceanographic Research Ship (Ship Classification)

AGOS Ocean Surveillance Ship (Ship Classification)

AGP Motor Torpedo Boat Tender (Ship Classification)

AGS Surveying Ship (Ship Classification)

AGSS Auxiliary Research Submarine (Ship Classification)

AH Hospital Ship (Ship Classification)

AI Artificial Intelligence; Airborne Intercept; Air Interdiction

AIAA American Institute of Aeronautics & Astronautics

AIC Atlantic Intelligence Center

AID Agency for International Development

AIM Airborne Intercept Missile

AIMD Aircraft Intermediate Maintenance Depot

AK Cargo Ship (Ship Classification)

AKB Auxiliary Cargo Barge/Lighter Ship (Ship Classification)

AKF Auxiliary Cargo Float-On/Float-Off Ship (ShipClassification)

AKR Vehicle Cargo Ship (Ship Classification)

ALCM Air Launched Cruise Missile

ALO Air Liaison Officer

AMC Army Material Command; Air Mobility Command (USAF)

AMRAAM Advanced Medium Range Air-to-Air Missile

AMW Amphibious Warfare

A/N Alphanumeric

ANG Air National Guard

ANGLICO Air Naval Gunfire Liaison Company

ANZUS Australia-New Zealand-United States Treaty

Ao Operational Availability

AO Oiler (Ship Classification); Area of Operation

AOE Fast Combat Support Ship (Ship Classification)

AOG Gasoline Tanker (Ship Classification)

AOR Replenishment Oiler (Ship Classification)

APC Armored Personnel Carrier

APD High-Speed Transport (Ship Classification)

APS Afloat Pre-Positioned Ship

APU Auxiliary Power Unit

AR Repair Ship (Ship Classification); Army Regulation

ARC Cable Repairing Ship (Ship Classification)

ARD Auxiliary Repair Dry Dock (Ship Classification)

ARDM Medium Auxiliary Repair Dry Dock (Ship Classification)

ARG Amphibious Ready Group

ARM Anti-Radiation Missile

ARPA Advanced Research Projects Agency (DoD)

ARS Salvage Ship (Ship Classification)

AS Submarine Tender (Ship Classification)

AS-(number) US Designation for Soviet Air-to-Surface Missile

ASARS Advanced Synthetic Aperture Radar System

ASAS All-Source Analysis System

ASAT Antisatellite

ASD Assistant Secretary of Defense

ASD(C3I) ASD (Command, Control Communications, and Intelligence)

ASD(FM&P) ASD (Force Management & Personnel)

ASD(LA) ASD (Legislative Affairs)

ASD(PA&E) ASD (Program Analysis & Evaluation)

ASD (P&L) ASD (Production & Logistics)

ASD(RA) ASD (Reserve Affairs)

ASDV Advanced Swimmer Delivery Vehicle

ASL Above Sea Level

ASLCM Advanced Sea Launched Cruise Missile

ASM Air-to-Surface Missile; Antiship Missile

ASN Assistant Secretary of the Navy

ASN(M&RA) ASN (Manpower & Reserve Affairs)

ASP Ammunition Supply Point

ASPJ Airborne Self-Protection Jammer

ASR Submarine Rescue Ship (Ship Classification)

ASROC Antisubmarine Rocket

ASUW Anti-Surface Warfare

ASW Antisubmarine Warfare

AT Antitank A&T Acquisition & Technology

ATA Advanced Tactical Aircraft; Auxiliary Ocean Tug (Ship Classification)

ATACMS Army Tactical Missile System

ATAF Allied Tactical Air Force (NATO)

ATC Air Traffic Control

ATF Fleet Ocean Tug (Ship Classification); Amphibious TaskForce

ATGM Anti-Tank Guided Munitions

ATO Air Task(ing) Order

ATR Automatic Target Recognition

ATSD Assistant to the Secretary of Defense

AUTEC Atlantic Undersea Test & Evaluation Center

AUTODIN Automatic Digital Information Network

AUTOSEVOCOM Automatic Secure Voice Communications

AUTOVON Automatic Voice Network

AV Air Vehicle; Aviation

AVN Aviation

AVM Guided Missile Ship (Ship Classification)

AVT Auxiliary Aircraft Landing Training Ship (Ship Classification)

AW Air Warfare; Amphibious Warfare

AWACS Airborne Warning & Control System

B Billion

B-1B Lancer Strategic Bomber

B-2 Stealth Bomber

BA Budget Activity/Authority

BAI Battlefield Air Interdiction

BAT Brilliant Anti-Tank

BB Battleship (Ship Classification)

BDA Battle Damage Assessment; Bomb Damage Assessment

BDE Brigade

BF Budget Function; Battle Force

BG Battle Group

BMD Ballistic Missile Defense

BMDO Ballistic Missile Defense Organization (Office)

BMDPM Ballistic Missile Defense Program Manager

BN Battalion

BP Brilliant Pebbles

BPI Boost Phase Intercept

BRAC Base Realignment & Closure

BRICKBAT Top Priority Program

BUR Bottom Up Review

BW Biological Warfare; Bandwidth

BY Budget Year

(C) Confidential

C2 Command & Control

C3I Command, Control, Communication, & Intelligence

C4I Command, Control, Communication, Computers & Intelligence

CA Combat Assessment; Heavy Cruiser (Ship Classification);Civil Affairs

C&C Command & Control

CAG Carrier Air Wing (Navy: From Carrier Air Group)

CAL Caliber

CALCM Conventional Air Launched Cruise Missile

CAP Combat Air Patrol

CAPTOR MK 60 Encapsulated Torpedo ASW Mine with MK 46Torpedo

CAS Close Air Support

CB Chemical & Biological

CBU Cluster Bomb Unit

CBW Chemical/Biological Weapon

CCDG Commander, Cruiser Destroyer Group

CCG Commander, Carrier Group

CDC Combat Direction Center

CDR Commander

CENTCOM U.S. Central Command

CENTURION Follow-on to SSN-21 Class Submarine

CEO Chief Executive Officer

CEP Circular Error of Probability

CG Guided Missile Cruiser (Ship Classification); Commanding General

CGN Guided Missile Cruiser Nuclear Propulsion (Ship Classification)

CI Counterintelligence

CIA Central Intelligence Agency

CIC Combat Information Center

CINC Commander-in-Chief

CINCCENT Commander-in-Chief, Central Command

CINCEUR Commander-in-Chief, European Command

CINCFOR Commander-in-Chief, Forces Command

CINCLANTFLT Commander-in-Chief, Atlantic Fleet

CINCNORAD Commander-in-Chief, North American AerospaceDefense Command

CINCPAC Commander-in-Chief, Pacific Command

CINCPACFLT Commander-in-Chief, Pacific Fleet

CINCSO Commander-in-Chief, Southern Command

CINCSOC Commander-in-Chief, Special Operations Command

CINCSPACE Commander-in-Chief, Space Command

CINCSTRAT Commander-in-Chief, Strategic Command

CINCTRANS Commander-in-Chief, Transportation Command

CINCUSNAVEUR Commander-in-Chief, U.S. Navy Forces Europe

CIPA Classified Information Procedures Act

CIWS Close-In Weapons System (Phalanx)

CJCS Chairman Joint Chiefs of Staff

CJTF Commander Joint Task Force

CLF Combat Logistic Force; Commander Landing Force

CLG Guided Missile Light Cruiser (Ship Classification)

CM Cruise Missile

CMC Commandant of the Marine Corps

CN Counter Narcotics

CNA Center for Naval Analyses

CNET Chief Of Naval Education & Training

CNO Chief of Naval Operations

CNR Chief of Naval Research

CNSP Commander, Naval Surface Forces Pacific

CNWDI Critical Nuclear Weapon Design Information

CO Commanding Officer

COA Course of Action

COD Carrier Onboard Delivery (Aircraft)

COE Chief of Engineers (Army)

COI Conflict of Interest

COM Communications

COMCARGRU Commander, Carrier Group

COMCARSTRIKEFOR Commander, Carrier Strike Force

COMCRUDESGRU Commander, Cruiser-Destroyer Group

COMDESRON Commander, Destroyer Squadron

COMDT Commandant

COMFIFTHFLT, Commander, Fifth Fleet

COMINEWARCOM Commander, Mine Warfare Command

COMINT Communications Intelligence

COMM Communications

COMMARCORSYSCOM Commander, Marine Corps System Command

COMMARFORLANT Commander, Marine Forces Atlantic

COMMARFORPAC Commander, Marine Forces Pacific

COMMIDEASTFOR Commander, Mid-East Forces (Now 5th Fleet)

COMNAVFOR Commander, Navy Forces

COMNAVSEASYSCOM Commander, Naval Sea Systems Command

COMNAVSPACECOM Commander, Naval Space Command

COMNAVSECGRU Commander Naval Security Group

COMSAT Communications Satellite

COMSEC Communications Security

COMSECONDFLT Commander, Second Fleet

COMSEVENTHFLT Commander, Seventh Fleet

COMSIXTHFLT Commander, Sixth Fleet

COMSTRIKEFLTLANT Commander, Striking Fleet Atlantic

COMSUBDIV Commander, Submarine Division

COMSUBFLOT Commander, Submarine Flotilla

COMSUBFOR Commander, Submarine Force

COMSUBLANT Commander, Submarine Force, Atlantic

COMSUBPAC Commander, Submarine Force, Pacific

COMTAC Commander, Tactical Air Command

COMTHIRDFLT Commander, Third Fleet

CONOPS Concept of Operations

CONPLAN Contingency Plan

CONUS Continental United States

COSCOM Corps Support Command

COTS Commercial off-the-Shelf

CP Command Post

CPA Chairman's Program Assessment; Closest Point of Approach

CQ Carrier Qualification

CRAF Civil Reserve Air Fleet

CRPTO Cryptographic

CS Combat Support

CSAR Combat Search & Rescue

CSS Combat Service Support

CT Counterterrorism

CTBT Comprehensive Nuclear Test Ban Treaty

CTG Commander Task Group

CTOL Conventional Take-Off and Landing (Aircraft)

CV Aircraft Carrier (Multi-purpose) (Ship Classification)

CVN Aircraft Carrier Nuclear Propulsion (Ship Classification)

CVT Training Aircraft Carrier (Ship Classification)

CVW Carrier Air Wing (Ship Classification)

CW Chemical Warfare; Chemical Weapon

CY Calendar Year

DAB Defense Acquisition Board

DASD Deputy Assistant Secretary of Defense

DASN Deputy Assistant Secretary of the Navy

DCI Director of Central Intelligence

DCNO Deputy Chief of Naval Operations

DC/S Deputy Chief of Staff

DD Destroyer (Ship Classification)

DDG Guided Missile Destroyer (Ship Classification)

DDI Deputy Director for Intelligence

DEA Drug Enforcement Agency

DEFSMAC Defense Special Missile & Astronautics Center

DEPSECDEF Deputy Secretary of Defense

DEW Distant Early Warning

DF Direction Finding

DIA Defense Intelligence Agency

DIS Defense Investigative Service

DISA Defense Information Systems Agency

DISCOM Division Support Command

DISN Defense Information Systems Network

DLA Defense Logistics Agency

DMA Defense Mapping Agency (Now National Imagery and MappingAgency)

DMSS Depot Maintenance Standard System

DNI Director of Naval Intelligence

DOD Department of Defense

DODD Department of Defense Directive

DODIG Department of Defense Inspector General

DOE Department of Energy

DOJ Department of Justice

DOL Department of Labor

DON Department of the Navy

DOS Department of State

DOT Department of Transportation

DSAA Defense Security Assistance Agency

DSARC Defense Systems Acquisition Review Council

DSB Defense Science Board

DSCS Defense Satellite Communications System

DSP Defense Support Program

DSRV Deep Submergence Rescue Vehicle (Ship Classification)

DS/S Desert Storm/Desert Shield

DSSP Deep Submerged Systems Project (Navy)

DSV Deep Submergence Vehicle (Ship Classification)

DTG Date Time Group

DTIC Defense Technical Information Center

DZ Drop Zone

E3 End-to-End Encryption

EA Electronic Attack

AC Echelons Above Corps

EAF Expeditionary Air Force

EAM Emergency Action Message

EDO Engineering Duty Officer

E&E Evasion & Escape

EFOG-M Enhanced Fiber Optic Guided-Missile

ELF Extremely Low Frequency

ELINT Electronic Intelligence

ELV Expendable Launch Vehicle

EM Electromagnetic

EMCON Emission Control

ENS Ensign

EOB Electronic Order of Battle

EOD Explosive Ordnance Disposal

EPA Environmental Protection Agency

EPW Earth Penetrating Weapon; Enemy Prisoner of War

ER Extended Range

EUCOM European Command

EW Electronic Warfare

EXCOM Executive Committee

FAA Federal Aviation Administration

FAC Forward Air Controller

FADM Fleet Admiral

FAE Fuel Air Explosive

FAR Federal Acquisition Regulation

FARP Forward Arming & Refueling Point

FAST Fleet Antiterrorism Security Team

FBI Federal Bureau of Investigation

FC Fire Control

FCC Federal Communications Commission

FEBA Forward Edge of Battle Area

FEMA Federal Emergency Management Agency

FF Frigate (Ship Classification)

FFG Guided Missile Frigate (Ship Classification)

FLEETEX Fleet Exercise

FLIR Forward Looking Infrared

FLTSATCOM Fleet Satellite Communications

FM Frequency Modulation

FMFLANT Fleet Marine Force, Atlantic

FMFPAC Fleet Marine Force, Pacific

FO Forward Observer

F/O Follow-On

FOB Forward Operating Base

FOG-M Fiber-Optic Guided Missile

FOG-S Fiber-Optic Guided Skipper

FOIA Freedom of Information Act

FON Freedom of Navigation

FORSCOM Forces Command (Army)

FOSIC Fleet Ocean Surveillance Information Center

FOSIF Fleet Ocean Surveillance Information Facility

FROG Free Rocket Over Ground

FRS Fleet Replacement Squadron; Federal Reserve System

FSS Fast Sealift Ship

FSSG Force Service Support Group (USMC)

FSU Former Soviet Union

FTE Full-Time Equivalent

FTI Fixed Target Indicator

FTRG Fleet Training Readiness Group

FW Fixed Wing

FY Fiscal Year

FYDP Future Years Defense Plan (Program)

GAO General Accounting Office

GCCS Global Command & Control System (DoD)

GBL Ground-Based Laser

GCC Gulf Cooperation Council

GENSER General Service

GP General Purpose

GPO Government Printing Office

GPS Global Positioning System

GSA General Services Administration

HAC House Appropriations Committee

HARM High Speed, Anti-Radiation Missile

HASC House Armed Services Committee

HAZMAT Hazardous Materials

HBC House Budget Committee

HE High Explosive

HELO Helicopter

HEMP High Altitude Electromagnetic Pulse

HEMTT Heavy Expanded Mobility Tactical Truck

HF High Frequency

HFDF High Frequency Direction Finding

HM Helicopter Mine Countermeasures

HMM Marine Medium Helicopter Squadron

HMMWV High Mobility Multipurpose Wheeled Vehicle (Humvee)

HMR Marine Helicopter Squadron

HNS Host Nation Support

HQDA Headquarters Department of the Army

HQMC Headquarters Marine Corps

HUD Heads Up Displays

HUMINT Human Intelligence

I&A Indications & Warning

IADS Integrated Air Defense System

IC Integrated Circuits; Intelligence Community

ICBM Intercontinental Ballistic Missile

IDA Institute for Defense Analysis

IFF Identification, Friend or Foe

IG Inspector General

IMCS Integrated Maritime Comm. System

INF Intermediate Nuclear Forces

INFOSEC Information System Security

INMARSAT International Maritime Satellite

INT Intelligence

IO Indian Ocean

IOC Initial Operational Capability

IR Infrared

IRR Individual Ready Reserve

ISR Intelligence, Surveillance, Reconnaissance

IUW Inshore Undersea Warfare

IW Information Warfare

IX Unclassified Miscellaneous (Ship Classification)

J1 Joint Personnel Staff

J2 Joint Intelligence Staff

J3 Joint Operations Staff

J4 Joint Logistics Staff

J5 Joint Planning Staff

J6 Joint C4I Systems Staff

JAG Judge Advocate General

JCS Joint Chiefs of Staff

JDAM Joint Direct Attack Munitions

JFACC Joint Force Air Component Commander

JFC Joint Force Command(er)

JIB Joint Information Bureau

JIC Joint Intelligence Center

JICPAC Joint Intelligence Center, Pacific

JROC Joint Requirements Oversight Council (JCS)

JRTC Joint Readiness Training Center

JS Joint Staff

JSOC Joint Special Operations Command

JSOTF Joint Special Operations Task Force

JSOW Joint Standoff Weapon

JSPD Joint Strategic Planning Document

JSTARS Joint Surveillance & Target Attack Radar System

JTF Joint Task Force

KIA Killed in Action

LA Legislative Affairs

LANT Atlantic

LANTIRN Low Altitude Navigation & Targeting Infrared for Night

LAV Light Armored Vehicle

LAW Light Anti-Tank Weapon

LCAC Landing Craft, Air Cushion (Ship Classification)

LCC Amphibious Command Ship (Ship Classification)

LCU Landing Craft, Utility (Ship Classification)

LGB Laser-Guided Bomb

LHA Amphibious Assault Ship-General Purpose (ShipClassification)

LHD Landing Helicopter-Dock Amphibious Assault Ship (ShipClassification)

LIC Low Intensity Conflict

LKA Amphibious Cargo Ship (Ship Classification)

LOC Lines of Communication

LOG Logistics

LPA Amphibious Transport (Ship Classification)

LPD Landing Platform-Dock Amphibious Transport Dock (ShipClassification)

LPH Amphibious Assault Ship-Helicopter (Ship Classification)

LR Long Range

LSD Landing Dock Ship (Ship Classification)

LST Tank Landing Ship (Ship Classification)

LT Lieutenant

LTJG Lieutenant Junior Grade

M Missions; Million

MAAG Military Assistance Advisory Group

MAB Marine Amphibious Brigade

MAC Military Airlift Command (Now Air Mobility Command)

MAD Mutually Assured Destruction

MAGTF Marine Air-Ground Task Force

MARCENT Marine Forces Central Command

MARCORPS Marine Corps

MARDEZ Maritime Defense Zone

MARDIV Marine Division

MARFORLANT Marine Forces Atlantic

MARFORPAC Marine Forces Pacific

MARG Mediterranean Amphibious Ready Group

MAU Marine Amphibious Unit

MAW Marine Corps Air Wing

MC Military Construction; Marine Corps

MCAS Marine Corps Air Station

MCB Marine Corps Base

MCCDC Marine Corps Combat Development Command

MCLB Marine Corps Logistics Base

MCM Mine Countermeasures; Mine Countermeasures Ship (Ship Classification)

MDZ Maritime Defense Zone

MEB Marine Expeditionary Brigade

MEC Marine Expeditionary Corps

MED Mediterranean

MEF Marine Expeditionary Force

METL Mission Essential Task List

MEU Marine Expeditionary Unit

MEU(SOC) Marine Expeditionary Unit (Special OperationsCapable)

MF Multifrequency; Medium Frequency

MHC Minehunter-Coastal Mine Countermeasures Ship

MIA Missing in Action

MILCON Military Construction

MILES Multiple Integrated Laser Engagement System

MINEWARCOM Mine Warfare Command

MINRON Mine Squadron

MIO Maritime Interception Operations

MIW Mine Warfare

MK Mark

MLRS Multiple Launch Rocket System

MM Millimeter; Minuteman (ICBM)

MMS Marine Mammal System

MOD Modification(s); Ministry of Defense

MOPP Mission Oriented Planning Posture

MOS Military Occupational Specialty

MOU Memorandum of Understanding

MOUT Military Operations in Urban Terrain

MP Manpower & Personnel; Military Police

MPA Maritime Patrol Aircraft

MPF Maritime Prepositioning Force

MPS Maritime Prepositioning Ship; MP Squadron

MR Medium Range

MRBM Medium-Range Ballistic Missile

MRC Major Regional Conflict

MSC Military Sealift Command

MSL Mean Sea Level

MTT Mobile Training Team

MV Motor Vessel

MW Mine Warfare

MX Peacekeeper ICBM

N8 Dep. Chief of Naval Ops for Resources, Warfare Requirements, and Assessment

N85 Director, Expeditionary Warfare Division

N86 Director, Surface Warfare Division

NA National Archives

NAS New Attack Submarine; Naval Air Station

NASA National Aeronautics & Space Administration

NATO North Atlantic Treaty Organization

NAV Navigational

NAVCENT Naval Forces U.S. Central Command

NAVEUR Naval Forces U.S. European Command

NAVFACSYSCOM Naval Facilities Engineering Command

NAVSEASYSCOM Naval Sea Systems Command

NAVSPACECOM Navel Space Command

NAVSPECWARGRU Navy Special Warfare Group

NAVSURFLANT Naval Surface Force, Atlantic

NAVSURPAC Naval Surface Force, Pacific

NBC Nuclear, Biological & Chemical

NCA National Command Authority(ies)

NCIS Naval Criminal Investigative Service

NCO Noncommissioned Officer

NDS Nuclear Detection Sensor

NDU National Defense University

NEACP National Emergency Airborne Command Post

NFO Naval Flight Officer

NG National Guard

NGF Naval Gun Fire

NGFS Naval Gun Fire Support

NGO Nongovernmental Organization

NIBWM (Inverse Operational Tempo) Nights in Bed With Mama

NMCB Navy Mobile Construction Battalion

NMCC National Military Command Center

NMD National Missile Defense

NOAA National Oceanic & Atmospheric Administration

(NOFORN) Not Releasable to Foreign Nationals

NOIC Naval Operational Intelligence Center

NORAD North American Air Defense

NOTAM Notice to Mariners

NPT Non Proliferation Treaty

NR Submersible Research Vehicle (Ship Classification)

NRF Naval Reserve Force

NRC Nuclear Regulatory Commission

NRF Naval Reserve Force

NRL Naval Research Laboratory

NRO National Reconnaissance Office

NSA National Security Agency

NSC National Security Council

NSG National Security Group

NSSN New Attack Submarine

NSWP Non-Soviet Warsaw Pact

NSWTG Naval Special Warfare Task Group

NTC National Training Center, Ft. Irwin, CA

NUCINT Nuclear Intelligence

NVG Night Vision Goggles

NW Naval Warfare

NWC National War College; Naval War College

OA Operational Area

OB Operating Budget; Order of Battle

OBE Overtaken by Events

ONI Office of Naval Intelligence

ONR Office of Naval Research

OOTW Operations Other Than War

OPCON Operational Control

OPFOR Opposing Forces

OPLAN Operation Plan

OPORD Operation Order

OPSEC Operations Security

OPTEMPO Operating Tempo (see NIBWM)

OSD Office of the Secretary of Defense

OSIS Ocean Surveillance Information System

OTH Over-the-Horizon

OUSD Office of the Under Secretary of Defense

PAA Primary Aircraft Authorization

PAC Pacific; Patriot Missile Advanced Capability

PAC3 Patriot Upgrade Program for ATBM Capability

PACAF Pacific Air Forces

PACOM Pacific Command

PAO Public Affairs Office(r)

PB Patrol Boat (Ship Classification)

PC Patrol Craft (Coastal)

PERSTEMPO Personnel Tempo

PG Patrol Combatant (Ship Classification)

PGH Patrol Gunboat (Hydrofoil) (Ship Classification)

PGM Precision Guided Munitions

PHOTINT Photographic Intelligence

PK Peacekeeper; Probability of Kill

PM Program Manager; Project Manager

POL Petroleum, Oil, & Lubricant

POM Program Objective Memorandum

POMCUS Prepositioned(Prepositioning) Material Configured toUnit Sets

POTS Plain Old Telephone System

PPBS Planning, Programming & Budgeting System

PRC People‚Äôs Republic of China

PSYOPS Psychological Operations

QRCC Quick Reaction Combat Capability

R Reliability

RADAR Radio Detection & Ranging

RADINT Radar Intelligence

RADM Rear Admiral

RAN Royal Australian Navy

RBOC Rapid Blooming Offboard Chaff

RCS Radar Cross Section

R&D Research & Development

RDF Rapid Deployment Force Radio Direction Finding

RF Radio Frequency

RFP Request for Proposal

RIMPAC Rim of the Pacific (Biennial Fleet Operation/Exercise)

RIO Radar Intercept Officer

RLG Ring Laser Gyroscope

RM Radioman

RMA Revolution in Military Affairs

ROE Rules of Engagement

ROK Republic of Korea

RO/RO Roll-On/Roll-Off

RPV Remotely Piloted Vehicle

RSTA Reconnaissance, Surveillance & Target Acquisition

RT Real Time

RV Re-Entry Vehicle

RWR Radar Warning Receiver

(S) Secret

SA Secretary of the Army

SAC Senate Appropriations Committee; Strategic Air Command

SACEUR Supreme Allied Commander Europe

SACLANT Supreme Allied Commander Atlantic

SAF Secretary of the Air Force

SAG Surface Action Group Saudi Arabian Government

SALT Strategic Arms Limitations Treaty

SAM Surface-to-Air Missile

SAR Synthetic Aperture Radar; Search & Rescue

SASC Senate Armed Services Committee

SATCOM Satellite Communications

SCIF Special Compartmented Information Facility

SCUD Soviet Short-Range Surface/Surface Missile

SDI Strategic Defense Initiative

SDV SEAL Delivery Vehicle

SEABEES Naval Construction Battalion Personnel

SEAD Suppression of Enemy Air Defense

SEAL Sea-Air-Land (Special Warfare Forces)

SECDEF Secretary of Defense

SECNAV Secretary of the Navy

SERE Survival, Evasion, Resistance & Escape

SF Special Forces

SHAPE Supreme Headquarters Allied Power, Europe

SI Special Intelligence

SIGINT Signals Intelligence

SINCGARS Single Channel Ground & Airborne Radio System

SINS Ships Interial Navigation Systems

SIPRNET Secret Internet Protocol Router Network

SITREP Situation Report

SLAM Standoff Land Attack Missile

SLAM-ER SLAM-Expanded Response

SLBM Submarine Launched Ballistic Missile

SLCM Sea Launched Cruise Missile

SLMM Submarine-Launched Mobile Mine

SLOC Sea Lines of Communication

SM Standard Missile

SM-2 Standard Missile 2

SOCOM Special Operations Command

SOFA Status of Forces Agreement

SOSUS Sound Surveillance System

SPACECOM Space Command

SPAWAR Space & Naval Warfare Systems Command

SPINTCOM Special Intelligence Communications

SRBOC Super Rapid Blooming Offboard Chaff

SS Submarine (Diesel Propulsion) (Ship Classification)

SSBN Ballistic Missile Submarine Nuclear

Propulsion (Ship Classification)

SSGN Nuclear-Powered Guided Missile Submarine

SSIXS Submarine Satellite Information Exchange Subsystem

SSM Surface-to-Surface Missile

SSN Nuclear Attack Submarine Nuclear Propulsion (ShipClassification)

S&T Science & Technology

STANAVFORLANT Standing Naval Forces Atlantic (NATO)

START Strategic Arms Reduction Treaty

STOVL Short Take-Off & Vertical Landing

STU-III Secure Telephone Unit — Third Generation

SUBLANT Submarine Forces, Atlantic

SUBPAC Submarine Forces, Pacific

SURTASS Surface Towed Array Surveillance System

SWA Southwest Asia

T Trillion

TA Target Acquisition

TACAIR Tactical Aircraft

TACAMO Take Charge & Move Out

TAD Theater Air Defense; Temporary Assigned Duty

TAGOR Military Sealift Command Oceanographic Research Ship

T-AGOS Military Sealift Command Auxiliary General OceanSurveillance

TAGS Surveying Ship

TAH Hospital Ship

TALD Tactical Air-Launched Decoy

T-AO Contract Operated Oiler

TARPS Tactical Air Reconnaissance Pod System

TASM Tomahawk Cruise Missile (Antiship Model)

TBD To Be Determined

TBMD Theater Ballistic Missile Defense

TDY Temporary Duty

TECHINT Technical Intelligence

TELINT Telemetry Intelligence

TENCAP Tactical Exploitation of National Capabilities Tera- Trillion

TF Task Force

THAAD Theater High Altitude Area Defense

TLAM Tomahawk Land Attack Missile

T/O Take Off; Table of Organization

TOT Time on Target

TOW Tube-Launched, Optically-Tracked, Wire-Guided Missile

TPFDL Time Phased Force Deployment List

TRADOC Training & Doctrine Command

TRANSCOM Transportation Command

TRAP Tactical Recovery of Aircraft & Personnel (USMC Team)

(TS) Top Secret

TSSAM Tri-Service Standoff Attack Missile

(U) Unclassified

UAE United Arab Emirates

UAV Unmanned Aerial Vehicle

UCP Unified Command Plan

UHF Ultra-High Frequency

UK United Kingdom

UN United Nations

UNOSOM United Nations Operations Somalia

UNREP Underway Replenishment

UNS Unspecified

UNSC United Nations Security Council

UNSECNAV Under Secretary of the Navy

USACOM U.S. Atlantic Command (Now Joint Forces Command)

USAF United States Air Force

USAID United States Agency for International Development

USCENTCOM U.S. Central Command

USCG United States Coast Guard

USCINC U.S. Commander in Chief

USCINCCENT Commander-in-Chief, U.S. Central Command

USCINCLANT Commander-in-Chief, U.S. Atlantic Command

USCINCPAC Commander-in-Chief, U.S. Pacific Command

USCINCSTRAT Commander-in-Chief, U.S. Strategic Command

USCINCTRANS Commander-in-Chief, United States TransportationCommand

USDA U.S. Department of Agriculture

USEUCOM U.S. European Command

USFK U.S. Forces Korea

USG U.S. Government

USIA United States Information Agency

USMC United States Marine Corps

USN United States Navy; Under Secretary of the Navy

USNAVCENT U.S. Navy, U.S. Central Command

USNR U.S. Navy Reserve

USO United Service Organizations

USPACOM U.S. Pacific Command

USSOCOM U.S. Special Operations Command

USSOUTHCOM U.S. Southern Command

USSPACECOM U.S. Space Command

USSR Union of Soviet Socialist Republics

USSTRATCOM U.S. Strategic Command

USTRANSCOM U.S. Transportation Command

USW Undersea Warfare

UUV Unmanned Undersea Vehicles

UV Ultraviolet

UW Unconventional Warfare

UXO Unexploded Ordinance

V Variant

VA Veteran's Affairs (Department)

VADM Vice Admiral

VCJCS Vice Chairman, Joint Chiefs of Staff

VCNO Vice Chief of Naval Operations

VF Fighter Squadron

VFA Fighter/Attack Squadron

VHF Very High Frequency

VL Vertical Launch

VLA Vertical Launch ASROC

VLF Very Low Frequency

VLS Vertical Launch(ing) System

VM Marine Aviation

VMA Marine Attack Squadron

VMA(AW) Marine All-Weather Attack Squadron

VMF Marine Fighter Squadron

VMF(AW) Marine All-Weather Fighter Squadron

VR Logistics Squadron

V/STOL Vertical/Short Take-Off & Landing

VTOL Vertical Takeoff & Landing

WAGB Icebreaker (USCG)

WESTPAC Western Pacific

WHEC High-Endurance Cutters (USCG)

WIA Wounded in Action

WMD Weapons of Mass Destruction

WMEC Medium-Endurance Cutter

WRSK War Reserve Spares Kits

WWMCCS Worldwide Military Command & Control System

WX Weather

XBT Expendable Bathythermograph

X-DECK Cross-Decked

XMIT Transmitter

XMTR Transmitter

XPONDER Transponder

YAG Miscellaneous Auxiliary Service Craft (ShipClassification)

YBD Bowdock (Ship Classification)

YD Floating Crane (Ship Classification)

YF Covered Lighter (Ship Classification)

YFB Ferry Boat or Launch (Ship Classification)

YFRT Range Tender (Ship Classification)

YHLC Salvage Lift Craft, Heavy (Ship Classification) 135

YLC Salvage Lift Craft, Light (Ship Classification)

YM Dredge (Ship Classification)

YP Patrol Craft, Training (Ship Classification)

YTB Large Harbor Tug (Ship Classification)

YTL Small Harbor Tug (Ship Classification)

YTM Medium Harbor Tug (Ship Classification)

YTT Torpedo Trials Craft (Ship Classification)

ZEOP Z-Electro-Optical Payload

Source: Department of Defense

Index

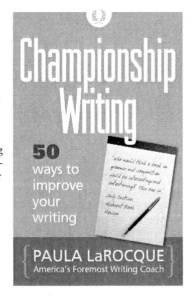